T0032932

DON'T
LOOK
BACK

DON'T LOOK BACK

A Memoir of War, Survival, and
My Journey from Sudan to America

ACHUT DENG AND KEELY HUTTON

FARRAR STRAUS GIROUX
NEW YORK

Farrar Straus Giroux Books for Young Readers
An imprint of Macmillan Publishing Group, LLC
120 Broadway, New York, NY 10271 • fiercereads.com

Our books may be purchased in bulk for promotional, educational,
or business use. Please contact your local bookseller or the Macmillan
Corporate and Premium Sales Department at (800) 221-7945 ext. 5442 or
by email at MacmillanSpecialMarkets@macmillan.com.

Library of Congress Cataloging-in-Publication Data
Names: Deng, Achut, author. | Hutton, Keely, author.
Title: Don't look back : a memoir of war, survival, and my journey from
Sudan to America / Achut Deng and Keely Hutton.
Description: First edition. | New York : Farrar Straus Giroux, 2022. |
Audience: Ages: 12–18 | Summary: "I want life. For ten years, Achut Deng
survived at Kakuma Refugee Camp in Kenya after her family was ripped
apart by the Second Sudanese Civil War. But Achut wanted to do more than
merely survive. She wanted to live. The twenty-two-year civil war essentially
orphaned over 20,000 children and drove them from their villages in southern
Sudan. Some of these children walked over a thousand miles, through
dangerous war zones and across unforgiving deserts. They are often referred
to as The Lost Boys. But there were girls, too. Achut Deng was one of them.
This is her story. It's a story of unimaginable hardship and selfless bravery, of
tormenting physical pain and amazing emotional resilience, of unbreakable
bonds of friendship and family. It's a story about what happens when your
dream comes true, only to give way to a new nightmare. It's about how hard
you will fight to save your own life" —Provided by publisher.
Identifiers: LCCN 2022007776 | ISBN 9780374389727 (hardcover)
Subjects: LCSH: Deng, Achut—Juvenile literature. | Refugees—Sudan—
Biography—Juvenile literature. | Refugees—United States—Biography—
Juvenile literature. | Sudan—History—Civil War, 1983–2005—Juvenile
literature.
Classification: LCC DT157.65 .D43 2022 | DDC 962.404/
3092 [B] —dc23/eng/20220420
LC record available at https://lccn.loc.gov/2022007776

First edition, 2022
Book design by Mallory Grigg
Printed in the United States of America

10 9 8 7 6 5 4 3 2 1

For my sons, Deng, Kuek, and Mayom. Being a mother to you amazing boys is the greatest gift in my life. Thank you for giving me the courage and strength to share my story with the world, and most importantly, to share my story with you. I love you unconditionally. —Achut Deng

To those who see reflections of themselves in Achut's story. You are not alone. —Keely Hutton

AUTHORS' NOTE

Some names have been changed, but the events portrayed in *Don't Look Back* are Achut Deng's memories to the best of her knowledge. The conflict depicted in this memoir is known as the Second Sudanese Civil War. In 1983, civil war sparked in Sudan when the military regime of the Government of Sudan (GOS) imposed laws mandating that all citizens adopt Arab culture, identity, and language. The controversial laws were viewed as a calculated move by the government in the north to control, through Arabization and cultural assimilation, southern Sudan, an area comprised mainly of Christians, while also securing access to the south's natural resources. Angered by the political ruling and fearing religious persecution, the Sudan People's Liberation Movement (SPLM) and its military wing, the Sudan People's Liberation Army (SPLA), were formed in southern Sudan. Support for the SPLM/SPLA spread throughout the region, with men and boys, most of whom were cattle herders knows as pastoralists, being recruited from the sixty-four ethnic groups in southern Sudan. The SPLA soldiers fought side by side against the GOS Army for eight years, but over time, tensions grew between SPLA leader Dr. John Garang from southern Sudan's largest ethnic group, the Dinka, and other SPLM/SPLA leaders, including Riek Machar from southern Sudan's second-largest ethnic community, the Nuer. Disagreements over the goals of the SPLM caused the group to fracture in 1991, creating two factions of the SPLA, one led by Garang, and one led by Machar. Fighting intensified following the split, resulting in bloody massacres of civilian populations. Although deadly conflicts continue in South Sudan today, the Second Sudanese Civil War officially ended on January 9, 2005, when the GOS and SPLA signed the Comprehensive Peace Agreement (CPA). The CPA provided the people of South Sudan the option to vote in favor of secession if unity between the north and south was not made an attractive option for them. Six years after the signing of the CPA, the people of South Sudan voted in favor of secession in the January 2011 referendum, and on July 9, 2011, they became the independent state of South Sudan.

The twenty-two-year civil war displaced an estimated four million people and caused the deaths of an estimated two million men, women, and children. The conflict forced over twenty thousand children from their families and villages in southern Sudan. The children walked over a thousand miles, through dangerous war zones and across unforgiving deserts, seeking sanctuary at refugee camps in the neighboring countries of Ethiopia and Kenya. Relief workers nicknamed them the "Lost Boys," after the group of orphaned boys who banded together in Neverland to create a family and take care of one another in J. M. Barrie's *Peter Pan*. Despite assistance from the Kenyan government, the International Rescue Committee (IRC), and the United Nations High Commissioner for Refugees (UNHCR), the camps struggled to provide basic necessities, such as food, water, shelter, and health care, for the surging number of people in their care. Many refugees, including Achut Deng, walked to Kakuma Refugee Camp in northwestern Kenya. Over the next decade, the number of refugees in Kakuma swelled, making it the world's largest refugee camp. With their homeland still gripped in war and more refugees arriving daily, conditions grew more dire for the children in Kakuma.

When the international community learned of the tragic exodus and continued suffering of the war-affected youth of southern Sudan, they demanded help for those trapped in refugee camps like Kakuma. In late 2000, a relocation program was established to help the Lost Boys in Kakuma start new lives in countries around the world. Of the four thousand Sudanese children relocated to the United States between the years 2000 and 2001, less than a hundred of them were girls. Achut was one of the girls brought to the United States with the Lost Boys of Sudan.

Twenty years later, in March 2020, Achut was interviewed by Caitlin Dickerson, who was working as an immigration journalist at the *New York Times*. Caitlin was writing an article on COVID-19's impact on employees at the Smithfield pork factory in Sioux Falls, South Dakota. Achut worked at the factory and shared her experiences with Caitlin. The article was read by millions, and Achut's interview touched the hearts of many readers, including staff at Macmillan Publishers. With Caitlin's help, editor Joy Peskin contacted Achut to discuss the idea of telling her story to the world.

Achut is a natural storyteller, but she wanted to be paired with a seasoned author to help tell her story, so in October 2020, Achut interviewed several writers and journalists for the collaboration. After careful consideration, she chose author Keely Hutton to partner with her as a cowriter on the project. Due to the COVID-19 pandemic and lockdown, Achut and Keely were unable to meet in person over the next ten months, but thanks to Zoom and cell phones, they spent hundreds of hours discussing Achut's life and her hopes for her memoir. The conversations took time and care. Achut had never shared her story with anyone before speaking with Keely. For many years, her physical and emotional survival depended upon Achut focusing on moving forward, but she realized to tell her story, she would have to look back and face her past. While Achut revisited memories of her childhood in Sudan and Kakuma and her adolescence in the United States, Keely researched Sudan, the Second Sudanese Civil War, the Lost Boys, Kakuma Refugee Camp, and the refugee relocation program by reading books and articles on the subjects and studying videos and photographs depicting the people, places, and events. And when Achut was ready to share her memories, thoughts, and feelings, Keely listened.

Don't Look Back depicts the life of Achut Deng, one

of thousands of children whose lives were irrevocably changed by the Second Sudanese Civil War. Although many of the experiences Achut shares in her memoir may be similar to those of other Lost Boys and Girls of Sudan, her memories and story are uniquely her own. In Achut's journey, we hope readers find the strength to persevere when facing obstacles in their own lives and the confidence to remember, despite where life takes them, to never forget who they are.

DON'T
LOOK
BACK

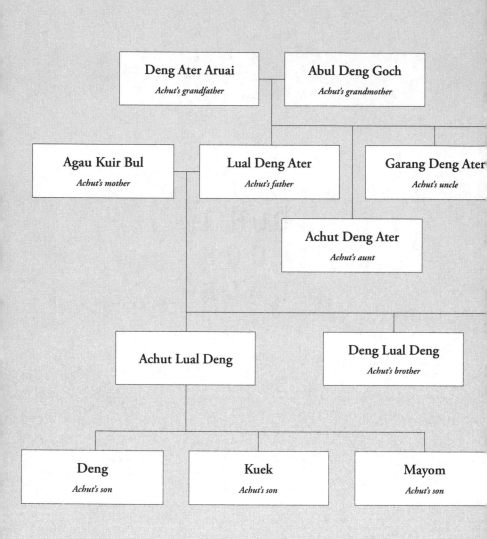

ACHUT DENG'S FAMILY TREE

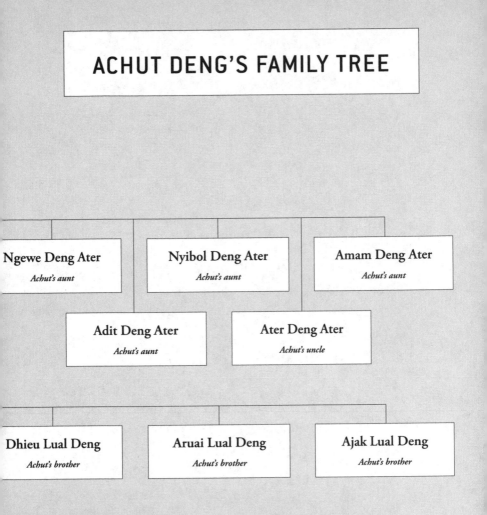

Ngewe Deng Ater
Achut's aunt

Nyibol Deng Ater
Achut's aunt

Amam Deng Ater
Achut's aunt

Adit Deng Ater
Achut's aunt

Ater Deng Ater
Achut's uncle

Dhieu Lual Deng
Achut's brother

Aruai Lual Deng
Achut's brother

Ajak Lual Deng
Achut's brother

CHAPTER 1

Houston, Texas—March 2001

They said I'd be safe here. They lied.

As I hid in the back corner of my bedroom closet, my breath seized at the sound of approaching voices outside our apartment building. They scrambled over one another, pushing and shoving, wrestling for control of the conversation and straining to be heard over the raucous peals of laughter punctuating their dialogue. As they drew closer, the voices charged through the open window of the second-floor bedroom, where I hid, throwing themselves against the worn plywood of my closet door. I considered sneaking out of my sanctuary to peek through the window to see who was coming and assess any potential danger they might pose, but my muscles refused to budge. So I remained in my corner of the closet, paralyzed in fear of the unknown, as well as the known.

I closed my eyes and listened, straining to determine whether the muffled, male voices used English or Dinka and praying they did not come inside. They spoke English. I recognized only two words in the jumble of their laughter and shouting: *no* and *home*. Finally, the unfamiliar voices, speaking their unfamiliar language, moved past our building and dissolved in the din of evening traffic.

I took a deep breath before easing open the closet door. The apartment was quiet. I peeked out to check the digital clock sitting on the plastic nightstand squeezed between the two single beds that crowded the narrow room. It was 5:53 P.M., almost two hours since I'd arrived home from school. I'd been hiding longer than I'd thought. The others would be home soon.

He would be home soon.

Time was running out. I had to make a decision before the decision was made for me. Again.

As I closed the door, echoes of my grandmother's voice whispered in my mind. "Not so fast, little one," my koko had cautioned me when, at five years old, I had slipped my small hand from hers and run through the open gate of the wooden fence encircling the thatched-roof huts, fields, and gardens of our home in southern Sudan. I had wanted to follow my uncle Abraham as he led our family's herd of cattle to drink from the lake outside our village. As I hurried after him, Koko scooped me into her arms before I accidentally startled a large black-and-white Ankole-Watusi bull, with long, curved horns and little tolerance for small children who did not heed their elders' warnings. "Achut, you must think before you move." She pressed a gentle finger against my forehead. "Good decisions take time and care. Always use both."

A suffocating ache radiated through my chest, and hot

tears escaped my eyes and burned down my cheeks. Even my happy memories were accompanied by pain.

They had called us Lost Boys when the others and I had arrived in Houston three months earlier from Kenya's Kakuma Refugee Camp, but I was not a boy, and I was not lost.

I knew exactly where I was and exactly how I'd arrived here. What I did not understand was why. But the why no longer mattered. Death had taken so much from me over my sixteen years, but life had taken more.

Bit by bit.

Piece by piece.

It had stolen everything until there was only one thing left to take.

CHAPTER 2

Wernyol, Sudan—1988

The first thing they took was my name.

Achut.

It had been passed down in my father's family for three generations to honor his great-grandmother, the first Achut of many. My great-great-grandmother had been the only child of seven to survive infancy.

"Let the name Achut be a blessing for all the children we have lost," my great-great-grandmother's parents announced when death did not claim their youngest child. Achut became revered in our family and village. Her name graced the lyrics of songs chanted at family gatherings in celebration of not only her life but, years later, the lives of her twelve children, including three sets of twins. For so much life to come after so much death, my great-great-grandmother Achut had truly been blessed. And so every firstborn daughter in our family to follow was given her name, including me.

Achut was the beautiful, vibrant note at the beginning of my song. A promise of life carried across the boundless blue Sudanese sky, on the voices of the Dinka people. It sang out with strength and clarity, sure of its place in the lyrics of my life.

Achut.

Spoken in soft, loving coos by my mother, it called to me.

Achut.

Its melody resonated through my soul with the echoes of my ancestors, binding me to my past and their future.

Achut.

For the first three years of my life, Achut was my name. And then, one day, it wasn't.

It was replaced by a strange, new name.

Rachel.

Discordant. Harsh. Off-key.

I tried to ignore it, but everyone in my family and village insisted on the new name. Everyone, except my koko.

Despite our family's constant reminders, my baba's mother, Abul Deng Goch, refused to call me Rachel.

"I am taking Achut to the garden," she would announce to Mama.

"Her name is Rachel," Mama would say for the hundredth time, but no annoyance or anger sharpened her tone. Mama loved and admired her mother-in-law. Mama and Baba had married in 1982, a year before Baba was conscripted into the Sudan People's Liberation Army (SPLA). Baba was Koko's firstborn child, and during his long deployment, Mama and Koko had grown close, working the land together, caring for my baba's younger siblings, and maintaining the Deng family homestead in his absence.

At five feet eight inches tall, my grandmother was considered short among the Dinka women in our village, but she carried herself with the confidence and courage of a woman who would never permit others to look down on her. Like most Dinkas, she was a devout Christian. She attended mass, recited her daily prayers, and paid her tithes, but she had refused a Christian name at her baptism and insisted on calling her family members by their traditional Dinka names. Her short hair, bleached in the Dinka custom from cow-urine rinses, hugged her head in a cap of tight sunset-orange curls. Her dark eyes, glistening with intelligence and curiosity, missed nothing. One stern glance could silence children and men alike, and one warm, dimpled smile could thaw the coldest heart.

"Come along, Achut," Koko would say, picking up her hand hoe and basket.

Mama would smile and shake her head as Koko pushed open the gate to the fence that enclosed the four huts and land that made up the Deng family compound. Two of the huts, with their round mud walls and steeped, conic straw roofs, housed our family, including our two dogs, as we slept at night. The third hut, identical in size and shape to our sleeping huts, served as a kitchen, where we stored our food and prepared our meals. The fourth, larger hut housed forty-one heads of cattle, which our family used for milk and currency.

Our compound was one of thirteen Deng family compounds located a thirty-minute walk from the center of the town of Wernyol. Each parcel of Deng land, with their thatched-roof huts, gardens, fences, wells, and grazing fields, created another link in the chain of family properties encircling a central family meeting area. Dozens of other Dinka families had similar groupings of family compounds situated in clusters around the town of Wernyol. Like crooked spokes on a wheel, well-worn dirt paths meandered from each family compound to the center of Wernyol, where thousands of villagers would meet to share meals, news, and gossip, as well as gather for prayers, dance, music, and important ceremonies celebrating rites of passage, such as boys reaching manhood, weddings, and baptisms.

"Be a good girl, Rachel," Mama would say, giving me a small, dull-edged version of Koko's sharp hand hoe, which my grandmother had crafted for me to use during our mornings spent in the garden.

"My name is Achut," I would tell Mama.

"Not anymore," Mama would say.

"My name is Achut?" I would repeat, confusion bending my words into a question.

With a patient sigh, Mama would place down the okra pods she was drying to use in soups and stews during the rainy season. Wiping her hands on her milaya, a colorful, beautifully embroidered sheet she wore wrapped around her body, she'd kneel and cup my small face in her hands. "Your name is Rachel now, little one. Rachel Achut Lual Deng." She'd say my full name, including my baptismal name, my great-great-grandmother's name, my baba's name, Lual, and his baba's name, Deng. Every Dinka child was gifted the names of their babas and their babas' babas. Even after a woman married, like when Mama married Baba, she did not take her husband's name. She retained the names of her family. You could trace a person's paternal lineage through the names that followed their first name. And the names that followed mine were Lual and Deng. Each name created another link to my family, forging an unbreakable chain through the generations that came before me and the generations that would follow.

"Rachel Achut Lual Deng," I repeated. My face scrunched up at the strange, new first name.

"You will get used to it soon enough," Mama would say, and then with a warm smile and no further explanation, she would send me to help Koko harvest potatoes and cassava.

It wasn't until years later that I heard stories of the white men who'd come to southern Sudan decades before I was born, preaching their God's word and persuading the Dinka people that worship of our creator, Nhialic, and our family names would never earn us a place in their God's heaven. They warned the villagers if they did not abandon their names, beliefs, and god, they would be damning themselves and their children to an eternity in hell. The key, they explained, was to choose a name from their holy text, for only biblical names could save us from such a horrible fate. Achut, much to Mama's dismay, was not a name found in their Bible.

So, when I was around three years old, in a baptismal ceremony I was too young to understand or remember, they replaced my great-great-grandmother's honored name with the name Rachel, which my aunt Elizabeth had plucked from one of the many stories found in the missionaries' holy book.

One afternoon, not long after I'd received the name that would grant me access to the Christians' heaven, Koko and I were working in the garden while Mama helped my aunt Amam, whose baptismal name was Monica, milk one of our cows in the cattle hut. Only five years older than me, Monica, who was eight, was more like an older sister than an aunt. Her older brother, my uncle Abraham, had taken the rest of the family's herd to cattle camp, a three-month-long cattle drive, during which time the men and older boys of our village accompanied their herds as they grazed the savannas of southern Sudan. The cattle camps offered an important education for the boys of our village. The majority of children in Wernyol did not attend schools to study reading and arithmetic. Occasionally, families would send one of their children to northern Sudan to receive a formal education, but to afford the schooling, they had to sell their cattle, which for most families was not an option. Girls, who stayed in Wernyol, were educated in gardening, cooking, and child-rearing by the women in their families to prepare them for their futures as wives and mothers, while the boys were taught how to hunt, fish, and care for their families' herds by the men of the village. Cattle camp provided intensive training for the boys and taught them how to be men. Uncle Abraham had left days earlier with our herd. It was his third time attending the annual cattle camp. As the oldest of my baba's younger brothers, Abraham, who was barely thirteen, had been the only father figure I had known in my three years of life. Despite Koko's and Mama's reassurances he would return home, I missed my uncle every time he left.

"When will Uncle Abraham be home?" I asked Koko.

"Your uncle *Garang*," Koko corrected me, using her son's traditional name, "will be home at the end of the dry season." She placed her empty basket in the dirt path between two rows of cassava plants.

During the wet season, when he wasn't talking about Adit, a girl from our village who had caught his eye, Abraham regaled Monica and me with stories of cattle camp. Although I'd never left our home or Wernyol, the stories of Uncle Abraham's months spent walking the southern Sudanese savannas with our herd gave me exciting glimpses of life outside our village. As he described his adventures, I'd imagine myself waking early each morning to pray and milk the cows before heading out with the herds in search of grazing ground. I would daydream of what the world outside Wernyol was like and what adventures and lessons might await me beyond its borders.

"When will that be?" I asked.

Koko drove her hand hoe deep into the ground. "He will return home when the rains come."

Shielding my eyes from the glare of the rising sun, I looked up at the cloudless blue sky. "When will that be?" I repeated.

Koko smiled. "He will be gone for three months."

I slapped at the narrow, palmlike groupings of cassava leaves crowding the sides of the path with my hand hoe. The leaves bobbed and swayed with each strike, but my dull blade left no damage on the plants. "That's too long."

When Monica and I would accompany Abraham to the fields as he tended to our herd, he would lift us onto the cows' backs and show us what he'd learned on his trips, from rubbing the ashes of cow dung, burned in the previous night's fire, into the hides of the cattle to protect them from flies and mosquitoes, to cutting and grooming their horns to grow into the Dengs' signature shape so everyone would recognize them as ours. When his friends visited, we'd listen to them discuss the markings on each bull and cow, and we'd laugh as Koko and Mama scolded the boys when their boastful arguments over who'd won the most wrestling bouts during the last camp devolved into rematches in our gardens. Before we retired to our huts at the end of the day, Abraham would reminisce about the nights he'd spent staring up at the stars, lying beside the crackling fire and the calves of our herd. His face would light up with such joy as he talked, I couldn't help but hope someday, when I was old enough, Uncle Abraham would take me with him when he ventured far from our home. But I would have to wait until I was ten before I would be allowed to join Abraham or any older male family member at cattle camp, and for a restless toddler, seven years felt like an eternity.

I smacked the cassava leaves again and wondered what exciting new things my uncle was experiencing without me.

"Patience, Achut," Koko said. "The wet season will arrive soon enough, and Garang will be home again." She handed me a cassava she'd freed from the soil. I dropped it into her basket.

But it was so hard to be patient, not when I knew Uncle Abraham would return home with another gift for me.

"I named him Majok," Abraham had told me when he'd returned home from his second cattle camp with a small clay bull he'd sculpted for me. It had the signature long, curved horns of the Deng family's herd. "After your baba's favorite bull."

As I watched Koko harvest another cassava tuber, I wondered if Abraham was making me a new clay animal, maybe a cow or calf to go with my bull.

With a frustrated huff, I slapped my hand hoe against another grouping of cassava leaves. Three months was such a long time to wait.

"I know you miss him. We all do, but your uncle had to leave to help our family and village, just like his brothers, including your baba. So, until we see them again, we will hold them in our hearts, just as they are holding us in theirs." Koko wiped away clods of dirt clinging to a cassava she'd dug up and handed the long brown root vegetable to me. "And leave my poor plants alone. Beating on them won't bring the rains or your uncle home any sooner."

"Yes, Koko," I said, putting the cassava in her basket.

As she continued to work the stubborn tubers free from the packed soil with her hand hoe, Koko hummed a song. Its familiar melody brought a smile to my lips and joy to my heart. It was my baba's favorite hymn. He'd told Mama he recited the hymn before every battle between the SPLA and the Government of Sudan (GOS) Army to give him strength and courage on the front lines.

As Koko's firstborn son, Baba, like firstborn sons across southern Sudan, had been forced to enlist in the SPLA in 1983 at the outbreak of the Second Sudanese Civil War. Due to the fierce, ongoing battles between the SPLA forces from the south and GOS forces from the north, Baba had been allowed only one visit to our village to see me, his firstborn child. I have no memory of the short time we spent together. I was only one year old, but Mama and Koko told me how Baba would sing the lyrics of his favorite hymn, 1 Timothy 6:12, as he cradled me in his arms, to remind me of his love and my strength when we were apart.

While Koko hummed Baba's hymn that day and rooted out cassava and potatoes to place in her basket, I followed her like a tiny shadow, scrambling along in the dusty wake of her bare feet as they plodded down the dry dirt furrows of our garden. When she drove her hand hoe deep into the earth, I'd press my dull tool against the ground. When she sang out lyrics from Baba's hymn, I'd mimic her sounds and tones. When she sighed with fatigue, arched her aching back, and wiped the sweat and dirt from her brow, I'd release a dramatic sigh, press my little fists into the small of my back, and wipe the imaginary sweat and dirt from my forehead. In my young mind, Koko and I were a formidable team in the garden. Surely, she could never complete the task of harvesting without me and my trusty hand hoe by her side.

As we continued digging into the hard-packed soil that day, however, I noticed my small hand hoe did not dig as effectively as Koko's. This would not do. So, when Koko placed down her sharp tool to carry the full basket of cassava and potatoes to our kitchen hut, I dropped my inferior tool and grabbed hers. Her hand hoe was much heavier than mine and too large for my small hands. It fell from my grip and landed, blade down, on my bare foot. The sharp edge sliced into the big toe of my right foot, splitting the nail in half and cutting deep into the nail bed. I cried out in surprise and pain.

Koko whirled around and saw blood spilling from my foot. She dropped the basket of tubers and called out my mama's Dinka name, "Agau!" as she pulled me into her arms and hurried from the garden to the fence surrounding our compound.

Mama rushed from the cattle hut. Monica followed close at her heels.

"What's wrong?" Mama yelled. "Is it enemy soldiers?" She stopped short when she saw me cradled in Koko's arms, and her eyes widened at the sight of my bloody foot. "What happened?" she asked, swinging open the gate for Koko.

"She sliced her foot on my hand hoe. I looked away for just a moment, Agau. It happened so fast."

"She'll be fine." Mama reached out to take me, but Koko would not let go. Mama could see the distress in Koko's eyes as she held me tight, and knew the best place for both of us in that moment was for me to remain in Koko's arms. "It's just a cut," Mama said, trying to reassure her mother-in-law. "I'm sure it looks worse than it is."

But Koko was not convinced. She carried me into the kitchen hut and held me on her lap. Monica fetched my clay bull to distract me while Mama tended to my wound.

"Will she lose her toe?" Monica whispered to Mama.

"No, no," Mama said, inspecting the depth of the cut.

"It is a deep wound, but she will be chasing you around again in no time."

Monica squatted beside Mama to get a better look at my injured toe. "Can I help?"

"You can help by finishing up with the milking, Amam," Koko ordered her daughter, using her traditional name.

"Yes, Mama." Monica pressed a quick kiss to the top of my head before hurrying out of the hut to complete her chores.

Mama gently wiped away blood oozing from a tender bit of exposed flesh. Sucking a breath through my teeth, I pulled back my foot.

"Does that hurt?" she asked.

I nodded but allowed her to take hold of my small foot again.

"What a brave girl you are." Mama smiled up at me as she cleansed the blood and dirt from my cut. "You haven't even shed a tear."

"She is brave and strong like her namesake," Koko said, wiping at the worried tears gathering in the corners of her own eyes. "Aren't you, Achut?"

My grandmother could endure her own pain. She had given birth to twelve children, survived the loss of her husband, mourned the deaths of five daughters, had two other daughters marry and leave home, and watched the SPLA take away three of her sons. Her love for her family was as strong and enduring as the White Nile River that flowed through Sudan, but what Koko could not bear was to watch the suffering of those she loved.

Mama finished bandaging my toe and pressed a tender kiss to my forehead. "Her name is Rachel," she reminded her mother-in-law, and before Koko could argue, Mama left to help Monica finish milking the cows.

Alone in the hut, Koko rocked me in her lap and hummed Baba's song. I snuggled my face into the warm crook of her neck and closed my eyes. I breathed deep her scent of cloves and thin leaves, which she added to the cow butter lotion she rubbed into her skin. She rested her cheek on my head. "No matter what anyone tells you, brave little one," she whispered as I drifted to sleep, "your name is Achut. Never forget who you are."

CHAPTER 3

Wernyol, Sudan—1990

Two years after I lost my name, a stranger arrived in our village.

The fighting had escalated over the seven years since the Second Sudanese Civil War had begun. Old alliances began to fracture as whispers of new alliances spread. Disagreements among the leaders in the SPLM/SPLA had led to tensions in the southern military as they struggled to hold back their enemies in the north. The strain on the SPLA troops had kept Baba from returning to our village and family. We had no photos of him, so I did not know what he looked like, but I knew my baba was in the army, and the stranger walking toward our village that afternoon wore a military uniform.

Monica and I were playing with our clay animals, including a new cow and calf Abraham had sculpted for me during his last two cattle camps. We were sitting beside the dirt path leading from our compound to our neighbors' when I spotted the soldier in the distance, walking the path that led to the center of Wernyol. Abandoning my play with Monica and our clay herd,

I ran over to where Mama stood farther down the path, talking with her best friend, Adual. Mama was wearing a vibrant red-and-black milaya. I wore a smaller version of the wrap, which she'd made from the same beautiful material.

"Mama!"

Adual stopped mid-sentence, and both women looked at me.

"Rachel," Mama said. "It's rude to interrupt."

"I'm sorry, Mama, but—"

"Apologize to Adual," Mama said.

I looked up at Mama's best friend. Adual was a tall, quiet woman. She had married our neighbor, a widower, two years earlier and moved in with him and his two children. After only a year of marriage, she received word her husband had been killed in the war. With her husband's death, his children went to live with their mother's family, leaving Adual alone in the hut next to ours. She and Mama had become close friends over the last two years. I liked Adual. Though she had no children of her own, she was kinder and more patient with me and the other children in our village than most. A timid smile graced her lips as she waited for my apology.

"Sorry, Adual."

Her shy smile widened, and she nodded once in acceptance of my apology.

"Now what was so important you had to interrupt our conversation?" Mama asked.

I pointed in the direction of the approaching soldier. "Is that Baba?"

I was eager to meet the man I'd heard so much about from Koko and Mama. Koko always talked with such pride of her firstborn child, and Mama's voice softened with tender affection whenever she spoke of Baba.

"Your baba gave my father *fifty-six* of his finest cows to wed me," she would reminisce with a sigh and smile. "He even gave up his most favorite bull to earn my father's approval."

"His bull, Majok, right, Mama?"

"That's right, which is why he gave you the nickname Majok, because you are now his most favorite."

"More favorite than all our cows?"

"More favorite than all the cows in all of Sudan," Mama would say, stretching out her arms. "In all the world."

My eyes would grow large at such an unbelievable claim. "That's a lot of cows, Mama."

"Yes, it is." Mama would laugh. "And your baba loves you more than all of them."

It was hard for me to comprehend how I could hold such a precious place in the heart of someone I'd only met briefly once and could not remember. I tried to imagine what my baba looked like and how his voice might sound. I'd often dreamed of meeting him someday when the war was over, and hearing him sing his favorite hymn and call me Majok. As the strange soldier neared our village, excitement swelled in my chest.

Mama and Adual looked in the direction I was pointing. The flicker of hope my question had lit in Mama's eyes dimmed at the sight of the soldier. "No, Rachel. That is not your baba."

"Is it Uncle Ater?" I asked.

The SPLA had returned to Wernyol a year after my baba's one and only visit and demanded the second-born sons of every family join the military to swell their dwindling ranks. My uncle Abraham, Koko's second son, should have been taken, but he was accompanying the men and older boys of the village on his first cattle camp. When the soldiers asked where they could find the boys, Koko and the other mothers claimed they did not know the location of the cattle camp or when their sons would be home with their herds.

Frustrated by the women's lack of help and unwilling to waste time searching the savannas for the villagers' second-born sons, the SPLA forced the next-oldest boy in each family to enlist and leave with them immediately for training. My uncle Ater, who was only ten years old, was among the boys taken that fateful day.

Three years after Ater was recruited, the SPLA returned again during cattle camp season. Unable to find Uncle Abraham, they left Wernyol with my uncle Andrew, who was my baba's half brother and only seven years old. The army claimed to be taking the young boys to a military school on the border of Ethiopia to receive a formal education, but news eventually reached our village that after a few short weeks of classes, the boys had been pulled from school and trained for the front line.

Andrew had been gone for several months, but at night, when Koko thought I was sleeping, I still heard her crying and praying for him. She had received no word about the fate of any of her sons since they'd been taken by the SPLA. As the years stretched on, the frequency and fervency of prayers for her sons fighting in the war increased with every whisper of news about battles fought between SPLA troops and the GOS Army.

"No, Rachel," Mama said, the color draining from her voice and face. "That is not Uncle Ater. Go get Koko! Tell her to meet us in the center of Wernyol right away!"

"Yes, Mama."

While Mama, Adual, and Monica hurried to follow the soldier into town, I ran as fast as my small legs would carry me in the opposite direction, to our compound, where I found my grandmother in the garden.

"Koko!" I yelled between labored breaths. "Mama needs you in the village!"

"What's wrong, Achut?"

"A soldier is coming."

"So soon again." Koko dropped her hand hoe and a bag of simsim seeds. The tiny seeds she'd harvested from her sesame plants spilled in a small pile at her bare feet as she looked around for Monica. "Where's Amam?"

"She went with Mama and Adual."

Taking hold of my hand, Koko hurried from our compound, down the two-and-a-half-kilometer-long dirt path that led to the center of the village.

By the time we arrived, news of the soldier had traveled through all the family compounds surrounding the village. Hundreds of men, women, and children had walked from their homes to gather in the center of the town, drawn from their work by curiosity and concern about the soldier's reason for visiting Wernyol.

We joined Mama, Adual, and Monica beneath a stand of large thëp trees. The trees' sprawling branches and thick foliage provided shade for the villagers clustered beneath them. We sat among a group of women who were speaking in tense, hurried whispers. Several of them were shaking. A few were crying. Mama sat silently next to Adual. Chin lifted and back straight, she stared at a hut at the far end of the village.

Koko sat down beside her, and Monica moved over to sit in front of her mother.

"Where is he?" Koko asked.

Mama did not look away from the hut. "He is speaking with the elders."

Koko nodded. "Has anyone seen the list?"

"No."

Koko reached over and placed a hand on Mama's arm. "Then all we can do is wait." She stared at the elders' hut. "We will know soon enough."

I did not understand what everyone was waiting for, but I could see the tension in their bodies and the fear in

Mama's and Koko's eyes. Their unnamed fear frightened me, and I began to cry.

Mama lifted me onto her lap. "Don't cry, Rachel. Everything will be all right." She wrapped her arms around me and pulled me close. I wanted to believe her words, but the fear shaking her body shivered through mine.

A tense hush fell over the gathered crowd when the door of the hut opened. Everyone watched in silence as the elders and soldier made their way to the center of town.

They stopped beneath the thëp trees, and the soldier unfolded a piece of paper. He cleared his throat and glanced out at the crowd of anxious faces. He didn't look much older than Uncle Abraham, and his voice cracked when he spoke.

"The following brave soldiers gave their lives in service to the SPLA in recent battles with the GOS Army."

Mama's hold on me tightened. Koko closed her eyes. Whispered prayers trembled on her lips as the soldier read out the first names.

"Mabior Mayen Rïng.

"Kuol Mayen Rïng.

"Marial Zarouq Bol.

"Alier Akol Nhial.

"Dut Akol Nhial."

Heartrending wails of mothers, falling to their knees at the sound of their sons' names, filled the air. Wives cried out in despair when they heard the names of their husbands. The new widows clung to their children and to one another in shared pain.

With each name and cry of grief, Mama's breathing hitched, but she did not look away from the soldier. I glanced at Koko, searching for some explanation or reassurance, but her eyes remained squeezed shut as she recited her prayers.

When he had read two dozen names, the soldier paused and looked up from the list. "Those are all the names of the soldiers killed in action."

Mama let out a muffled cry, and Koko paused in her prayers. She took hold of one of Mama's hands and nodded.

"I will now read the names of those wounded in action," the soldier continued.

Koko closed her eyes again and resumed her prayers, but she did not let go of Mama's hand as the soldier returned to his list.

"Jok Dhuka Bior.

"Thon Chan Ajang.

"Chol Agar Dit.

"Lual Deng Ater."

Mama gasped.

"My son's hurt?" Koko interrupted the soldier.

The young man looked up from his list. "Is your son Lual Deng Ater?"

"Yes," Koko answered. "He is my eldest child."

The soldier referred to his paperwork.

"Lual Deng Ater suffered two bullet wounds," he read, "one to the leg and one to the shoulder. He sustained additional injuries when the military vehicle transporting him to a field hospital flipped. He was thrown from the vehicle and landed in a swamp, where he suffered a python bite to his leg."

Mama covered her mouth in horror. "But he's alive?"

"At the time of this report," the soldier said, "Lual Deng Ater was listed as wounded, not dead."

The tension in Mama's body deflated, and her head and shoulders collapsed under the weight of her relief. Trapped in her arms, I squirmed to break free.

"Your baba is alive, Rachel," she whispered. "He is alive."

As the soldier continued reading the names of the wounded, Koko prayed not to hear the name of her son Ater, or the name of her stepson Andrew, both of whom had been recruited into the SPLA when they were just boys, and both of whom she loved dearly. The women of Wernyol seldom received news of their sons and husbands fighting for the SPLA. Occasionally, a soldier returning home for a short visit would relay news of other men and boys whom they'd fought alongside in battles, but most of the time, families were left with only silence and their imaginations to fill in the long waits between updates. When a soldier with a list arrived at the village, however, everyone prayed not to hear their loved ones' names. It was a case of "no news is good news," and Koko was praying the soldier brought no additional news of her missing sons.

The soldier finished reading the names of the wounded. Ater and Andrew were not among them. Koko said one final prayer of thanks before opening her eyes.

"The soldiers I named as wounded are being treated at a military hospital in the town of Torit," the soldier explained. "One woman from each soldier's family is ordered to travel to Torit to help care for their injured husband or son. I will accompany the women on foot to Pawel, where a military vehicle is waiting to transport you to Torit. The drive will take nine hours, so bring water and food for the trip." He checked his watch. "I am leaving in thirty minutes. Be back here before then if you plan to join me."

"You should go, Agau," Koko told Mama. "Lual will need your help to heal from so many injuries."

Mama looked down at me. "What about Rachel?"

"I will watch over Achut while you are gone," Koko said, standing up. "She will be safe with me. Come. Amam and I will pack you some food and supplies for the trip. You will need to leave right away."

While Monica filled and corked dried, hollowed gourds, called aduɔks, with fresh milk, water, and peanut paste, and Koko packed strips of dried beef, aduɔks of dehydrated corn kernels, dried medicinal leaves, and an extra milaya

31

in a handwoven sack for Mama's trip, Mama walked me to the garden. She held my hand and did not let go when we stopped in a section of freshly planted soil.

"Rachel," she said, kneeling before me, "I have to go away for a while. Baba is hurt and needs me to help him heal."

I stared down at my bare feet. Though the deformed nail on my right big toe showed the severity of the accident with Koko's hand hoe two years earlier, Mama's care had kept any infection from taking hold and helped heal my wound. She would do the same for Baba. If anyone could help heal Baba, it was Mama, but I didn't want her to go. My chin quivered at the thought of her leaving.

Mama had never left me before. All my life, she had been there. Her smile was the first to greet me every morning, and her lips were the last to kiss me good night before I drifted to sleep. Her hands had tended to every cut and scrape I'd suffered from the moment I'd learned to crawl to the moment I'd started to run. Her voice had reached out to me in the dark of night with gentle reassurances when fear gripped my imagination, and her arms had embraced me with warmth and love when sadness gripped my heart. Mama was my heart, and I was hers.

Tears spilled down my cheeks. "Can I go with you?"

"A hospital is no place for a child, Rachel."

"But I can help."

"You can best help by being the brave girl I know you are and staying here with Koko. She will need your help in the garden and preparing meals for Aunt Monica and Uncle Abraham when he returns home. You are her best helper. Can you do that for Baba and me?"

I cast my eyes to my bare feet and nodded. Fresh tears, like the first, intermittent drops of rain before a storm, fell onto the dirt. "When will you be home?"

"When Baba is better."

I watched a line of small brown ants scurrying over a mound of freshly dug earth, one of many Mama and I had packed down while planting sunflower seeds a day earlier. Row upon row of the mounds lined the far edge of the garden. Mama had told me those little seeds would push up from the soil and grow four times taller than me in just three months' time. I couldn't imagine anything could grow that tall that fast, accept maybe Uncle Abraham, but I believed my mama, and I had been excited about marking the sunflowers' growth with her.

Maybe, I thought, *when she comes home, she will bring Baba, and we can all watch the sunflowers grow together, as a family.*

"When will he be better?" I asked, delighted by the sudden prospect of having both my parents with me.

"I don't know," Mama said, sadness pinching her words. She cupped my face with her free hand and tilted my chin so I had to look into her deep brown eyes. "As soon as Baba is well, I will come home." She wiped the tears from my cheeks and wrapped me in a tight embrace. "Don't cry, Rachel. I promise. I will come back to you."

Koko appeared at the edge of the garden with the sack of supplies for Mama's trip.

Mama gave me a final, loving squeeze before releasing me. I grabbed hold of her hand, not ready to let her go. Koko smiled at us, but it held no happiness. Koko would miss Mama, too. "Take care of my son," she said, handing Mama the sack.

Mama tried to smile but failed. "I will." Fighting back tears, she surrendered my small hand to Koko. "Watch over my daughter."

Koko held my hand tight. "Always."

CHAPTER 4

Wernyol, Sudan—November 1991

The sunflower seeds I'd planted with Mama grew several feet above Uncle Abraham's head. The flowers had blossomed with long, silky petals in cheery shades of yellow surrounding round centers packed tight with brown seeds. After they reached their tallest height, the flowers bowed their weighty heads, dropped their seeds, withered, and died. Monica and I helped Koko gather the seeds and replant them in our garden, and still, Mama had not returned.

In the weeks after she'd first left to care for Baba at the military hospital in Torit, I'd ask Koko every night before bed when we'd see Mama again. Her reply was always the same: "We must trust in God's plan, Achut."

I assured her I did, and it wasn't a lie. Not exactly. I did trust in God's plan. I just didn't understand his timetable. What could be taking Mama so long? She had cleaned and bandaged my hurt foot in a matter of minutes. It had taken only weeks for it to heal. How much longer could it take for her to help Baba get better?

Every few months, a new, strange soldier, with a new

list of names, would visit our village. Sometimes, he left with more young boys to replace the names on his list. For each visit, I sat with Koko and Monica as they prayed not to hear the names Ater, Andrew, or Lual on the list of the dead or the name Abraham on the list of the new recruits. Abraham was sixteen now, much older than many of the boys who'd been forced into the ranks of the SPLA, but Abraham had been fortunate. Every time the SPLA returned to Wernyol, looking for new recruits, he'd been accompanying our herd on the village cattle drives and avoided detection and forced conscription, but Koko feared it was only a matter of time before Abraham was discovered and she lost another son to the SPLA and our bloody, never-ending civil war with the north.

After each soldier's visit, we returned to our work at the Deng family compound. I did everything Mama had asked of me and more. She had said it was the best way I could help Baba heal, and I wanted him better, so Mama could come home. Each morning, when the first blush of sunlight kissed the endless horizon of the night, I woke and followed Monica to the cattle hut to help her milk the cows. When we were done, I'd grab my hand hoe and join Koko in the garden to assist with any planting or sowing. As the sun reached its zenith in the cloudless blue sky, I'd help Koko and Monica prepare the food for dinner. Some days, if there wasn't much to do in the garden, I joined Abraham on his walks around the perimeter of our property, to inspect the fencing and watch him mend any damaged sections or patch any holes.

It was important work that required vigilance, for there was no lack of predators and scavengers in southern Sudan. Villagers were in a constant battle to protect their cattle from wild dogs, leopards, hyenas, cheetahs, and lions. It was dangerous enough to travel beyond the borders of the village in the light of day, but everyone knew you did not leave the safety of the fencing encircling your family's compound after sunset. The moon and stars provided little guidance in the dark of night for one to see where to safely walk. Cobras and vipers hid in tall grasses, crocodiles lay in wait just beneath the dark waters of swollen rivers and lakes, and pythons coiled in the shadows of their muddy banks, ready to strike any bare feet that wandered too close.

In the quiet of night, before sleep pulled you under, you could hear the scratchy rustlings of wild dogs charging through fields of Sudan grass in pursuit of their next meal, the deep, guttural roars of lionesses taking down their prey, and the high-pitched, hysterical yips of hyenas fighting over the remains of some other predator's kill. When the sounds reached my ears on my mat in the thatched-roof hut I shared with Koko, I prayed to God, thanking him for the protection of my family, home, and our dogs, Alel and Panyliap.

Koko's baba had given her Alel, a large black dog, six years before I was born. The old dog slept at her feet every night. When I was four, Koko gave me a brown-and-white puppy she'd found abandoned and near death on her walk home from town. I had been playing outside, attempting, unsuccessfully, to sculpt a small lump of clay into a cow, when Koko placed the puppy in my arms. She named him Panyliap, which means "the world turned upside down." Curled up in my lap, the orphaned puppy nuzzled his small nose under my arm and fell asleep. He was so tiny and malnourished, Koko worried he might not survive, but like the sunflower seeds, Panyliap flourished under our care. Two years later, he stood taller than me. When my loyal dog was not helping Alel protect the cattle in the fields with Uncle Abraham during the day, Panyliap curled up beside me at night to keep me safe from any harm.

Lying in the darkness, my thoughts often returned to Mama. My heart ached in her absence. Burrowing my fingers into Panyliap's fur, I'd close my eyes and listen for the slow, steady rumbling of Alel's snores and the familiar words of Koko's whispered prayers. I'd let the calming sounds cocoon me from the frightening noises outside our hut. With Koko and our dogs snuggled close, I would eventually drift to sleep without fear of the wild animals prowling the darkness beyond the borders of our home.

But I was only six years old and did not know there were far more dangerous predators than lions and leopards lurking in the darkness of southern Sudan. I was unaware that Koko and Abraham had been shielding Monica and me from conversations about politics and the war. I was ignorant of the news, passed from village to village in the nervous whispers of adults, that Riek Machar had returned to his Nuer community and was amassing a rebel militia of adolescent boys to attack Dinka villages north of Wernyol. I knew nothing of his plan to send his rebels south into Twic East County, in an attempt to capture SPLA leader Dr. John Garang's home territory of Bor. I did not understand it was those growing concerns that kept Koko tossing and turning at night. I did not notice her burying her worries beneath our daily routines and hiding her fears behind forced smiles. I did not see Koko's struggles to take an increasingly imperfect world and make it perfect for me for just one more day.

They attacked at night.

Koko woke me with the first sounds of gunfire.

"Come, Achut!" She pulled me up from my mat. "We must go!"

"Where?" I asked, rubbing the blurriness of deep sleep from my eyes.

"There's no time for questions. Come with me!" The darkness in the hut hid Koko's face, but I sensed her fear in every frantic word she spoke and flinched at the sound of the loud, rapid pops of guns firing in the distance.

The familiar scent of sandalwood filled the air. Koko kept pieces of the fragrant wood in each of the huts. She loved the scent, and so did I. It smelled of home. But that night, another scent permeated the darkness. Smoke.

Without another word, Koko pulled on her cream milaya, dressed me in the red-and-black milaya that Mama had made me, and rushed me from our hut. Panyliap and Alel followed close at our heels, their heads low and hackles raised. Uncle Abraham and Aunt Monica were waiting outside the hut they shared. The gunfire had yanked them from their sleep as well.

"What's happening?" Monica asked.

Abraham squinted into the darkness. "Is it the Nuer?"

"Yes," Koko said. "There were Nuer attacks in Duk County a couple nights ago."

Duk County was located to the north, not far from Wernyol. Koko and the elders of our village had heard news of the battles between the Dinka of Duk County and the Nuer rebels. "They'll be after the herd, Garang," Koko told her son.

It was nearing the end of the wet season. The rain-soaked soil squished and slid beneath our bare feet as we hurried across the compound to the cattle hut. Between volleys of distant gunfire, the low bellows of our forty-one cattle rumbled behind the hut door.

"Hurry!" Koko ordered Abraham as she glanced north, her eyes wide with fear. "We must drive them into the fields."

Monica held my hand as Koko and Abraham entered the hut and worked their way behind the sleepy herd, clapping their hands loudly, waving their arms, and shouting. The startled herd shifted, pressing up against one another in their confusion until the first bull breached the open door and ran out into the fields. The rest of the herd followed.

When the cattle hut was cleared, Koko and Abraham rejoined Monica and me by the closed fence gate. Koko lifted me into her arms. The sound of gunfire was drawing closer, and it was now accompanied by screams and desperate cries. I covered my ears against the deafening noise. Koko tightened her hold.

Glints of moonlight chased the trails of angry tears streaming down the hard lines of Abraham's face as he watched the herd he had tended to for most of his youth disappear in the darkness of the open field. "That should keep the rebels busy for a while," he said.

Flashes of bright light dotted the dark horizon as another volley of sporadic gunfire tore through the night air.

"Let's hope so," Koko said.

Uncle Abraham fetched a long wooden stick with a sharp knife fastened to the end, which he used as a spear for fishing and hunting. He gripped the spear with both hands, stepped back into a fighting stance, and aimed the point of the knife in the direction of the approaching threat. "Take Monica and Rachel and run, Mama. I will protect our home."

Koko grabbed the spear from her son and threw it to the ground. "No, Garang. This is not a fight you can win."

News of Machar leaving the SPLA and building a

militia had monopolized conversations between the village elders for weeks, but no one knew when or what his rebels' next move in the war would be. Early rumors circulated in the area that the Nuer rebels were only interested in stealing cattle from Dinka villages, and though everyone agreed losing their livestock would be devastating, it was preferable to losing their lives.

When word had reached Wernyol of the attack on the neighboring village of Duk County, it was followed by the disturbing news that the focus of the Nuer attacks had broadened. They were no longer only stealing the Dinkas' cattle, they had started killing the Dinkas' teenage sons and abducting their teenage daughters. Koko was aware of the rumors and was not going to wait to see if they were true.

She handed me to Abraham. "Carry Achut. We must go. Now."

"Where?" Monica asked.

"South."

Without another word, Koko opened the gate and led Monica, Abraham, and me through the protective fencing surrounding our home. Alel and Panyliap followed. Koko's old black dog stayed by her side while Panyliap kept pace with Abraham's long strides.

Over Abraham's shoulder, I watched my home fall farther away. The sharp, rapid pops of bullets firing ripped through the darkness as angry voices barked commands over panicked cries for help and mercy. My eyes stung with tears, and though the night air was warm against my skin, shivers seized my body. Like venom, fear spread through my veins with every panicked heartbeat. My breaths came short and shallow. Panyliap's cold nose butted against the bottom of my bare foot. I looked down at my furry, faithful protector, grateful he was with me as we fled our home.

By the time we had reached the dirt road leading south from our village, thousands of men, women, and children fleeing Wernyol had joined us. I recognized some of the voices, but it was difficult to make out faces in the dark. Adjusting his hold on me, Abraham turned his head to search the growing crowd of people behind us.

"Don't look back," Koko ordered. "It will slow your steps."

Tears glistening in her big brown eyes, Monica placed a hand on her brother's arm. "Adit will be all right. Her family will have fled with the others."

Abraham nodded. He had made no secret of his interest in Adit, a fifteen-year-old girl from our village. I had met Adit a few times when she had joined Abraham and other teenagers from the church choir at our homestead to practice their hymns. Monica loved to tease Abraham when she caught him staring longingly at Adit or showing off in front of her. She told me she thought Abraham would one day ask to wed Adit, even though Koko would not entertain the idea of her sixteen-year-old son marrying anyone for several more years.

The volume and frequency of the gunfire behind us

increased as we walked, and the glow of growing flames pulsed on the northernmost edge of our village.

"If we are to survive," Koko told her son, the hard edge of her voice softening, "we must keep moving forward."

"Yes, Mama." Securing his hold on me, Abraham picked up his pace, but moments later, he was glancing behind us again.

Despite Koko's warning, I, too, looked back, but not in search of Adit or anyone else. Fear kept pulling my gaze back to our homestead. With every step Abraham took, our home grew smaller and more distant. Tears spilled from my eyes and fell onto Abraham's bare shoulder.

"Don't be scared, Rachel," Abraham said, squeezing me tight. "Everything will be all right."

I wanted to believe him, but what would happen when Mama came home? How would she find us if we were not there waiting for her?

How would she find me?

As we continued to walk down the narrow dirt path, I stared at the four thatched-roof huts, carefully tended gardens, and sprawling fields of the Deng family compound until the darkness stole it all from my sight.

It was the last time I ever saw my home.

CHAPTER 5

Wernyol, Sudan—November 1991

The pursuing Nuer rebels spurred the villagers into a panicked run. The dirt path connecting Wernyol to Pawel, a village to the south, was too narrow for the frightened crowd, pushing and shoving their way to the front of the line. Several men, who had refused to leave their cattle behind to be stolen, drove their herds off the path. The bulls pressed their large bodies through the tall Sudan grass and thick vegetation, creating a trail for the men to walk.

With our home no longer visible, Koko stepped from the dirt path to follow the men and their cattle.

"Where are we going, Mama?" Monica asked.

"It is not safe to walk out in the open," Koko answered. "We must travel through the forest and hope the rebels do not follow."

Abraham and I nearly collided with Monica when she stopped short. She stared at the dark expanse of tall, densely packed trees standing between us and Pawel. There was no safe path to follow through the forest. The tight spaces between the trees were overgrown with grasses, shrubs, and underbrush. "We can't go in there at night," Monica told Koko. "It's too dangerous."

"We have no choice, Amam," Koko said, taking her daughter by the hand. "It is more dangerous to remain out here."

Night was darker in the forest. Light from the moon and stars could not penetrate its heavy foliage and high canopies. Despite Koko's warning that our home was no longer safe, I wanted nothing more than to return to the confines of our compound. I imagined being back in our hut, safe and secure on my mat with Koko and Alel on one side and Panyliap curled up next to me.

Instead, I walked beside Abraham, holding tight to my uncle with one hand and the scruff of Panyliap's fur with the other, my eyes struggling to make out the silhouettes of the people walking all around us. Stumbling through the forest, we navigated the darkness by listening for the sound of bare feet treading over the grass and underbrush. But Monica was right. It was too dangerous to be outside at night.

Because we were not the only ones in the forest listening in the dark.

Beyond the frantic whispers of villagers and the rustle of feet tripping over the uneven ground and tree roots that had broken the surface of the forest floor, the familiar sounds of wild animals stalking their prey reached my ears. The darkness amplified their every breath, step, and growl, making it impossible to determine their location.

Afraid some unseen predator would hear us, I tried to walk quietly, but it was impossible to do so and keep up with Abraham's long strides.

I bit down on my lip to keep myself from crying. The salty tang of blood touched my tongue. Ahead of us, I heard a deep growl rumble in Alel's throat as he walked alongside Koko and Monica. Beside me, Panyliap echoed Alel's warning with his own low, angry growl. Had they heard a pride of lionesses prowling through the underbrush behind us or a cheetah's coiled body shifting in the branches above our heads? My panicked mind could not help but wonder what unfortunate creature was about to become these predators' next prey.

Somewhere in the darkness ahead of us, a woman screamed. It was the first of many voices to cry out, only to be suddenly silenced, as we continued our walk through the dark forest. Their cries were followed by vicious growling and thunderous roars. It was then that I realized the moment we had stepped into the predators' hunting ground, we had become their prey.

Behind us, the sound of fighting grew louder. Looking back toward the village, the flash of bullets firing could be seen through small gaps between the trees. The rebels were getting closer. The cattle and belongings we'd left behind had done little to slow them. They were not here for our possessions. They were here for us.

Despite the darkness and wild animals, the villagers started to run. The men who'd driven their herds into the forest spurred them forward. The frightened cattle charged through the dense foliage, trampling anything and anyone in their way. More than one child fell beneath their stampede of hooves.

Abraham pulled me into his arms as a startled bull charged past us. "I've got you, Rachel," he said, holding me close.

"Stay together!" Koko yelled over her shoulder as she lifted Monica into her arms.

We pressed forward, but all around us terrified voices cried out as families were torn apart in the chaos.

"Mama!"

"Baba!"

"My child! I can't find my child!"

The voices bled into one another, filling the darkness, as mothers, fathers, and children called out for lost loved ones. But we could not stop. The constant crack of guns firing behind us kept our feet moving, despite the unseen dangers lurking ahead. We stumbled blindly forward, hoping we were still heading south and praying we were not the next person to fall beneath a stampede of cattle, step on a poisonous snake, find ourselves surrounded by a pack of wild dogs, or be chased down by a hungry pride of lions.

Clinging to Abraham, I squinted into the darkness, trying to find Koko and Monica. It was then I realized Panyliap was no longer by my side.

"Panyliap!" My voice joined the others screaming for

their lost family members. "Panyliap!" I cried, hitched sobs breaking my voice.

No answering bark or yip met my ears, and no cold nose pressed against my foot.

The gunfire grew louder and more rapid. The rebels had entered the forest.

Koko stopped. I thought she was looking for Alel, who was also missing, but she put down Monica and grabbed me from Abraham's arms. "Take your sister and go!"

"What?" Abraham said, disbelief siphoning the strength from his voice.

"I'm slowing you down. Take Amam and run!"

"Mama, is this a good idea?" Abraham asked.

"There's no time to argue, Garang," Koko told her son. "Go!"

Abraham reached out for me. "I can carry Rachel."

"No," Koko said. "You won't be able to run with two little ones on your hands."

"But, Mama—"

"The rebels are not coming for me and Achut, Garang. They have no use for the old and young. They will not hurt us. We will be fine. But you won't. If they catch you, they will kill you and abduct your sister. You must run! Take her now and go!"

"No!" Monica cried, clinging to Koko. "I'm not leaving you."

Gunfire and screams tore through the forest, and the acrid smell of smoke pressed through the foliage.

Koko grabbed Monica's arm and shoved her toward Abraham. "Take your brother's hand, Amam, and run. Do not look back!"

Abraham grabbed hold of his sister's hand. "We will find you when it's safe," he promised, and then he and Monica sprinted into the darkness.

CHAPTER 6

Pawel, Sudan—November 1991

Death stalked our every move. Koko and I tried to keep pace with the other villagers, but my legs were too small and my strides too short. I tripped over exposed roots and thick clumps of grass. After my second fall, Koko lifted me into her arms and carried me until she could no longer bear my weight. When she put me down, she grabbed hold of my hand.

"Don't let go, Achut."

I held tight to Koko's hand and ran as fast as my legs would carry me, but no matter how fast we ran, a steady stream of terrified villagers continued to flow past us, fleeing the forest and its predators. Koko and I fell farther and farther behind, until the rustling of bodies pressing through the dense vegetation before us grew distant. It was then, between the sporadic pulse of gunfire and the desperate cries from fallen villagers, I first heard their voices.

The Nuer rebels.

As they pursued us through the forest, they yelled to one another. Though I could not understand their words, the excitement in their voices and the sharp edges to their tone sliced through the darkness like pangas, the lethal machetes they carried.

Behind us, to our right, a man's voice cried out for help in Dinka. The taunting voices of rebels quickly descended upon him. As the man begged for his life, a dog barked. It was the fierce, warning bark of a dog protecting its owner. Panyliap used the same bark anytime a wild animal ventured too close to our hut at night. Darkness hid the man and his dog from my sight, but I could imagine the scene. The injured man cowering on the ground, desperate and frightened, as the armed rebels approached. The dog, his hackles raised, ears pinned back, and teeth bared, standing between his owner and the rebels threatening him.

In the flash of my imagination, the brave dog protecting his owner had brown-and-white fur, like my Panyliap. My labored breathing hitched at the thought of my dog, lost in the dark, surrounded by predators. Struggling to keep pace with Koko, I prayed Panyliap had escaped the forest and the dangers lurking there and was waiting, safe and unharmed, for me at home.

Behind us, the barking grew louder, more ferocious, burying the man's pleas.

The flash of a muzzle and two gunshots punctured the darkness.

The pleas and barking fell silent.

My legs froze. I turned and stared back in the direction of the shooting.

Please bark, I thought. *Please bark.*

But the only sounds to reach out from the darkness were the rebels' laughter and the steady padding of their footsteps drawing closer.

"Come, Achut," Koko whispered. "Before they find us." She gathered me into her arms and ran.

As I clung to Koko, tears burned in my eyes for the man with his unanswered pleas and the loyal dog protecting his owner, and hatred burned in my chest for the rebels with their cruel guns and even crueler laughter.

Koko carried me until we reached the edge of the forest. Her skin slick with sweat and her chest heaving with quick, shallow breaths, she eased me to the ground.

My knees buckled. It took two unsteady steps before I found the strength to stand.

Gunshots continued to echo through the night. I glanced back as a fresh wave of fear surged through my body with the realization that, though we had escaped the dangers of the forest, we had not escaped the rebels.

Koko grabbed my hand. "We must keep moving. Can you run for a while?"

I nodded.

Her dark eyes held mine, and a small but reassuring smile graced her lips. "We'll be all right, Achut. I promise."

I nodded again, afraid if I opened my mouth to speak, I would cry.

"That's my brave girl."

But I did not feel brave. I couldn't stop shaking, and my legs were weak with fear. I flinched with each pop of bullets exploding from their chambers, and I didn't want to run anymore. I didn't want to move anymore. I wanted to cover my head and close my eyes. I wanted my home and my hut and my dog, but more than anything, I wanted my mama. It had been over a year since I'd watched her leave to help Baba. I had tried to be brave in her absence. Baba had needed her, but I needed her, too. I needed her to hold me in her arms. I needed her to tell me everything was going to be all right. I needed to hide in her embrace, to feel her warmth, and smell her scent, until the sun drove the rebels, darkness, and death away.

I needed her.

But I could not tell Koko I needed Mama, because Koko needed me to run, so I ran.

We continued south. Gentle light from the moon, diffused through wispy clouds stretching high across the night sky, leached all color from the world, leaving only hazy outlines in deepening shades of grays. Far ahead, we could make out the silhouettes of a sea of people flowing through clusters of thatched-roof huts and Dinka family farms.

"That's Pawel," Koko said, giving my hand a reassuring squeeze. "We'll find help there. Just a bit farther, Achut."

Hope lifted her words and strengthened my strides. Koko had promised we'd make it to Pawel, and we had.

A fresh volley of gunfire tore through the forest behind us. I glanced back as the first rebel stepped from its shadows, his gun raised. He was followed by line after line of armed rebels spawning from the darkness.

"Don't look back, Achut!" Koko said, pulling me along the dirt path toward the village.

By the time we reached the first grouping of huts on the outskirts of Pawel and joined the mob of people fleeing, the rebels were close enough that I could see their faces and bodies in the muted moonlight. Like Uncle Abraham and the other Dinka boys from our village, their heads were shaved, except for a circle of short hair resting on the tops of their heads like crowns, and their faces still retained the roundness of youth. Though they carried weapons like the SPLA soldiers who visited our village with lists of names, these warriors did not wear military uniforms, and no heavy boots adorned their feet. Ragged shorts, torn pants, and tattered shirts hung from their tall, lean frames, and bare, calloused feet pounded the ground as the rebels charged into the village. The only indicator that they were Nuer were the six raised, horizontal lines stretching across each rebel's forehead, traditional markings from the scarification ritual every thirteen-year-old Nuer male underwent to mark their transition into manhood. If not for the unique markings on their foreheads and deadly weapons in their hands, the rebels looked just like us, and if you were close enough to see the rebels' markings in the dark of night, it was too late for you to flee.

As the rebels infiltrated the crowd of hundreds fleeing the village, the darkness and chaos made it impossible for me to determine who was Dinka and who was Nuer, who was my friend and who was my enemy.

Only when they raised their weapons and fired did the distinction become clear.

The crowd scattered after the first shot. People pushed and shoved to get away from the rebels and their guns. Many people fell. Some were brought down by the stampede of bodies. Some were felled by bullets. Rebels dragged screaming women into huts while others beat elderly villagers with the butts of their rifles or cut them down with their pangas.

Pawel was no longer safe.

Koko's grip on my hand tightened as she fought to navigate us safely through the sea of people. My fingers hurt, but I didn't dare pull my hand free.

"Where are we going?" I asked as we followed the crowd out of the town.

"We must keep going south until the rebels stop chasing us or until we find SPLA troops to help."

I didn't know how far it was to the next village and prayed we wouldn't have to walk through another forest to get there.

Gunfire pursued our every step. Struggling to keep pace with the fleeing villagers and outrun the rebels, we passed the last hut on the outskirts of Pawel when another bullet fired in the darkness and Koko fell.

No one had bumped into us, so I assumed she had tripped. Distracted by the gunfire and rebels, I did not see the gaping wound from where a bullet had torn through

Koko's calf, nor did I notice the blood streaming down her leg.

"Are you hurt?" I asked, helping her to her feet before we were knocked to the ground by the frantic villagers running past us.

"No," she answered, favoring her right leg. "I'm fine."

Holding hands, we started to walk again, but Koko's steps were slowed by a noticeable limp.

More bullets ripped through the crowd behind us. Koko glanced back at the rebels, slowly stalking the people of Wernyol and Pawel, like dogs herding cattle.

I pulled on Koko's arm, urging her forward. "Don't look back."

After several pained steps, she led me from the mob of fleeing villagers, off the narrow dirt path, and toward a cluster of trees. "I can't go any farther, Achut."

"But you said we had to keep moving south."

"I know," Koko said, "but I need to rest awhile." Clutching my hand, she hobbled under the low branches of a large tree. Time and weather had hollowed the old tree's massive trunk. She led me inside the narrow opening, where we crouched low together, tucked away from the view of any rebels passing on the dirt path.

The inside of the old tree smelled of damp and rot. The stench tickled my nose, and I started to sneeze.

Koko clamped a hand over my nose and mouth and held a finger to her lips.

"You cannot sneeze," she whispered. "You cannot cry. You cannot make a sound, or they will find us."

Rubbing the bridge of my nose to quell the sneeze, I nodded.

The young rebels sang and laughed as they sauntered down the dirt path in their unhurried pursuit of the Dinka villagers fleeing Pawel. When the largest group of rebels had passed our hiding place and their voices had faded, Koko whispered, "When the rest are gone, we will walk back to Pawel."

I shook my head, afraid to leave our hiding place. The rebels had not spotted us, even when they were only meters away. It was a good hiding place. I didn't want to risk leaving it.

While we waited, Koko examined my feet. They had swelled during our run through the forest, and cuts and abrasions marred the painfully tight skin. Koko carefully peeked her head outside the hollowed tree. Glancing back at me, she held her hand up, signaling me to stay hidden, and then raised a single finger to her lips. I nodded.

Crouching low, Koko crept out from the tree over to a nearby bush. Scraps of torn material, ripped free from one of the fleeing villagers, clung to the bush's thorny branches. Koko untangled the material and then knelt by a villager lying on the muddy ground just past the bush. From the hollowed tree, I could not tell if the villager was a man, woman, or child. Their body lay stretched out at odd angles on the wet ground, their face buried in the mud. Koko bowed her head and said a hasty prayer above their still body before removing the cowhide coverings from their feet and hurrying back to our hiding place. She tore the soiled cloth into two long strips and wrapped them around my sore feet. She then tried to secure the cowhide coverings over the bandages, but my feet were still too small. Tossing the coverings outside the hollowed tree, Koko took me into her arms.

Grimacing against the pain in her hurt leg, she whispered against my ear, "We will hide in one of the huts back in Pawel, where we can lie down and rest."

"What if the rebels find us?" I asked, my voice trembling with fear.

Koko shook her head. "They'll continue to follow the villagers south, just like they followed us from Wernyol. We'll wait out the night in a hut, and in the morning, help will arrive."

I looked south, down the path, to the villagers fleeing the armed rebels, and then I looked north to the villagers who'd been unable to escape the rebels' bullets. They lay sprawled along the dirt path that cut through Pawel. The same dirt path Koko and I had just traveled. Death had not claimed all the people who had been cut down in the barrage of gunfire. Some still moved, writhing in pain, or trying to crawl to safety, but most of the bodies lay motionless on the ground. From the shelter of our tree, I could not tell if they remained still out of fear or if death had taken them, too.

I watched as the last of the rebels walked by their fallen prey. Their steps were leisurely, and their gaits swung with the confidence of unchallenged predators. A few young rebels set the thatched roofs of huts lining the main path ablaze with burning sticks. They did not loot the homes first or check to see if they were empty. They did not stop when an anguished chorus of screams from men, women, and children trapped inside cried out for help. They did not even stay to watch them burn.

The rebels were not warriors seeking out enemy soldiers on a battlefield. They were not predators stalking their next meal, nor were they prey fighting for survival. They were a force of nature unleashed on our villages. They were a wildfire in the dry season, sparked by heated political rhetoric, fed on the tinder of mistrust and lies, fueled by hate and prejudice, and spread on the winds of war. They swept through our villages devouring everything and everyone in their path and leaving only death and destruction in their wake.

As I watched the last of the rebels follow their comrades out of Pawel in pursuit of the fleeing villagers, I knew Koko was right. It was dangerous to keep walking in the dark, and the sun wouldn't rise for hours. I was tired, and she was hurt. Our only choice was to find a hiding place to wait out the night. We carefully made our way back into the burning village of Pawel. Koko shielded my eyes as we navigated through the minefield of massacre victims.

"Don't look," she said, but her voice caught in shock and grief at what she saw, and I feared no matter where we hid or how long we waited, there would be no escaping the growing inferno burning through southern Sudan.

CHAPTER 7

Pawel, Sudan—November 1991

I followed Koko to her sister-in-law's hut on the northern edge of Pawel. From the cover of the cornfield separating two family compounds, we waited and watched the three huts and gardens for nearly thirty minutes before Koko deemed there were no rebels in the area and it was safe to approach one of the smaller huts.

She raised her fist and released a long, slow breath before knocking gently twice and calling out in Dinka, "Awak, are you in there?"

After several seconds of silence, a female voice replied, "Abul? Is that you?"

Koko's shoulders lifted and fell in a relieved sigh. "Yes," she said, smiling down at me. "It is me and my granddaughter, Achut. May we come in? We need a place to hide."

A tense exchange of whispered words inside the hut was followed by the shuffling of feet and the scrape of something large being moved on the other side of the door. The door opened a few inches. I could see the slice of a man's face through the narrow crack. His eyes scrutinized Koko before dipping lower to look at me.

"Are there any rebels around?" he asked.

"No," Koko said. "They followed the villagers south."

"Let them in," a voice whispered from inside the hut.

The man opened the door just wide enough for us to enter. Koko pushed me inside first and then followed. The man quickly closed the door behind us and began barricading it with large pieces of wood.

Ten adults and two children huddled in the darkness in the center of the home. The boy looked to be my age. The girl was no older than two.

"Thank you," Koko whispered, addressing the group. "We had nowhere else to go."

One of the women stood and swept her arm toward a bare portion of the dirt floor next to her. "Of course," she said in a quiet voice. "Please, come sit down."

Still holding fast to my hand, Koko hobbled toward the woman.

The woman's forehead creased with worry. "Abul, you're hurt."

"It's nothing I can't tend to." Koko lowered herself gingerly to the ground. She took hold of the bottom of her milaya and tore a strip of cloth from her wrap. "Come, Achut."

I knelt beside Koko as she inspected her right leg. Blood ran down her ankle and foot in crooked streams from a small hole on the inside of her calf.

The man who had opened the door sat down next to Awak. "Did the bullet go through?"

"I think so," Koko said, carefully inspecting a larger exit wound on the other side of her leg.

"Koko?" I asked. "You were shot?"

"It's nothing to worry about," Koko said, looping the length of cloth around her right thigh, just above the knee. "But I need your help to tie this. Take hold of the ends."

I took the ends of the strip in each hand. The material was wet with Koko's blood.

"Pull as hard as you can," she said through shallow breaths. "It needs to be tight enough to stop the bleeding."

I looked up at her, tears welling in my eyes.

"You can do this, Achut. I know you can."

I yanked the strips of cloth as hard as I could in opposite directions.

A quick intake of breath hissed through Koko's clenched teeth. Her eyes squeezed shut and every muscle in her body tightened, but she did not cry.

"I'm sorry, Koko," I whimpered.

After a moment, she let out a long, ragged breath and opened her eyes.

"It's all right," she whispered. "You did well." Keeping the ends of the cloth pulled taut, she took them from me, and, crossing them again, she fed one side through a loop she'd created and, with a firm pull, finished the knot. The flow of blood from the bullet wound slowed. A feeble smile wavered on her lips. "See. All better."

Koko was not the only person in the hut suffering from a gunshot wound. An elderly woman had a cloth tied tight around her upper left arm to stanch the bleeding from two wounds caused by rebel bullets. One had torn through her forearm. The other had shattered her elbow. The arm hung limp by her side as she leaned against an elderly man caring for her.

Across from us, a young woman knelt over a man lying on the ground. She was crying as she pressed a large wad of cloth into his side. Both the cloth and ground were dark with blood. The man's whole body shuddered with each pained breath he pulled through his pale, trembling lips, and blood gushed from his wound with each weak exhale. I wondered, as I watched the young woman work to stop the bleeding, why she didn't tear a strip of her milaya and tie it tightly around the man's waist, like Koko or the old woman had above their bullet wounds, but as the expanding puddle of darkness crept across the dirt floor, I doubted there was enough cloth, even if we used all our milayas, to stop that much blood.

"Are you sure the rebels are gone?" the man next to Awak whispered to Koko.

Koko shook her head. "We saw many leave, but some may be hiding in other huts."

The man folded his hands in his lap and bowed his head. "Then we will stay here and remain quiet until morning, and we will pray that God will send the SPLA by then."

Everyone nodded in agreement to his plan and prayer.

Koko pulled me onto her lap and wrapped her milaya around us both. "Remember, Achut," she whispered against my ear, "we cannot make a sound. We must be patient and silent."

I nodded and snuggled against Koko's chest. She rested her cheek atop my head, but the harder I tried to stay quiet, the louder every small sound grew. Her heartbeat pounded against my face. The tense silence amplified my every breath. And any movement—a shift in someone's position or stretch of a leg or arm—grated against my ears, rubbing away what little courage I had left. When the two-year-old girl grew restless in her mother's arms, I wanted to scream, "Be quiet!"

Didn't she know the rebels might be listening? Didn't she understand the danger her whining could lure to the hut?

But as the night stretched on, it wasn't the singing or laughter of rebels we heard outside. Drawn to Pawel by the scent of blood, the growls of wild dogs and yips of quarreling hyenas filled the night air. As the scavengers fought over the dead and dying, Awak's husband quietly crept over to the hut door and added another piece of timber to the barricade.

I covered my ears against the sounds outside the hut, and Koko held me tighter.

"We just have to make it through the night," she whispered against my small hand. "We just need to survive until morning." She pressed a kiss to my hand and, rocking me gently, began to pray.

In the darkness of the hut, I heard the whispered prayers

of other voices, including the young woman still pressing the cloth into the bleeding man's side. When the toddler began to fuss again, the mother gave her hungry daughter her breast. She let her nurse for hours. It was the only way to keep her quiet.

As I watched the toddler in her mother's arms, I thought of Mama and wondered where she was and if she was thinking of me. I thought of Uncle Abraham and Aunt Monica. Had they been with the villagers running down the dirt path? I wondered if they had passed the tree where Koko and I had hid or if they were huddled together in one of the huts of Pawel, silently praying for morning to come and wondering what had happened to Koko and me.

Night and the sounds of death stretched on for what felt like days. When the frenzied sounds of the scavengers dragged my imagination into dark corners where thoughts of Abraham, Monica, and Panyliap, lying among the fallen villagers, spawned, I pressed closer to Koko and listened to her strong heartbeat.

Lub-dub.

Lub-dub.

Lub-dub.

Lub-dub.

I focused all my attention, every thought on the beat pulsing deep in her chest.

Con-stant.

Car-ing.

Lov-ing.

Ko-ko.

I concentrated on the rhythm, repeating the pattern in my weary mind until every other sound in the world disappeared and Koko's heartbeat was all that remained. My eyes grew heavy under the reassuring repetition of my grandmother's heart and the rhythmic rocking of her warm lap. Eventually, all thought and fear dissolved in the haze of sleep.

I don't know how long I slept or if Koko slept at all, but when I woke, she was smiling down at me, her dark eyes glistening with unshed tears.

"We survived until morning, Achut," she whispered.

I squinted toward the door. Planks of wood still barricaded us inside, but beneath the door, a shaft of soft hibiscus-red sunlight reached toward us. I smiled.

It was the most beautiful light I had ever seen.

CHAPTER 8

Pawel, Sudan—November 1991

"Can we go home now?" I asked Koko.

She cupped my face in her hands. "Not yet, little one," she whispered. "We must wait here a while longer."

"How much longer?"

"Until the SPLA arrives," Koko said.

"When will they get here?"

"Soon, I hope. Until then, we need to be patient."

"Will Baba be with them?"

Koko smiled and kissed the top of my head. "That's enough questions for now," she whispered. "We have to stay quiet, remember?"

But I was tired of being quiet. I wiggled around on her lap, trying to find a comfortable position.

"Stay still, Achut," Koko whispered.

"I need to pee. Will you take me outside?"

"We can't go outside. Not yet."

"But I really need to go," I whined, bouncing on her lap.

Koko glanced around the hut. The sunlight stretching beneath the door provided enough illumination to better see the people hiding with us. The other children were sleeping, even the fussy toddler, but most of the adults were awake. They sat on the dirt floor, silent and still, their eyes staring toward the door, waiting. The only adult who was not awake was the bleeding man on the floor. His eyes were closed, and he was no longer writhing and moaning in pain. He was as still and silent as the others. The young woman, who had been pressing the cloth to his side all night, sat beside him, holding his hand. She was no longer crying. She stared at the door, her eyes wide and unblinking.

"Koko," I whispered. "I have to go . . . now." I bit down on my bottom lip, afraid if she didn't take me outside right away, I would have an accident in front of everyone. My cheeks warmed with embarrassment at the thought.

Koko leaned close to Awak. "Do you have an empty bowl or aduɔk Achut may use?" she whispered in her sister-in-law's ear. "She has to go."

Awak glanced at me, pity pinching her brow. She nodded and handed Koko a bowl.

Koko placed the bowl in my lap. "Use this."

I looked around at the people in the hut. No one was paying attention to Koko or me, but I still did not want to pee in front of them. "Can't I go outside? I'll stay close to the hut."

"No," Koko said, her voice firm. "It's not safe."

"But it's morning."

"You are not to leave this hut until the SPLA arrives, Achut. Do you understand?"

"Yes, Koko," I whispered.

As the sunlight burning beneath the door warmed from simmering red to blazing white, the rest of the sleeping villagers in the hut began to stir. All except the man with the bleeding side. His eyes remained closed.

After a whispered discussion between a few of the other men and the young woman holding the sleeping man's hand, the young woman leaned down, kissed the man's forehead, and let go of his hand. She watched through tears as the other men carefully lifted the sleeping man into their arms and carried him from the hut. He never stirred or opened his eyes, and when the men returned minutes later, their arms were empty.

"Why did they leave him outside?" I whispered to Koko. "You said it's not safe."

"He did not survive until morning," Koko answered, sadness weighing down her words. She hugged me closer. "He is with God now. Nothing and no one can hurt him anymore."

I did not question Koko further. Back in our village, I had heard Koko and Mama talk about people who had died. Relatives and family friends. Young and old. Some taken by time. Some by disease. Too many by the war. But I had never been so close to a dead person before, and even though the man had been left outside the hut and out

71

of view, I could still see his face and closed eyes and was struck by how much death looked like sleep.

Only two other people left the hut that day. As morning stretched on and no SPLA soldiers arrived, two women snuck over to the larger hut on the compound, where Koko's sister-in-law kept her cooking supplies. They hurried back with a bundle of burning sticks and a basket full of corn. Lighting a fire in the center of the hut, the women placed the ears of corn directly into the flames. During the chaos and carnage of the attack the night before and the long hours of anxiously awaiting for help to arrive the next day, fear had left no room for thoughts of hunger and thirst. My stomach complained in rumbling growls at the smell of the roasting corn. I was so hungry, I would have eaten the corn raw, but I waited quietly on Koko's lap as the women cooked. When the kernels had browned, Awak removed the ears of corn from the fire and gave one to each person in the hut. The tender kernels burst with sweetness in my mouth as I bit along the cob. When we'd finished eating, we returned our cleaned cobs to the fire and continued our silent vigil of watching the hut door and waiting for the SPLA.

As the sunlight beneath the door dimmed from bright white to the dark orange of dying embers, our hope, which had buoyed our spirits at dawn, also dimmed, and my fears of the dangers that would return with the night resurfaced.

"What if they don't come before dark?" I asked Koko.

Koko rested her cheek on the top of my head and sighed. "Then, together, we will make it through another night, Achut. Together, we will survive until morning."

As night fell over Sudan, the women doused what remained of the cooking fire with handfuls of dirt from the floor, and darkness once again filled the hut. Cuddled against Koko's chest, I closed my eyes and listened to the comforting rhythm of her heart. Its steady beat was just pulling me toward sleep when another sound outside the hut yanked me back.

It was a voice calling out in Dinka.

My eyes popped open. I strained to listen, trying to make out what the voice was saying.

"Do not be afraid! We are here to help!"

"Come out!" a second voice yelled in Dinka. "We are with the SPLA!"

I twisted in Koko's lap to tell her help had arrived. It was night, and they were late, but the SPLA was finally here.

I'd expected to see my excitement over the joyous news reflected in Koko's face, but instead, her brow was furrowed with concern. She held a single finger pressed against her lips, and as she stared into my eyes, she slowly shook her head.

The voices outside grew louder as they drew closer to our hut. "If you are injured, we can help you!"

Confused by Koko's reaction, I looked to the other people in the hut. They all wore the same expression of fear and concern. I did not understand. We had been waiting in this hut for the SPLA to arrive all night and day. Now they were here, and no one was moving.

"It's safe to come out!" the voices said. "We will protect you!"

I started to stand, but Koko held me firm in her lap and shook her head again.

Outside, another voice answered, "Over here! Please, we need help! My father is wounded."

Seconds later, the same voice cried out in fear, and gunfire ripped through the village.

We sat in the dark huddled together, listening as the rebels lured people from their hiding places with lies spoken in our language. They took no prisoners and left no witnesses. And when their lies no longer worked, they started going from hut to hut in search of Dinka villagers.

At some huts, they kicked in the doors before firing inside. At others, they didn't bother with the doors. They stood outside and shot their bullets through the hut walls.

As the voices drew closer, Koko began to rock me and silently recite her prayers, asking for God's protection.

God must not have heard her over the gunfire and screams. I covered my ears with my hands to quiet the deafening sounds.

"Come out if you want to live!" a voice outside our hut door yelled in Dinka.

No one moved. No one even breathed.

I flinched at the pounding of bodies ramming into the

door. The hastily constructed barricade of wooden beams shook with every kick of the rebels' feet outside.

Bam!

Bam!

Bam!

I pressed my hands tighter over my ears but could not block out the sound of the rebels fighting to enter our hiding place. Finally, the barricade failed, and the door swung open. The shadowy figures of men holding rifles stood in the breached doorway.

It was the only exit. There was nowhere to run. Nowhere to hide.

The rebels aimed their guns into the hut, and Koko pulled her milaya over my head.

She held me tight against her chest and wrapped her body around me like a protective shell. She wanted to shield me from seeing the worst of people. She wanted her scent to be the last I smelled and her words to be the last I heard.

"You are strong," she whispered against my ear.

From the protection of her arms, I heard desperate voices cry out for mercy.

The rebels answered with bullets.

I don't know how long they fired their weapons inside the hut. Koko's body jerked once and her tight hold loosened, but she remained bent over me, shielding me from the rebels and their bullets. Time lost all structure in the terror. Seconds stretched into minutes, and minutes into hours. And then, as suddenly as it began, the gunfire stopped.

I remained hidden, waiting for the rebels to leave. When their voices and footsteps faded into silence, I peeked out from beneath Koko's milaya.

I squinted into the darkness. The hut was so quiet. I could not see the others.

I looked up at my grandmother. "Koko," I whispered. "Is it safe now?"

She didn't answer.

She couldn't.

CHAPTER 9

Pawel, Sudan—November 1991

Time shattered with the firing of the rebels' guns, leaving me only fractured memories of the two days that followed. Each jagged shard, with its razor-sharp edges, remained lodged deep in my mind and heart like shrapnel.

Koko's unblinking eyes staring down at me.

The waning warmth of her embrace.

The sudden stiffening of her body, unforgiving and unyielding.

The traumatized tears of the boy sitting across the hut.

The anguished moans of the survivors.

The silence of the others.

And the toddler's piercing cries, unending and unanswered.

Fearful that the baby's screams would draw the rebels back to the hut, I burrowed deeper into Koko's lap, hiding again beneath her milaya, breathing in the scent of sandalwood, cloves, and thin leaves. Seeking sanctuary in memories of home.

Closing my eyes, I pressed my ear to Koko's chest, searching for the soothing rhythm that had guided me safely through the previous night, but the only sound I found was the ragged breath of my own fear.

Sunlight crept beneath the closed door of the hut twice more before we were discovered. Distant gunfire and explosions heralded the return of voices outside. They called out in Dinka, just like before, and just like before, they promised help.

"Is anyone here?"

"Call out if you can!"

"We're with the SPLA!"

Behind the voices, the sounds of a fierce battle rumbled in the distance.

I peeked out from Koko's milaya. No one in our hut spoke. No one moved.

The boy and I locked eyes. The toddler had crawled over to him in the night. After several restless hours, she had fallen asleep in his lap, but the voices outside stirred her from her slumber. The boy tried to rock her back to sleep, but she wailed out in hunger. He covered her mouth with his hand, but it was too late. The hut door swung open, and a man holding a rifle stepped inside.

He wore the same camouflage uniform and army-green beret as the soldiers who had visited our village over the last several years with their lists of names. Hope bloomed in my chest. The SPLA had come, just like Koko had promised.

The soldier stood frozen in the center of the hut, his eyes wide in horror as he took in the brutal scene before him. He was tall and thin, like Abraham, but unlike my uncle, many years had wrinkled the skin surrounding the soldier's weary eyes and hues of gray tinted his short black hair, as well as the stubble on his face. He spotted me peeking out behind Koko's milaya and lowered his weapon. As we stared at one another, two more soldiers entered the hut.

The youngest took a step back at the sight and mumbled a prayer beneath his breath.

Red and gold stripes adorned the collar of the third soldier's uniform. "Any survivors?" he asked.

"Three children," the older soldier replied, "and a man and woman."

"Grab whoever is alive and can walk, but hurry! The fighting is getting closer." Then he turned and exited the hut.

As the young soldier checked on the boy and toddler, the older soldier slowly approached Koko and me. He knelt beside us. Sunlight, streaming in from the open door, glistened on trails of tears streaming down his cheeks. "It's going to be all right." He reached out for me.

My gaze traveled from his tears to the six raised, horizontal scars lining his forehead. I pulled away from his outstretched hands and ducked back beneath Koko's milaya.

"Don't be scared." The soldier slowly lifted my cloth

covering. Fresh tears shone in his eyes. "I'm here to help. Are you hurt?"

I shook my head.

His scarred brow furrowed in disbelief as he stared at my milaya. "Are you sure?"

I nodded.

He started to lift me into his arms, but I held tight to Koko.

"We're going to take you somewhere safe," he said, "but we have to hurry."

"What about Koko?" I asked.

"I'm sorry," the soldier said. "She's gone. There's nothing we can do to help her now."

I didn't understand. Koko's eyes were not closed like the man the others had left outside the hut. She had survived until morning. We both had. We had waited quietly until help arrived, just like Koko had said we should.

"No," I argued. "Koko's eyes are open. I am staying with her."

The battle raging in the distance grew louder.

"She's dead," the soldier stated, leaving no room for misunderstanding or hope.

I stared at him. He was wrong. He had to be. My mind went blank, and my body grew numb. I cannot recall the sights and sounds in that hut in the moments that followed. Everything faded into nothingness. Everything except one smell.

Blood.

Its scent, like rusted metal after a soaking rain, hung in the still air of the hut. I pressed closer to Koko, seeking her comforting scent, but all I could smell was blood. It clung to everything and everyone, even Koko.

The soldier lifted me from her lap. As he carried me across the room, my eyes remained locked on Koko, waiting for her to follow, waiting for her to stop him, but she did not move and she did not speak.

On the other side of the hut, the young soldier was holding the crying toddler and explaining to the six-year-old boy that his parents were gone. The boy did not argue as I had. He did not say a word.

"I need the baby's milaya," the older soldier told his younger SPLA comrade.

"Why?"

The older soldier jutted his chin toward me. "Her milaya is soaked in blood."

I looked down at my favorite milaya, the one that matched Mama's. It was stained dark red.

"Is it her blood?" the young soldier asked.

The soldier holding me glanced behind us. I followed his gaze to where Koko remained, hunched over and still. Darkness stained her milaya and pooled beneath her.

"No," the soldier said, angling me so I could no longer see Koko, "but she can't wear this. The smell will draw predators."

Explosions trembled in the air outside the village.

The soldier holding the toddler hurried over to where

the child's dead mama lay and quickly removed her juɔk, a long cloth mamas used to secure their babies to their chests. He then removed the little girl's milaya. "Change her into this," he said, tossing the milaya to the older soldier. "But hurry," he added, wrapping the juɔk around the toddler. "Or none of us is getting out of here alive."

I stood there, in the middle of the hut, staring at Koko as the older soldier quickly removed my bloody milaya, tore the baby's clean milaya into a single strip of cloth, and wrapped it around my waist to make a hasty covering. He then turned to a man and woman lying on the floor. Like me, they were covered in blood. Like Koko, their eyes were open.

"Can you walk?" the soldier asked.

"No," the man said in a weak, breathy voice.

"Leave us," the woman said through her tears. "Take the children and go."

The soldier did not hesitate. "We'll send help when we can," he told the couple as he lifted me into his arms.

"No!" I screamed. "We can't leave Koko!"

"She's gone," the soldier repeated. "I can't save her, but I can save you."

"You're lying," I told the soldier. "Look! Her eyes are open! She is not dead."

"That happens when a person dies," the soldier said. "Their eyes remain open until someone closes them."

My shocked gaze traveled from Koko's blood-soaked milaya to her lifeless eyes.

"Can you close her eyes?"

Gunfire and cries for help echoed outside the hut.

"I'm sorry," the solder said. "There's no time."

"Please don't leave her!" I cried as the soldiers carried the boy, the baby, and me to the open doorway. I reached out for my grandmother. "Koko!"

But she did not look up or reach for me.

She did not move.

She remained seated on the floor, her unseeing eyes staring at her empty lap.

As the soldier carried me from the hut, I could no longer escape the painful truth. The soldier had not lied to me. I had lied to myself. For two days and two nights, I had refused to accept the reality I now knew to be true.

My koko was dead.

We walked south for hours in the rain, fleeing the battle raging between the SPLA and Machar's rebel militia just north of Pawel. While their comrades fought back the rebels, four soldiers escorted us to Paliau, a town occupied by the SPLA. One soldier carried the toddler, who was too young to walk on her own. The other three soldiers and six men and women, whose injuries from the massacre were not severe, took turns carrying me and the other eighteen children they'd rescued from Pawel. The rain muffled our footsteps and hid our tears.

My swollen, cut feet ached with every pained step,

causing me to limp along behind the others. As I walked, the cloth strips Koko had gently wrapped around my feet when we'd hidden in the hollowed tree began to unravel. I tried to fix them, but I didn't know how. Clutching the soiled, torn rags in my hands, I sat on the muddy path and cried.

They were gone. Panyliap, Alel, Monica, Abraham, Baba, Mama, Koko. I did not know if I would ever see them again. I did not know if they had all been killed by the rebels, like Koko. Sitting in the pouring rain, there were only two things I knew for certain.

My family was gone.

And I was alone.

The older soldier with the Nuer markings on his forehead rushed over to where I sat. He held a young boy, who he'd been carrying for several kilometers.

"You must keep up," he ordered.

When I did not respond, he put the boy down and told him to catch up with the others.

"What is your name?" the soldier asked me in a gentler voice.

"Rachel."

"This is not the time to cry, Rachel." He glanced back in the direction of the heavy artillery and gunfire. "There will be time for tears later, but for now, if we are to survive, we must hold on a bit longer. Can you do that for me?"

I stared at the bandages in my lap.

The Nuer soldier knelt before me and spoke in a voice

heavy with the burden of his own grief. "You need to keep going, Rachel. Can you do that for your koko?"

With tears in my eyes, I looked up at him and nodded.

Fighting back his own tears, he placed my bandages on the side of the path and lifted me into his arms.

CHAPTER 10

Paliau, Sudan—November 1991

Word of the massacres in Wernyol and Pawel reached Paliau before our small, weary group trudged into the Dinka town early the next morning. Stories from survivors passing through as they fled south, combined with the constant sounds of battle raging in the north, had spurred many of Paliau's villagers to leave with the growing groups of refugees. I wondered if Uncle Abraham and Aunt Monica were among them. The remaining villagers, who had chosen to stay behind, opened their homes to us, offering what little food and shelter they could spare.

The battle between the SPLA and the rebels continued for days. At night, the sound of explosions echoed through the darkness. During the day, thick columns of white smoke were visible north of Paliau. Yet, despite the constant reminders of the war, I felt safe in the care of Paliau's villagers and under the protection of the SPLA soldiers.

Over the next two days, our SPLA guardians gathered what little information they could about the children they had rescued in Pawel, including our names and the names of our families and villages.

The older soldier with the Nuer markings added my parents' names to his list.

"We're going to inform the SPLA in Torit that you were rescued in Pawel, Rachel, so they can notify your parents that you are safe."

I didn't know how long it would take for the soldier's letter to reach my parents, or how long it would take Mama to walk from the hospital in Torit to Paliau, but I knew she would come for me as soon as she could, just as she'd rushed to Baba's side when he needed her help. She would find me, and then we would go home. I just needed to be patient and wait with the soldiers and villagers in Paliau for her to come for me.

The next morning, dozens of battle-weary SPLA soldiers arrived with troubling news of the war. They had lost their battle with the Nuer rebels and could no longer hold back the enemy forces marching on Paliau. Everyone in the village was ordered to evacuate.

Rumors of the events that had precipitated the rebel attacks dominated hurried conversations as villagers frantically collected what few possessions they could carry from their homes. They mentioned the name Riek Machar often as they spoke. I did not know who Riek Machar was, but his name was spoken with fear and anger, and words like "blame," "traitor," and "murderer" accompanied it in every mention, even among the SPLA soldiers. I didn't learn until years later about the high-ranking position Riek Machar had held in the SPLA and how his decision to break from their ranks and form a new, Nuer-led faction of the army had led to the devastating events, which had irrevocably changed the lives of so many people in southern Sudan, including mine.

As the soldiers urged us to hurry with the evacuation of Paliau, tensions ran high and trust fractured among the Dinka and Nuer soldiers in the SPLA, who had served on the front line of the Second Sudanese Civil War against the GOS Army for years. Following Riek Machar's split from the SPLA and the attacks on Dinka villages at the hands of his rebels, the SPLA soldiers suddenly found themselves questioning the loyalties of their brothers-in-arms. Dinka soldiers worried about their families and villages and wanted to return to their homes to protect their loved ones from the rebels. Nuer soldiers worried about the Nuer defectors and struggled with facing a new enemy on the battlefield, an enemy born from their own villages and families.

The soldiers argued about the next best course of action. Following a heated exchange, they agreed their only option was to walk the survivors to the Pinyudo Refugee Camp in Ethiopia, where we would be safe from Machar's rebels and the GOS Army.

I did not understand how far or dangerous the journey would be, but I knew I did not like the plan to leave. I needed to wait in Paliau for Mama. Every step I took away from danger also took me farther away from my home and family. If I followed the soldiers to Ethiopia, if I left

Sudan, how would Uncle Abraham and Aunt Monica find me when it was safe again? How would Mama find me when she received the soldier's letter about my rescue in Pawel? If given the choice, I wanted to stay.

But I was six and I was not given a choice. The rebels were coming. To escape their guns and pangas, we had to leave. To survive to see another morning, we had to keep moving.

As night and the rains fell once again over southern Sudan, we began our two-day walk south to the town of Bor, where the SPLA said we would rest for a few days before continuing our trek across southern Sudan to Ethiopia. With the addition of the new SPLA soldiers and Paliau villagers, our small group of twenty-six refugees grew to almost two hundred. I overheard soldiers telling villagers that the walk to the refugee camp would take months. Stories of people who'd attempted the walk and never reached Ethiopia ran rampant among the villagers, but the soldiers assured us our large numbers would deter most wild animals from attacking and promised to use their weapons to protect us from any predator foolish enough to try. For added security, the SPLA armed any man healthy enough to walk on his own and strong enough to carry and fire a rifle. As we left Paliau, our protectors took their positions at the front and the back of the line to lead the way and make sure no one fell behind.

We walked in silence. The only sound announcing our

presence was the soggy squelch of nearly four hundred bare feet and military boots trudging in a long, single-file line along the narrow, rain-soaked path. The scabs on my feet tore free in the first kilometer. The mud stung as it pressed into the newly opened wounds with every squishy step, but I kept walking. We all did.

The adults took turns carrying the children. Every kilometer, they would put down the child they were carrying and pick up another. A young soldier, no older than nineteen, alternated between carrying me and another boy. He and many of the young SPLA soldiers, who'd fought the Nuer rebels near Pawel, had been sent to the region from the SPLA military school on the border of Ethiopia. Most had never fired a weapon until they faced Machar's rebels in Pawel. The horror of those battles haunted them on our walk. It was evident in their trembling hands as they gripped their weapons and in their vacant eyes as they scoured the darkness for danger.

But not my soldier. If he was scared, he shielded me and the other children from his fear with reassuring smiles and a calm voice. He was tall and lean. His back and arms must have ached from carrying us over so many hours and kilometers, but he never complained. I stared at his face as he carried me. His kind eyes held great sadness. When he caught me staring, he would smile, but the pain never left his eyes. He looked too young to be a father, but he must have had younger siblings or young nieces and nephews back home because he was so patient with us children. He reminded me of Uncle Abraham. As I walked beside the soldier, I thought of the many walks I had taken with my uncle to check the fencing around our family compound. And when the soldier lifted me into his arms, the memory of my uncle carrying me through the forest the night of the attack whispered in my mind: *I've got you, Rachel.*

I liked the soldier with the kind smile and sad eyes, so I remained close to him during the long walk and prayed when we reached the safety of Bor, Uncle Abraham and Aunt Monica would be waiting for me.

The driving rains softened as we reached the Dinka village of Manydeng. After twelve hours of walking, our stomachs were hungry, our clothes were drenched, and our bodies were exhausted. The rebels pursuing us, however, did not have the burden of the elderly, the injured, and children slowing their pace. They continued to gain on us, so stopping for a day or two, in order to recover our strength, was no longer an option. We stayed in Manydeng just long enough to rest our tired feet, refill our water and milk supplies, and eat whatever the generous Manydeng villagers had to spare. But even when we were not moving, my body could not rest. My senses were always alert, listening for danger, ready to run.

More villagers joined us when we left Manydeng. Dark clouds hung in heavy sweeps across the morning sky as our SPLA escorts led over three hundred men, women, and children south toward Bor. I remained by the young

Dinka soldier's side the whole walk. He became my protector.

By late afternoon, we reached a wide river. As we stood on its muddy banks, my soldier pointed across the water.

"It's not much farther. We'll be to Gakyuom by evening. We can rest there for the night. Then it is only another twenty kilometers to Bor." He smiled down at me. "We're almost there, Rachel."

I looked to my right. The swift-moving river flowed until it disappeared over the horizon. I looked to my left. The river stretched just as far in the opposite direction. It would take us days to walk around it.

An older SPLA soldier with red and gold bars sewn onto the collar of his uniform addressed the villagers. "We have to cross the river."

Anxious whispers skittered through the crowd. The river had swelled during the rainy season. I stepped closer to my soldier, leaning my weight against his leg.

As I stared at the water, an old woman reached over me and grabbed hold of my soldier's sleeve. The fabric of a yellow milaya brushed across my face. I peeked up at her from beneath her milaya, but she did not look down at me. Her eyes were locked on the young soldier, whose sleeve she clutched.

Tears followed the crooked paths of her wrinkled skin, and her voice trembled when she spoke. "I don't know how to swim."

The soldier gave her hand a gentle, reassuring squeeze. "Don't worry. We will get you across."

The old woman smiled tentatively, but her tears did not stop as she released her hold on his sleeve.

There were far more villagers than soldiers in our group. Many admitted they, too, could not swim. It would take time for the soldiers to help us safely cross the swollen river, and with the rebels in pursuit, time was not a luxury we could afford. Panic seized the crowd. I pressed closer to my soldier.

The commanding officer attempted to calm everyone's fears. "One of my soldiers scouted ahead. The water is not deep here, but the current is strong." He paused to make sure he had everyone's attention. "Walk slowly and stay on your feet. If the current takes you, we won't be able to help."

Several people stepped away from the river. There had to be a safer way to get to Bor. Behind us, like distant thunder, explosions rumbled beneath the clouds. The constant reminder of the threat hunting us across southern Sudan lured the villagers back to the riverbank. Given the choice between certain death at the hands of the rebels and possible death in the currents of the river, they chose to take their chances in the water.

The SPLA officer waved his soldiers forward. "Carry as many children as you can."

One by one, we entered the river.

CHAPTER 11

Gakyuom, Sudan—November 1991

My soldier lifted a boy, who looked to be around three years old, onto his back so the boy's mama could attempt to cross the river without the extra weight of her son.

He glanced over his shoulder and smiled at the frightened toddler. "Hang on tight."

The boy wrapped his small arms around the soldier's neck, and the soldier pressed a hand on the boy's back to secure him in place.

I held my breath as the soldier entered the river. Within two steps, the water reached his waist and lapped at the feet of the boy he was carrying.

I took a tentative step toward the edge of the water. I did not want to be left behind, but just like the old woman, I could not swim. If I tried to walk across the river, like my soldier, the water would be far above my head. Mama and Koko had warned me from the time I could walk to stay away from the rivers. The waterways of southern Sudan were feeding grounds for poisonous snakes, crocodiles, and pythons. Staring into the murky waters separating me from the safety of Bor, I didn't see any snakes or crocodiles, but I knew they were there, lurking just beneath the surface, waiting to strike.

My soldier glanced over his shoulder to where I waited on the riverbank. "Don't worry. I will carry you, too."

Assuming he planned to take the little boy across and then return for me, I stepped away from the edge, but instead, my soldier twisted his torso toward me and leaned down, so his bent arm holding the toddler on his back was within reach. "Grab on to my arm and lock your fingers together."

I stretched up on my toes, looped my arms around his bicep, and intertwined my fingers.

"Lock them tight."

I squeezed my fingers together.

"Whatever you do, Rachel, no matter what happens, do not let go. If you do, you'll be lost. Understand?"

I nodded and tightened my grip as he pulled me off the riverbank. He walked cautiously, testing each step before shifting his weight from his back foot to his front. Within minutes, the river reached his chest and was creeping toward the toddler's shoulders and splashing around my jaw. I lifted my chin as high as I could to keep my nose and mouth out of the water, but my ears dipped below the surface, and the water rushed in, drowning out the panicked cries and desperate screams of the others struggling in the strong currents.

Despite their best efforts to stay on their feet during our crossing, many succumbed to the river. All around us, people slipped beneath the water, never to resurface. Men and women. Young and old. Soldiers and villagers. The river did not discriminate.

"Don't look," my soldier told us as the river pulled a man beside us under. "Just hold on. If you keep holding on, you'll make it to the other side."

Carrying the boy and me on his arm and back, the young soldier trudged through the rising waters, navigating past the drowning people reaching out for help. As we neared the middle of the river, an old woman struggling in the current grabbed the soldier's arm. She wore a yellow milaya. She held tight to his arm and pulled down, fighting to break free from the river's hold.

The soldier lost his footing and stumbled to the side. Water flowed into my mouth and nose as my head dipped beneath the surface, but I did not let go. The soldier lurched forward, pulling my head free from the river. I surfaced, choking and coughing, terrified the woman clinging to the soldier's arm would drag us down again. The boy on the soldier's back cried out for his mama.

The soldier dug his feet into the riverbed and leaned into the flow of water, fighting to stay upright against the pull of the river and woman. The muscles in his arms and neck strained as he fought to keep us all above the surface. His entire body shook from the effort. A frustrated scream tore through his throat as the old woman and river began to pull us down. His hand holding the boy on his back trembled as he stared into the woman's terrified eyes. "I'm sorry," he said.

Looking away, he wrenched his arm free, and she was gone.

He adjusted his hold on the boy and me and stepped forward. "I'm sorry," he repeated to no one and everyone as he continued across the river. "I'm sorry."

Nearly three hundred of us entered the river that day. Barely two hundred and fifty escaped its swollen waters and unforgiving currents. I was among the lucky ones who survived the crossing. The SPLA commander, who had led us from Paliau, was among the missing.

My soldier lifted the little boy and me onto the river's muddy banks before pulling himself to safety. All along the riverbank, soldiers and villagers broke free from the water's pull. Some lay on the ground, struggling to reclaim their lost breaths. Others stood on the edge, scouring the river's surface for missing loved ones. Voices, hollow with disbelief, and cries, raw with grief, filled the air.

"He was right beside me."

"She's gone!"

"Mama!"

The rebels, who had chased us from Paliau, stood on the other side of the river, arguing among themselves. Occasionally, one would fire at us across the water, but they made no move to enter the river.

"Start walking!" my soldier ordered the survivors.

Those who had not lost anyone to the river formed a line behind three armed soldiers and began walking south. Reluctantly, others followed.

A young woman remained behind, pacing beside the river, searching its waters.

My soldier approached her. "We need to leave."

"But my mama," she cried. "I can't find her."

"Whoever is missing is missing," the soldier said, pulling her away from the river and the rebels firing at them from the other side. "We have to go."

I thought of the old woman in the yellow milaya I saw slip beneath the water and wondered if she was the young woman's mama. As the young woman continued to frantically search the swiftly moving water, I realized even if the old woman wasn't her mama, she was someone's, and now she was gone, just like my koko. To survive, we had to leave her behind.

Tears streamed down the young woman's face as she glanced back to the river one last time before joining the line of refugees.

My soldier escorted the toddler and me to the front of the line, where he left us in the care of a group of women. Then, removing the weapon slung across his back, he walked to the end of the line to protect us if the rebels decided to cross the river.

We walked for hours. The stranglehold fear had maintained on me for a week eased with every exhausted step I took away from the river and rebels and toward the safety of Bor. I was sure Abraham and Monica were waiting for me there. They had to be. Or maybe they were in Gakyuom. All the villagers from Wernyol, Pawel, and Paliau who had survived the rebels had walked south. My uncle and aunt had survived, I assured myself when doubt pushed forward thoughts of Koko and those who had not. Abraham and Monica had run far ahead of Koko and me. They had to have outrun the rebels.

We reached the Dinka village of Gakyuom at dusk, just as my soldier had predicted. The villagers had been welcoming survivors of the massacre for days, and though their homes were already crowded with people fleeing the rebels, they welcomed us, too. As our line of tired, hungry, and grieving refugees limped into Gakyuom, they met us with understanding smiles and gentle words. They led us to the center of the village, where other Dinka, who had arrived in the days before us, waited. The moment they saw us, they rushed down the line, searching every face.

Cries of joy rose above the crowd as families and friends were reunited. All around me, people were hugging and crying. Their happiness rose in my chest, buoying my sinking hope. I leaned around the woman standing in front of me and pressed up on my toes to better see. I scoured every face we encountered, searching for Uncle Abraham and Aunt Monica.

I found only strangers.

Several people grabbed my face for a better look, hoping

I was their lost child or grandchild, but there was no recognition in their desperate eyes as they stared into mine before moving on to the next child. Scared and dejected, I wandered to the back of the line, looking for my soldier, but he was no longer there.

The frayed thread of hope holding me up snapped. I sank to the ground.

I was truly alone now. The war had taken them all.

Everyone who'd loved me.

Everyone who'd protected me.

Everyone who'd known me.

They were gone.

And I was left.

I sat, silent and numb, near the back of the line, as women and children begged us for any information about the homes and families they'd left behind.

"What village are you from?"

"Where is my son?"

"Do you know what happened to my daughter?"

"My mama was hurt. Did the rebels spare her? Did they spare anyone?"

"Have you seen anyone from Paliau?"

"Pawel?

"Wernyol?"

"Please, can you help me?"

I did not look up or reply. I could not help them. I had no answers. Only questions. My head hurt from the insistent, unanswered questions pulsing through my brain. I cradled my head in my hands, wanting to hide from all the questions, theirs and mine.

I did not want to speak. I did not want to move. I did not want to think anymore, so I kept my head bowed.

I did not look up when a woman knelt before me, or when she gently lifted my chin with her finger and gasped.

I did not look up until I heard her voice.

"Rachel?"

CHAPTER 12

Gakyuom, Sudan—November 1991

I stared into the familiar eyes of Mama's best friend, afraid if I blinked, she would disappear.

Adual pulled me into her arms. "Rachel! You're alive!"

I heard her voice and sensed her embrace, but they felt muted and distant.

"You know this child, Adual?" an older woman standing behind her asked. The strange woman wore a long white tunic, a white headwrap and veil that hung down her back, and a thin red cord of rope around her neck. A silver cross hung from the cord.

With tears in her eyes, Adual smiled up at the woman. "This is Rebecca and Michael's daughter," she said, using my parents' Christian names.

The woman in white pressed her cross to her lips and knelt before me. "What is your name, child?"

"Rachel."

She smiled and took my face in her hands. "My name is Martha."

When I did not respond, she explained. "My given

name is Adau Lual. We are family. I'm your baba's first cousin."

I stared at the woman in white claiming to be my family, but I had never seen her before.

"I left Wernyol before you were born," Martha explained, "to spread the word of God. I built a church here in Gakyuom. It is my home now." She studied my face. "I see your baba in your eyes, Rachel, but you favor your mama." She glanced around at the women standing nearby. "Where is Rebecca?"

I did not answer. I did not know where Mama was. I looked to Adual for help.

"Rebecca left for Torit over a year ago to help Michael after he was wounded in the war," Adual said. "She was not in Wernyol when the rebels attacked."

"Praise God," Martha said. She looked down at me. "Then who did you come here with, Rachel?"

Again, I did not answer. I knew none of the names of the people I'd followed from Pawel, not even the name of my soldier.

Adual glanced around us, perhaps noticing for the first time that I was alone. "Rachel, where is your koko?"

At the mention of Koko, the numbness smothering me burned away, exposing raw pain. "They left her behind," I said through stuttered breaths, "in a hut with the others."

"Who did?" Adual asked. "Where?"

"The soldiers. In Pawel. They told me she was gone,

that they could not help, but her eyes were open." I started to cry. "Her eyes were open, and they left her."

Adual held a trembling hand to her mouth. "What about Abraham and Monica? Are they with you?"

I shook my head. "Koko told them to run. We were slowing them down. They didn't want to leave us, but Koko said we would be safe . . ." My voice trailed off as the memory of our last moment in the forest with my aunt and uncle resurfaced. If Adual was asking if they were with me, it meant she did not know where they were either. They had not made it to Gakyuom. "Koko said the rebels would not hurt us." I looked up at Adual. "Why did they hurt us?"

Adual's embrace tightened around me. "I don't know." She held me as she, Martha, and I cried.

When everyone who could be reunited with their families had been found, Adual picked me up, and we followed my auntie Martha to her home. She lived in a small thatched-roof hut in walking distance from a larger hut she'd built as her church. Dozens of refugees were seated in clusters in front of her hut, preparing dinner and talking. She explained how a steady stream of refugees, fleeing the massacres in Wernyol and Pawel, had arrived in Gakyuom over the last week. Mama's best friend, Adual, had been among the first. Adual's parents had been killed in the massacre. Auntie Martha had welcomed Adual and every person seeking sanctuary into her home. Adual had been staying with Martha ever since, helping with the flood of refugees and looking for any survivors from Wernyol.

Adual prepared me a bowl of corn porridge and a gourd of cow's milk. She sat down near a fire that several refugees were using for cooking. She pulled me onto her lap and handed me the gourd.

"Drink slowly," she cautioned as I gulped down the warm milk. "Or you'll make yourself sick."

I tried to slow down, but I was so hungry. As I ate, Adual tended to my cut, swollen feet.

"Will Mama find me here?" I asked as she wrapped my feet in clean bandages.

"I don't know," she said, tying off the last bandage. "But I promise you, Rachel, when it is safe, we will find your mama, and we will go home again."

With her promise fresh in my mind, and my feet clean and my stomach full for the first time in days, I snuggled into Adual's lap and watched the dying flames of the fire retreat into the charred logs as the men and women discussed the attacks on the Dinka villages and what it meant for the war.

"The GOS have been killing our husbands, brothers, and sons for years," one woman said, "but they've always kept the fighting between armies and the war to the battlefields. They did not kill civilians."

"I fear with the attacks in Wernyol and Pawel," another

woman said, "all of southern Sudan is now the rebels' battlefield, and we are all now their enemy."

"There is no honor in attacking unarmed, innocent civilians." A young man threw a small rock into the fire, disrupting the pile of burning wood. "In killing women and children!"

A spray of sparks exploded into the darkness. I watched them sway and swirl on warm currents of air, drifting in lazy paths into the night air, where they joined the stars.

"The Nuer leaders must condemn the rebels' actions and vow no further harm will come to any civilian," another young man stated, his voice rising with the embers. "We must make it clear if the Nuer continue to massacre our Dinka people, we *will* retaliate. If they kill us, we will kill them!"

"We must pray it does not come to that," Auntie Martha said. Using a long stick, she poked and prodded at the scattered pieces of flaming wood, carefully reorganizing them once again into a whole, contained burn. "I have sisters and brothers who married Nuer men and women. They have children with both Dinka and Nuer blood running through their veins. Are they no longer my family? Are they now my enemy?" She stood before the fire and addressed the refugees like a minister preaching to her congregation. Her white dress glowed with soft golds and warm oranges from the flickering light of the fire. "Dinka. Nuer. Us. Them. Are we not all Sudanese? Are we not all human beings? Are we not all God's children?"

No one answered.

"This war has already taken so much," she continued. "Do not willingly give it more. We must not allow it to strip us of who we are or dictate who we are destined to be." She then led the refugees and soldiers in prayer, asking God to welcome our lost loved ones into his home in heaven and praying for guidance in leading our hearts toward forgiveness and our country toward healing.

The angry young men sat with their heads bowed. I could not tell if their heads hung in prayer or shame. Perhaps both.

After Auntie Martha's prayers, the conversation around the fire returned to a calmer discussion of the war and the decisions of its leaders. They spoke of Riek Machar, Dr. John Garang, Salva Kiir, and Omar Hassan Ahmad al-Bashir, men I did not know and names I did not recognize. I understood nothing of the politics of the war beyond all it had taken from me. Confused by their conversation and bone-weary, I closed my eyes and drifted to sleep.

Nightmares invaded my dreams. I was alone, surrounded by darkness. The familiar sounds of predators, stalking in the shadows outside our hut in Wernyol, echoed from every direction.

Prowling footsteps.

Hungry yips.

Angry snarls.

Menacing growls.

As they drew closer, they twisted into the now-too-familiar sounds of new, more lethal predators.

Barking orders.

Taunting lies.

Cruel laughter.

A gunshot. Sharp and thunderous.

And then another.

And another.

Adual shook me from my sleep. Securing me in her arms, she scrambled to her feet. "Run!" she yelled to the people around the fire.

Another gunshot punctuated her panicked command.

We followed the SPLA soldiers, refugees, and villagers sprinting for the cover of the trees outside of Gakyuom, but it was too late. Men with guns blocked our escape.

We turned to run in the opposite direction but found more armed men walking toward us. We were surrounded.

When I first saw the soldiers, with their uniforms and weapons, stepping out from the darkness, I thought the SPLA or maybe Baba had received my soldier's letter and sent help. It was not until the strange fighters aimed their guns on the SPLA soldiers standing with the villagers and refugees that I realized my mistake. It had not been the dangerous waters of the river that stopped the rebels from pursuing us. It had been their knowledge of who awaited us on the other side. Knowledge, at age six, I did not possess. Knowledge I would not gain or fully understand until I was much older.

For years, SPLA soldiers from the Nuer and other ethnic groups across southern Sudan had fought alongside the Dinka against a common enemy, the GOS Army, but in recent weeks, SPLA defectors had joined Machar's faction, and along with his new rebel recruits, had turned their anger and guns on us, a betrayal signed in Dinka blood with the massacres at Wernyol and Pawel. There was no sanctuary to be found in Bor. The rebels had driven us directly into a GOS ambush.

Images of the rebels aiming their weapons into the hut in Pawel burned before my eyes. I knew what came next.

The pleas.

The bullets.

The silence.

I covered my ears and burrowed my face into Adual's embrace. She pulled me closer and turned her body, shielding me from the GOS soldiers and their guns.

A brief exchange of bullets tore through the night air. The SPLA soldiers tried to protect us, but they were outnumbered and outgunned.

In the darkness and chaos, I did not see my soldier fall, but he was not among the captives the GOS troops marched at gunpoint to Bor that night.

None of the SPLA soldiers who had guided us from Paliau were.

CHAPTER 13

Bor, Sudan—November 1991

The first thing I noticed about the town of Bor was not its large size, military occupants, crowded streets, or cramped quarters. It was the bones.

Human remains, at varying stages of decay, were scattered throughout the town. The GOS troops left their victims where they fell, refusing them the dignity of even the simplest of burials, allowing wild animals and time to eat away at the bodies until all that remained were piles of bones.

Adual, who had carried me from Gakyuom, tried to shield my young eyes, but the bones were everywhere. I burrowed my face into the crook of her shoulder, but as we were led into the GOS-occupied town, a soldier ripped me from her arms.

"Rachel!" Adual screamed, reaching out for me.

"Stand there and be quiet!" the soldier told her in Sudanese Arabic. "Move again, and I will shoot you and the girl."

Adual's arms fell to her sides. Though we spoke Dinka in Wernyol, everyone in Sudan knew enough Sudanese

Arabic to understand the GOS soldiers' commands, and the bones littering the street were a stark warning that their commands were to be heeded.

When the GOS troops had ambushed us in Gakyuom, they had allowed the villagers, including Auntie Martha, to remain in their homes. The refugees, however, were told it was not safe for us in Gakyuom and the soldiers would be taking us to a refugee camp in Bor, for our protection. But as the soldiers shoved their way through the hundreds of refugees gathered in the center of Bor, sorting us into groups based on our ages and health, I felt neither safe nor protected.

They wasted no time in deciding who would stay and who would go, who would live and who would die. To save bullets, the soldiers used pangas and batons to dispose of those they deemed too old or injured to be of use. Their bodies were left with the other piles of bones.

Soldiers pulled families apart. Mothers begged for mercy and fell to their knees as soldiers tore crying children from their arms, but their pleas fell on deaf ears and cold hearts. Adual was shoved toward an area with other women and men as soldiers dragged terrified teenage girls and young women into nearby buildings. Huddled with the other young children, I covered my ears to block out their anguished screams, but I could not escape the desperate pleas crying out in my mind. The world was not safe. I was not safe.

The soldiers herded the rest of the children into a line.

I stood next to the young boy who had hidden in the hut with me in Pawel. His was the only face I knew. A soldier with many colorful ribbons adorning his uniform stalked back and forth in front of our group. I stared down at my bruised and battered feet, afraid to look at the man prowling before us. He stopped in front of the boy from the hut.

"What is your name?"

The boy answered in a trembling voice, barely louder than a whisper. "Dut."

I glanced over at the boy I'd hid with for three days and nights. It was the first time I'd heard his name.

Dut.

Knowing it somehow made him more real. It was probably a family name, one his parents had chosen for him at his birth, one that bound him to those who came before, one that would remind him of who he was even when everyone else was gone.

"No," the commander spat at the boy. "Your name is Mohammad."

His declaration made, the commander moved down the row of children, assigning Muslim names to every boy, age six and older. A young soldier followed the commander, pulling each boy from the line, including the boy who had been named Dut.

After stripping the boys of their identities, several soldiers escorted them to the White Nile River, where boats waited to transport them north, deep into GOS territory.

I learned years later that when the boys reached northern Sudan, the GOS Army broke them down physically, mentally, and emotionally during weeks of brutal training. If Dut survived, he would emerge without a trace of who he was. He would be a soldier, loyal only to the GOS, which would send him into southern Sudan to kill his people and claim their land.

With the boys gone, the soldiers walked the remaining girls over to where Adual and the women waited. As soon as I was within reach, Adual drew me into her arms and held me tight.

"Are you all right?" she whispered.

I nodded.

"We will take you to the refugee camp now," a soldier announced.

They escorted our group of fifty women and children through Bor. The large Dinka town situated next to the White Nile had been divided into two sections after the GOS had seized control. One side housed the GOS soldiers. The other side had been declared a refugee camp by the northern army, but we were not refugees with the freedom to come and go as we pleased. We were prisoners. GOS soldiers patrolled the perimeter of the camp day and night.

When we arrived at the plot of land declared a refugee camp, we found little food and no shelter, just a handful of simple tools, a few pots for cooking, and more skeletal remains.

"No one sleeps until the entire area is cleared of the bones," a soldier ordered.

"When we're done," an older woman asked, "where will we sleep?"

"If you want somewhere to sleep, you have tools and people, build it yourself. Now get to work."

It took us over an hour to remove all the bones. We carried them to a spot several meters outside our assigned patch of earth, leaving the piles for the next new group of refugees to move. When we were done, Adual and the other women built a fire, prepared corn porridge for everyone, and kept watch over us children while we slept. Then Adual wrapped me in her milaya and curled up next to me on the ground.

Despite the intense physical exhaustion begging my body to rest, my mind refused. Images of the rebel attacks, the river crossing, and the bones of Bor flashed in my mind every time I closed my eyes, sending spikes of adrenaline surging through my body and causing me to twitch awake and cry out in fear.

"Shhhhh," Adual hushed me gently. "It's all right. I'm here, Rachel. You are not alone."

Lying in Adual's arms as the sounds of unseen predators, gnawing on the bones we'd moved hours before, lurked in the darkness, I thought of Koko and how she'd comforted me in the hut in Pawel when fear trembled through my body in uncontrollable shivers.

We just have to make it through the night. We just need to survive until morning.

With Adual's words whispering in my ears and the memory of Koko's words whispering in my mind, I closed my eyes and drifted to sleep.

The next day, Adual and the other women rose with the sun to gather wood and mud to begin the construction of three thatched-roof huts. The other children and I were instructed to collect wood for the fire. The women worked tirelessly for days, only stopping to cook food and sleep for a few hours before waking to begin another day of arduous work.

When they were finished, each hut had one door, no windows, and enough space to sleep ten to fifteen children. The women did not sleep inside with us. They slept by the fire each night, armed only with large sticks, to make sure no wild animals broke into the huts while we slept. Every evening before bed, Adual cleansed the wounds on my feet, made sure I'd been fed, and helped me get settled on the floor of one of the huts before she joined the women by the fire.

When I was reluctant to close my eyes for fear of the memories and nightmares that awaited me in sleep, I'd listen for the sounds of the women. During the day, they would bury their heartache and pain while they worked to keep us children fed, protected, and hopeful, but in our absence, during the darkness of night, the women laid their anguish to bare. From my small patch of ground in the hut, I listened to them, crying over their missing and dead husbands, murdered relatives, abducted sons and daughters, lost homes, and stolen virtue. Their pain was raw and heartbreaking, but I did not cover my ears and hide from their despair. I embraced it. Their tears brought me comfort. The sound of their grief meant they were still outside the huts, protecting us from the world and all who would hurt us. It meant, despite all I had lost, someone who cared was still there. Adual was there, and I was not alone.

In the mornings, I would wake when it was still dark, while the other children slept, and I would peek out the hut door to make sure Adual and the others had survived another night. As dawn painted the retreating night in softening hues of ripened-mango red and tangerine orange, I would quietly watch the women. Before the dying embers of the fire, these women, from whom the war had taken so much, stood together, and embraced. Their broken bodies and spirits clung to one another for strength, making whole their shattered pieces. They began each new day this way, holding one another up in support and prayer, and I began each new day watching them and drawing hope from their collective strength.

CHAPTER 14

Bor, Sudan—January 1992–May 1992

Over the next few weeks, the GOS soldiers brought more women and children to share the land and resources in the refugee camp. With each new group, the piles of bones were moved farther out, increasing the perimeter of our prison. While the women built shelters for the new refugees, we welcomed the children into our huts. The limited sleeping space became more cramped with the additional bodies, but we always made room. As the weeks stretched into months, the number of refugees confined in the GOS-run refugee camp swelled to over ten thousand.

Food and medicine were scarce in the camp. Occasionally the United Nations (UN) would deliver desperately needed supplies to Bor, but the soldiers hoarded the majority of the provisions. Our movements were limited to the camp with few exceptions. Every several days, the GOS permitted us to walk to the White Nile to fetch water and bathe. They also allowed small groups of refugees to travel to the neighboring towns of Gakyuom and Yomchiir to attend mass and purchase produce.

"Rachel!" Auntie Martha would pull me into her arms

for a tight hug every time Adual and I came to visit. "I am so glad you are here. The other children are practicing a hymn for this Sunday's mass. They could use your lovely voice to make their song soar. Why don't you join them?"

While I ran off to sing and play with the other children in Auntie Martha's congregation, Adual and Martha would sit and talk. Our days spent in Gakyuom provided us a brief escape from the horrors of life in the GOS refugee camp, but our stays were never long enough.

When the sun hung low in the late-afternoon sky, Adual would beckon me to join her and Auntie Martha. "It's time to go, Rachel."

I hated to leave, but I knew she was right. It was dangerous to walk back in the dark, and if we didn't return to Bor before nightfall, the soldiers would come looking for us. Adual would squeeze my hand when she saw the disappointment on my face as we left Auntie Martha's church. "I'll try to get us permission to come back soon."

I knew our trips to Gakyuom were not free. Nothing in Bor was, but I did not know how high a price refugees paid for a few hours of freedom, especially the women. Those who did not have the money or valuables to pay the soldiers were forced to pay with their bodies.

As word of the assaults on the female refugees in Bor reached the SPLA, outrage in the Dinka communities of southern Sudan grew to a fever pitch. SPLA leader Dr. John Garang wanted to attack the GOS troops occupying Bor and save the refugees, but he could not lead an assault without risking massive casualties within the population he hoped to free, so he changed tactics. Instead of military pressure, he applied public pressure on Omar Hassan Ahmad al-Bashir, leader of Sudan and head of the GOS Army, to stop the inhumane abuses and crimes perpetuated by his soldiers in Bor. Garang's tactic worked.

Days after Al-Bashir imposed a new rule prohibiting attacks on female refugees, Adual and I were walking to bathe in the river when a group of GOS soldiers dragged a young soldier into the center of town. Their captive was handcuffed and struggling to break free. They threw the young man to the ground in front of a group of soldiers, citizens, and refugees.

A GOS commander stood before the gathering crowd. "This man was caught assaulting a woman in the refugee camp!"

He held a straight-edged razor above the soldier's head. In the weeks following the attack on Wernyol, I had witnessed too often the atrocities committed by soldiers wielding blades.

I took hold of Adual's hand and pressed closer to her as the commander grabbed the man by his jaw and tilted his head back. "In accordance with the directive declared by our leader, Omar Al-Bashir," the commander announced, "he will now face the punishment for his crime." Positioning the edge of the razor at the front of the young soldier's hairline, he scraped the blade along the curve of the man's skull, shaving off his hair. He pressed down with each pass, deliberately slicing into the soldier's scalp. The guilty man did not cry out or beg for mercy. When his head was shaved clean of everything but the blood running from several deep cuts, the officer signaled for another soldier to bring him a small bag. The officer reached into the bag and lifted a fistful of salt into the air for all to see.

"Any soldier discovered assaulting or raping a refugee will face the same punishment and forever bear the marks of his crimes." He then poured salt into the man's long, open wounds.

That was when the soldier screamed.

"Come, Rachel," Adual said, ushering me away from the torturous scene.

As we hurried to the river, I could still hear the soldier's wails of pain. Despite the agony I heard in his screams, I felt no pity for him. His cries were nothing compared to the cries I'd heard every night from the women seated around the fire in the refugee camp, the same cries I'd heard calling out for help from behind closed doors in Pawel, the same cries of women pleading for mercy from the shadows of every Dinka town the rebels and GOS attacked. The soldiers offered their victims no compassion, so I had no compassion to offer them.

In the weeks that followed that first public punishment, dozens of soldiers with shaved, scarred heads walked around Bor, bearing the mark of shame for all to see. They were shunned by refugees and soldiers alike, and eventually the daily assaults on the female captives ceased, but the show of punishment did nothing to alleviate the other threats we faced.

The killings of Dinka men captured by the GOS continued, and every Dinka boy abducted by the soldiers was torn from his family and put on boats for northern Sudan. With mounting pressure from the SPLA and rumors of an imminent attack, the GOS started making plans to clear out Bor and move everyone north to a refugee camp deeper in GOS territory. They did not hide their plans. They asked for volunteers to register for transport, but they did not say what would happen to those who chose to stay.

Fearful of being taken north into enemy territory, and certain execution was the alternative, escape attempts among the refugees increased. Some succeeded. Some failed.

When Adual and the other women took me to visit Gakyuom and Yomchiir, I would hear whispered conversations about the escapes.

"They were heading to Pinyudo in Ethiopia."

"No, I heard they were walking to Kenya. There is a new refugee camp there."

"But how would they get there? There's no safe way to Kenya. They'd have to cross swamps and deserts."

"Is the journey to Ethiopia any safer?"

"Yes. Thousands have already made it. The SPLA took

my son there for military school. If I were strong enough to make the trip, that's where I would go."

Adual and the other women never joined these conversations. They would listen but refused to voice their opinions. After mass, they would talk to Auntie Martha quietly for a few minutes before buying produce for the week and walking us back to Bor. Their silence about the topic, which seemed so important to every other refugee and villager in and around Bor, made me anxious. Everyone had a plan but us, so one evening, when Adual was preparing me for bed, I asked her if we were leaving Bor.

"Why are you worrying about that?" she asked.

Tears blurred my vision as I stared up at her. "I don't want to become a pile of bones."

Adual took me in her arms and rocked me to sleep. "I will never let that happen."

CHAPTER 15

Bor, Sudan—May 1992

Six months after the GOS ambush in Gakyuom, Adual and I followed the other women and children from our small grouping of huts to a table the soldiers had set up on their side of Bor. I thought we were waiting in line to ask for permission to visit Gakyuom again, but my excitement over the possibility of seeing Auntie Martha and the others in her church vanished the moment the first woman in our group spoke.

"We are here to register to be transferred north," she announced to a soldier seated behind the table.

Confused, I looked up at Adual, but she was staring straight ahead, focused on the interaction between the woman and soldier.

"The next boats north leave in two weeks," the soldier stated.

The woman nodded. "We understand."

One by one, the women and children from our group added their names to the list. When Adual stepped up to the table, I prayed she would ask about visiting Gakyuom for the day. Keeping her head bowed respectfully before the soldier, she said, "We also want to volunteer to be transported north."

I stepped back, but Adual took hold of my hand. My legs ached to run, but I didn't know where to go. I did not want to be separated from Adual and the others, but I also did not want to be taken farther from Wernyol. I was already too far from home, and I didn't know how to get back.

Having added Adual's name to his list, the soldier cast an annoyed look at me. "Name?"

My heartbeat broke into a panicked gallop. How would I ever be reunited with Abraham and Monica if the GOS took me away? How would Mama and Baba find me?

I took another step back from the table, but Adual's grip on my hand tightened.

The GOS soldier released an impatient sigh. "What . . . is . . . your . . . name?"

Adual looked down at me and gave my hand a gentle squeeze. "Go ahead. You can tell him."

I cast my gaze to my bare feet and the split big toe-nail from the accident with Koko's hand hoe when I was three. I remembered Mama cleaning and bandaging my toe. Every day for weeks, she'd tended to my hurt foot until it had healed. Adual had done the same for my blistered, cut feet when she'd found me in Gakyuom. Adual was Mama's best friend. Mama had trusted her, so despite my confusion and fear, I needed to trust her, too. Fighting back tears, I stepped up to the table. "My name is Rachel."

The soldier added my name to the list and then motioned to the woman waiting behind us. "Next!"

But Adual did not move. "Could you please tell me if our request to attend the church celebration in Yomchiir for the weekend has been granted?" she asked the soldier.

"I don't know."

The soldier again waved the woman behind us forward, but Adual stood her ground with me positioned directly in front of her. "We have been helping at the church for weeks in preparation for the celebration. They are expecting us."

The soldier set down his pen, sat back, and crossed his arms over his chest.

"Please, sir." Adual placed her hands on my shoulders. "The children have been rehearsing their songs and dances for the mass and will be so disappointed if they were not allowed to attend. It will be our last opportunity to see everyone before we're transported north."

With some reluctance, the soldier stood and carried his list of volunteers over to where an officer was talking with a group of soldiers. The soldier motioned to Adual and me and pointed at the list. The officer barely glanced at the paper, nodded once, and then dismissed the soldier.

"You may attend the ceremony," the soldier said when he returned to the table.

Adual smiled. "Thank you."

"When will you be back?" the soldier asked.

"The ceremony ends Sunday afternoon. We will return by evening."

The soldier did not question Adual further. The GOS soldiers seldom did. During our six months in Bor, Adual and the women in our group had worked hard to earn the soldiers' trust through unflappable obedience. That, coupled with their willingness to volunteer for transport to the refugee camp in northern Sudan, quelled any suspicions regarding their requests to travel outside the perimeter of Bor.

As we walked back to our huts, I could not help but think of the choice Adual had made for us. She had always made the right choices for me, even at the expense of her own safety, but her decision to register us for transfer north twisted in my stomach like spoiled milk, and troubling questions swarmed my mind like locusts.

How could Adual keep her promise to find Mama and return home someday if we left southern Sudan? Would the GOS assign me a new name, like they did with Dut? If they did, how would Mama ever find me if I were living in a strange place with a strange name? What if the GOS separated Adual and me in the new camp? Who would care for me?

These weighty thoughts slowed my steps as the beginning of tears burned in the back of my nose and behind my eyes. I didn't want Adual to think I didn't trust her. I did trust her, but I did not trust the GOS soldiers. I'd heard their lies many times over our half a year of captivity, starting with the lie that they were taking us to Bor for our safety. We had never been safe in their camp. Death threatened us day and night. It burned in the hate-filled leers of the soldiers. It growled from the empty bellies of over ten thousand refugees huddled on small patches of barren earth. It fortified its grip on us from the growing piles of bones lining the boundaries of the camp. And at night, it whispered from the depths of my nightmares.

Adual noticed me worrying my lower lip with my teeth. "Rachel, are you excited about the church celebration?"

I nodded, afraid if I parted my lips to speak, every doubt and fear surging through my mind would spill out, and my tears would follow.

Adual picked me up. "Me too."

As we made our way through the refugee camp, she reviewed what would take place over the three-day celebration, and despite my doubts about her decision to register us for transfer and my fears over what awaited us in the GOS refugee camp in the north, I couldn't help but feel excited to attend the celebration in Yomchiir. Any chance we had to leave Bor and the GOS soldiers' constant monitoring of our every move felt like a gift, and the church celebration at Yomchiir was to last three days. That meant seventy-two hours of freedom.

As I fell asleep that night, I focused on the hope those three days stirred, pushing the despair of our upcoming transfer north from my mind with thoughts of seeing Auntie Martha, and singing, dancing, eating, and praying with the other children, villagers, and refugees, away from the ever-watchful eyes of the GOS. There would be time for tears later.

The Wednesday prior to the celebration, the GOS Army began allowing small groups to leave for Yomchiir. The women in our cluster of huts started escorting two or three children at a time to help with preparations. By Friday morning, larger groups were leaving for the popular church event. Yomchiir was an hour walk from Bor, and as more women and children left for the celebration, my patience frayed.

"When do I get to go?" I asked Adual as we watched two women lead twenty children from the refugee camp. "I want to go to the celebration, too."

"Soon," Adual promised.

By Saturday afternoon, two of our three huts were empty, and I was pouting over the fact that there was only one day left of the celebration weekend, and I was still stuck in Bor. Finally, as the sun sank toward the horizon, Adual and five other women gathered twenty children, including me, by the fire.

"It's time to go," Adual announced. "We have a long walk ahead of us, and it will be getting dark soon, so we must move quickly and stay together."

Moving quickly would not be a problem. I was so excited to get to Yomchiir, I could have run the whole way. I grabbed hold of Adual's hand and started pulling her toward the GOS Army checkpoint.

"We will see you tomorrow," Adual told the remaining forty women and children from our section of the camp.

"Safe travels," one of the women said, waving us goodbye.

We made our way through Bor to the checkpoint, where nearly a hundred refugees had gathered.

"You are to be back here by Sunday evening," a soldier warned before allowing the refugees to pass. "If you are not back before the sun sets tomorrow, we will send patrols to hunt you down." Resting his hands on the hilt of a panga tucked in his belt, his eyes narrowed on the women escorting the children to Yomchiir. "You do not want that to happen."

Despite the soldier's threat, a current of excitement flowed through the crowd as we left Bor. For the refugees, the few gatherings outside of the confines of the camp that we were permitted to attend were small glimpses of life before the rebel attacks. Moments when we could forget about the despair of our present and the uncertainty of our future. Moments when we could remember the joy of our past. These rare times were more than an escape. They were hope. Hope that someday we would be able to return to the lives and families we had left behind. Hope that somewhere, they still existed, waiting for us to come home.

Though our anticipation for the church celebration

urged our small feet to run ahead, the children and I reined in our impatience and walked behind Adual and the other women. Dusk was deepening into night, and a child who ventured too far from the group would be easy prey for any wild predators watching from the shadows.

Occasionally, Adual would walk ahead to talk in hushed voices with women who were not from our small group. I could not hear their conversations, but the women looked concerned by Adual's words. Some nodded in agreement. Others shook their heads and walked faster. These short, tense discussions continued until we were several kilometers from Bor. When Adual finally rejoined the five women and twenty children from our huts, we stopped walking.

"Did they agree?" one of the women asked.

"Not all of them," Adual replied, disappointment weighing down her words.

I bounced on the balls of my feet, wishing they would save their conversation for when we arrived in Yomchiir. Auntie Martha would be there, and I couldn't wait to hear more of her stories about Baba and her when they were little.

"How many agreed?" another woman asked.

"Less than half," Adual answered.

The women exchanged worried glances.

"What do we do?" an older woman asked. "It's getting late."

As the women continued their tense discussion, I watched half of the larger group continue their walk toward Yomchiir. Only forty or so women and children waited with us. As the distance between us and the other group grew, my excitement about getting to Yomchiir soured into impatience and panic. The older woman was right. It was getting late. The sun would be setting in the next hour, and it was not safe to be outside if you were not with a large group to keep predators away.

"Maybe we should wait a little longer?" one of the women said.

What are they waiting for? I thought. The women and children we'd left back at the camp? They weren't due to leave until the next morning. If we waited for them, we'd miss another night of the celebration.

I glanced behind us in the direction of Bor, hoping to see more refugees walking our way, but there was nothing behind us but an empty dirt path and the darkening evening sky.

"Maybe they just need a little more time," another woman said.

No, I thought. We need to catch up to the others.

I took hold of Adual's hand. I wanted to pull her along. The others would follow, I was sure of it, and the refugees left back in the camp would meet us at Yomchiir in the morning.

To my relief, Adual shook her head. "No. We don't have time to wait."

The knot twisting in my stomach began to loosen. I took a step in the direction of Yomchiir and tugged on

Adual's arm. If we hurried, we could catch up with the others.

Adual did not move. When I turned back, she was staring off to our left, her brow furrowed in thought. I followed her gaze but saw nothing but trees and darkness.

I tugged on her arm again. "Aren't we going to the celebration?"

She knelt before me so she was looking directly in my eyes. "You trust me, don't you, Rachel?"

I nodded.

"Here's the truth. We were never going to the celebration."

I dropped her hand. "But Auntie Martha is waiting."

"She knows we're not coming."

I stared at her. I did not understand. Of course Auntie Martha knew we were coming. She had helped us prepare for the celebration. For weeks, she and Adual planned for today.

"Going to the celebration was never our plan," Adual explained. "Neither was going north."

"Are we going back to Bor?" I asked, panic vibrating through my chest.

"No." She glanced back as the women in our group began to guide the other children off the dirt path leading to Yomchiir and toward the trees.

"We are going to Ethiopia."

CHAPTER 16

Keyala, Sudan—May 1992

For months, between their tears and prayers around the fire, Adual and the other women had been plotting our escape. While the GOS soldiers had been watching us, Adual and the women had been watching them. They'd monitored the soldiers' patrols of the refugee camp to determine the safest times to leave without immediate detection. They'd listened closely to the stories of other escape attempts, learning much from those who had succeeded and more from those who had failed. They'd determined the best time to travel was at night, when darkness would cloak our movements. And they'd waited patiently for the perfect opportunity to flee.

When Auntie Martha and the church leaders from Yomchiir started discussing plans for their weekend-long celebration, Adual and the women found their opportunity. We walked right out of Bor, with permission from the GOS Army and with any suspicion of our motives for attending the celebration squashed by our willingness to register for the transfer north.

"They won't notice we're missing and start tracking

us for twenty-four hours," Adual explained as we left the path to Yomchiir. "But we can only safely travel at night, which gives us barely eleven hours to put as much distance between Bor and us as possible, so we have to move fast."

My heart pounded so loudly as I followed Adual and the others, I was sure the soldiers in Bor would hear it. I had thought we would be spending the night and next day celebrating with Auntie Martha and the others, but now we were on the run, fleeing to another country. I struggled to understand what was happening and why everything had changed. Ever since we'd been captured and taken to Bor, Adual had been adamant that we follow the GOS soldiers' every command, even the small ones. Obedience meant survival. When the GOS realized we had lied and escaped, they would send soldiers to track us down, just as the Nuer rebels had hunted us when we'd fled our home in Wernyol. My body trembled as memories of those terrifying days of running from the rebels resurfaced, the sound of their guns and threat of their blades stalking our every step.

Adual took my hand and held it tight. As we hurried into the deepening night, my mind filled with questions about the groups of women and children who had left Bor for the celebration before us. Had they, too, abandoned the path to Yomchiir? What about those who'd remained in Bor? Did they hope to escape after us? How many of them had been part of Adual's plan? And how many of us would survive?

It was nearing the end of the dry season in Sudan. Unlike when we'd fled Pawel six months earlier, we did not have to walk in the rain or trudge down muddy paths. It allowed us to keep a faster pace, but months with little rain had left the sodden earth to bake under the sun, creating hard, uneven paths that battered our bare feet. When we could, we kept to the woods and tall grasses so we had somewhere to hide should GOS soldiers come looking for us.

With only the light of the stars and crescent moon to guide us, we headed south. No one spoke as we walked. Everyone was listening for the rustling of bodies pressing through the coarse, dry grasses or the crunch of booted feet on the hard dirt paths. Our senses were vigilant, and our muscles were tightly coiled, ready to fight or flee the moment danger pounced. Adual and the women carried large sticks, the only weapons we had to protect ourselves from attack, whether from human or animal.

My feet, which had healed under Adual's care during our time in captivity, swelled from the hours of walking. Adual carried me when she could, but there were more children than women in our group, so we were forced to take turns walking during the long trek. The rough, rocky ground tore into my swollen feet, leaving bloody footprints behind every pained step. When the night sky lightened along the horizon, we took cover behind a grouping of trees, where the women fed us what little food they had managed to smuggle past the soldiers.

Adual uncorked an aduɔ̈k, and, using the curved edge of a dried snail's shell, she scooped out a mouthful of peanut butter from the hollow gourd.

"I'm sorry. I can't give you much, or you will be too thirsty," she explained as I scraped the paste free with my small finger. "We need our water to last for several days. I can only give you enough to put something in your stomach, so eat slowly."

Despite Adual's warning, I ate the scoop of peanut butter in one bite. It did nothing to calm the hunger gnawing at my stomach, but there were many small mouths to feed. While Adual continued to hand out snail-shell scoops of peanut butter to the other children seated around me, I sucked on my finger, working the tip of my tongue beneath my fingernail, desperate not to waste any of my portion. Only when all the children had been fed did Adual and the women finally sit and share what meager rations remained.

After she'd finished eating, Adual lifted me onto her lap. "Let me see your feet, Rachel."

She took them in her hands and gently inspected the fresh cuts, where the taut, swollen skin had split. She apologized every time I winced when she touched a painfully tender spot, but she did not stop working until she had removed all the dirt and grass. "We need to cover these, or they'll become infected."

She looked around, but aside from the milayas we were wearing, we had no cloth to use as bandages, so Adual turned her gaze to the trees and grass hiding us from anyone passing through the area. She searched the ground until she found two small, flat pieces of wood. She then tore several long green leaves from a nearby bush. Holding my right foot on her lap, she carefully placed one of the pieces of wood against the sole of my foot. She secured the wood by winding the long leaves around my foot and tying knots to create a basic shoe. She then repeated the process on my left foot before searching for more pieces of wood and leaves so she could tend to the other children.

With the wood and leaf shoes strapped to my feet, I curled up on the ground and fell asleep. The women and Adual took turns keeping watch as the children slept throughout the day. When the sun finally dipped below the horizon again, Adual woke me.

"It's time to walk again, Rachel."

We repeated this process for several days, hiding from the sun, and walking under the moon. We traveled southeast of Bor, bypassing the town of Juba, which the women had overheard was also occupied by GOS forces. With each new dawn, Adual would make me a new pair of shoes to replace the ones that had worn out on the previous night's walk. They helped protect my feet from the ground, but they made walking difficult. I was not used to wearing shoes, even simple ones made of wood and leaves. The inflexible wooden soles did not move with the natural heal-to-toe rolling motion of my feet. They slipped and shifted beneath my steps. By the third day of walking, the cuts on my feet had darkened to a beefy red and began to ooze.

"The leaves are making them worse," Adual said, removing the shoes. "I think their oils have caused an infection." Using a corner of her milaya, she gently patted the weeping wounds clean. "I will carry you as far as I can tomorrow. By morning, we should arrive in Keyala, where I will look for better material to wrap your feet."

She lay down beside me, holding me close. We had no blankets and relied on one another for warmth. "Try to sleep, Rachel. You need your rest."

I closed my eyes, but every time sleep attempted to settle in my body and mind, hunger and fear set in, leaving me awake with my thoughts.

I thought of Mama and wondered why she hadn't come for me yet. Everywhere we went, people knew of the massacre at Wernyol. The stories from fleeing refugees always arrived before we did. Mama had to have heard them by now. She had to have learned what happened to our village and home. She must be worried. It made no sense that she would not come for me unless . . .

"Adual?" I whispered.

"Yes."

"Is Mama alive?"

Adual shifted her body so she was facing me. "Yes."

"How do you know?"

"When my husband was killed in the war," she explained, "I knew he was gone because someone told me he had died. Has anyone told you your mama is dead?"

"No, but—"

"Then until someone tells us otherwise, your mama is alive." Adual wiped the tears from my cheeks. "I miss her, too, Rachel. We will find her when we are safe in Ethiopia."

"Are we almost there?" I asked.

"No, it will take us a couple months to walk there."

"Months?" My feet ached at the thought of having to walk that long.

"Yes, but with each step, no matter how small or painful, we are one step closer. Closer to Ethiopia. Closer to safety. Closer to seeing Abraham and Monica again." She smiled at me. "And closer to finding your mama. We must keep moving forward."

I fell asleep that morning, hopeful that with Adual's help, I would reach Ethiopia, find my aunt and uncle, and be reunited with Mama. I just had to keep walking.

Adual carried me most of the next night, and by morning, we had reached the town of Keyala. It was a large town, crowded with refugees. Although the villagers were sympathetic to our plight, they were not happy to see us. Wave after wave of people fleeing the rebels and GOS soldiers had descended upon Keyala over the months since the massacres in the Dinka villages to the north. Their food and water supplies, already sparse due to the dry season, had been stretched too thin with the additional demands of the starving and thirsty refugees.

"Could you give us just enough for the children?" Adual begged a man.

The man shook his head. "I'm sorry, but if I feed your children, mine will starve."

Throughout the town, we received similar apologies. A few townspeople gave us what small offerings they could afford to spare, but it was never enough.

"We will find more in the next town," Adual tried to reassure me, but doubt frayed the confidence in her voice.

Though we did not find much food or water in Keyala, we did find many familiar faces. We reunited with several of the groups of women and children who had left Bor in the days before our escape. They had waited for us to arrive before continuing their walk. Unfortunately, the forty women and children we'd left behind in Bor never arrived. When I asked Adual if we would be waiting for them, she shook her head.

"The GOS soldiers must have discovered we did not reach Yomchiir and stopped anyone else from leaving."

As I lay in Adual's lap, I thought of the women and children who had been scheduled to leave Bor the morning after we escaped. I prayed they were not being punished for our deception and wondered if the GOS Army had already loaded them onto boats and transferred them north. Both possibilities played out in my imagination, bringing forward memories of all the people we had been forced to leave behind. The men, women, and children in the river. The injured villagers in Pawel. And Koko, sitting in that hut, forever staring at her empty lap.

Hiding my tears from Adual, I cried until sleep quieted my thoughts.

We left Keyala the next night with far less food than we'd hoped and far more refugees than we'd expected.

"We need to head to Kapoeta next," a man from Keyala said as we left town, "if we are to get to Kakuma before the GOS Army or rebels take over all of southern Sudan."

Adual stopped walking. "Kakuma? But we're not going to Kenya, we're going to the refugee camp in Ethiopia."

"There is no refugee camp in Ethiopia," the man said.

"Of course there is," another woman from Bor argued. "Every refugee we've met was headed to Pinyudo."

The man shook his head. "Then they will be disappointed. If they don't die on the way, they'll be killed when they reach the border."

"Has the GOS taken control of the border, too?" Adual asked.

"No. The Ethiopian government emptied the camp months ago. They are no longer allowing refugees from Sudan to cross into Ethiopia."

"What about Uganda?" another woman asked. "We are much closer to their border."

"Uganda is dealing with its own civil war and refugee crisis," the man explained. "They will not welcome ours."

"So, Kenya is our only hope," Adual said.

The man nodded. "We just have to pray they don't close their borders to us, too."

CHAPTER 17

Keyala and Nadapal, Sudan—June–August 1992

There was no safe path to Kenya.

We had no map to guide our way, only stars.

We had no weapons to protect us, only sticks.

And we had no guarantee we would survive the journey, only hope.

We continued southeast from Keyala. In every village and town along the way, more men, women, and children joined our group. The larger numbers helped protect us from predators as we walked during the night but made it more difficult to hide from the rebels and the GOS soldiers during the day. The additional people also ate into our limited food and water supply.

We refilled our aduɔks at streams and rivers as we walked, but after six months of little to no rain, water sources became scarce. Those we did find held stagnant water and muddy puddles, teeming with unseen parasites. We drank it anyway. The only other option was to die of thirst.

As we traveled through villages in the three Equatoria regions, the southernmost portion of the country and home to over two dozen ethnic groups, desperation drove us to steal crops from the farmers' fields and water from their wells. Although some in the Equatoria regions had joined the SPLM, many rejected involvement in the movement and avoided being pulled into the escalating fighting between the Dinka and Nuer. But the surge of refugees fleeing south through their territory pushed the warring factions of the SPLA's problems to their homes and lands. To protect their crops and families, they shot at refugees pillaging their fields and water sources. Most of their bullets missed, but occasionally, they hit their marks. We had no choice but to leave the injured behind.

Despite gaining more refugees at every village and town, we lost many during the weeks of walking. Some died of hunger. Some died of thirst. Some succumbed to dysentery or malaria. And some simply stopped.

Weeks after we'd left Keyala, we were walking through a field of tall grass when a woman stopped. Her legs had swollen to the point you could no longer distinguish her knees from her thighs, and her ankles and feet were covered with painful blisters caused by guinea worms working their way through the soft tissue of her legs.

Every day, when we stopped to rest, Adual would use a sharp stick to lance any swollen bumps forming on my legs and feet. The larvae of the guinea worm, ingested by drinking stagnant water, penetrated the abdominal and intestinal walls, burrowing into the soft tissue, where they grew up to one meter in length before erupting from the skin through ulcers that itched and burned.

The crude incisions Adual made on my feet often revealed the tips of the white stringlike worms. When enough of the thin worm was visible, Adual would grab hold of the tip and gently pull. It was an agonizingly slow process. The momentary relief of pressure the incision brought was quickly replaced by searing pain, but the worms had to be removed. Despite the care Adual took to work the parasites free, sometimes the fragile worms broke apart before she finished, and the remaining portion continued to grow in my legs, only to reappear beneath a new blistering ulcer days or weeks later. Even the ones she successfully removed were soon replaced by new worms when we took our next drink of dirty, stagnant water. She tried her best to remove any guinea worms before they caused debilitating swelling or secondary infections and blood poisoning, but for some refugees, it was a losing battle.

Unable to bend her swollen legs, the woman gingerly lowered herself to the ground, where she sat and watched our group walk past her. I recognized the woman. She had been with us in Bor. She was not much older than Adual. I had heard her crying by the fire at night and had listened to her pray for her husband and children, killed by the rebels.

I tugged on Adual's milaya and pointed to the woman.

Adual released my hand. "Stay here. I'll be right back."

She walked over to where the woman sat in the grass. I could not hear what she said, but the woman glanced up at Adual and then, without a word, returned her unfocused gaze to the refugees walking away. Adual bent down and hugged the woman. When she returned to where I waited, tears wet her cheeks.

"We must keep going."

"What about her?" I asked. "It's not safe to be alone."

"Her journey has ended," Adual said. "But we have much farther to go." She took my hand. "Come along, Rachel, or we'll be left behind."

I cast one last glance over my shoulder at the woman sitting alone in the grass, and then I quickened my pace to catch up with the others.

The woman from Bor was the first to stop, but she was not the last.

After months of pain and loss, the fragile flames of hope many refugees had carried with them were extinguished. The light in their eyes dimmed first, and then their steps slowed. As the rest of us continued walking, they would sink to the ground, sitting in the middle of a dirt path. Against a tree. Beside a riverbank. Among the tall grass. Their faces void of expression, and their eyes empty of emotion, they sat, and they waited.

Death was merciful. It never made them wait long. If hunger, thirst, or illness did not claim them, wild animals did. Lethal predators, like lions and wild dogs, followed us, day and night, eager to pick off the sick, the weak, and the hopeless. They were not alone. Drawn to the scent of the dying, large vultures, like hunchbacked harbingers of death, lurked near those who stopped and waited for them to draw their final breath.

Despite the escape from pain and hunger death promised, I kept walking. I knew every step brought me closer to the next village or town, and in every new place we reached, I would find hundreds and thousands of new faces. Each new face held the promise of hope. Hope that one of those faces might be Mama's. It was that hope that urged my tired legs and aching feet forward, even when they begged to stop.

After weeks of walking, we reached the town of Kapoeta. I searched every new face we passed for Mama, but she was not there. We didn't find Abraham or Monica either, but we did find thousands of new refugees on their way to Kenya and the Kakuma Refugee Camp. Some of the refugees, like Adual and me, had fled rebel attacks in the north, but many had been ousted from the Pinyudo Refugee Camp in Ethiopia. Among them were young SPLA soldiers, who, like my uncles, Ater and Andrew, had been taken from their homes when they were just boys and sent to the SPLA military school on the Ethiopian border for a brief time before being armed and ordered to the front lines of the war. They provided our group a new level of protection with their training and weapons, and they shared their stories of the atrocities committed at Pinyudo.

"They forced us out in the middle of the night, at gunpoint."

"They threatened to shoot us if we did not cross the Gilo River and leave Ethiopia. Many of us did not know how to swim."

"They waited until we entered the river, and then they started shooting."

"There were bodies everywhere. The river ran red with blood."

"The blood drew crocodiles from the riverbanks. It is a miracle anyone survived."

Listening to the young SPLA soldiers tell their stories, my mind reeled. When we had escaped Bor, I had hoped Uncle Abraham and Aunt Monica had made it to Pinyudo.

With every step, no matter how small or painful, we are a step closer, Rachel. Closer to Ethiopia. Closer to safety. Closer to seeing Abraham and Monica again.

Adual's words repeated in my mind as we left Kapoeta, but I couldn't stop thinking about the soldiers' stories of the bodies, the crocodiles, and the red river. Their horrifying tales unearthed memories I'd tried hard to bury. Memories of my river crossing as we'd fled the rebels on our way to Bor. Of clinging to my young soldier's arm as water flooded my nose and mouth. Of terrified faces slipping beneath the surface. Of the words "I'm sorry" being spoken, over and over again, to those who would never answer. The memories shivered through my body.

"Are you cold?" Adual asked. She felt my forehead and cheeks for signs of fever. She and the other women had dug too many shallow graves for children stricken down by malaria. She pulled down my lower eyelids to check if the whites of my eyes had yellowed with jaundice. "Do you feel sick?"

I didn't know how to answer. I always felt sick. There was not a time my head didn't hurt from thirst, my stomach didn't ache with hunger, and my vision didn't blur with dizziness from both. My legs and feet burned and itched from painful guinea worm blisters that had yet to rupture, and thick, cracked calluses had formed on the soles of my feet, making every step agony. Adual would pull out the guinea worms and clean the wounds on my feet whenever we stopped for the day, but every night's walk split them open again. The only thing worse than the constant physical agony was the crippling pain in my heart.

The moment the rebels had attacked our village, grief had coiled around my chest like a python, relentless and patient. With each loss, it ensnared me with another constricting loop. And in those rare moments, when the peaceful pull of sleep or the merciful lull of imagination allowed me to forget, grief squeezed, reminding me it was still there. I missed Koko and Mama with an ache, so deep and suffocating, at times it was difficult to breathe.

With every new village that wasn't home, with every new face that wasn't Mama's, with every new loss that wasn't mourned, grief strengthened its hold, tighter and tighter, until I thought my heart would break and my breaths came in short, shallow gasps.

"You don't have a fever," Adual said, studying my face. "I think you're just exhausted." She lifted me into her arms. "I will carry you for a while."

Clinging to Adual, I thought again of the soldiers' stories of Pinyudo and prayed my uncle and aunt had never reached Ethiopia and were safe at the Kakuma Refugee Camp. But as we slowly walked through the night with thousands of refugees, I could not help but worry. What if, like Pinyudo, Kakuma was not safe? What if with every step we took toward Kenya, we were moving closer to our deaths?

Besides protection, the SPLA soldiers brought our group another helpful skill, navigation. The young soldiers had trained and served throughout southern Sudan. They knew the territory, where to find water, and how to avoid towns and villages held by the GOS Army or Machar's growing militia, which had gained support and additional fighters from other ethnic groups in southern Sudan. They also knew the most direct route to Kenya, so they took the lead. Their pangas carved paths through dense foliage and tall grasses until the forests and savannas we'd traveled through since escaping Bor ended, giving way to the deserts of southeastern Sudan.

We continued to walk only at night, not just to avoid being spotted by the rebels and GOS soldiers, but to avoid the sun. During the day, the sun baked the desert sands. The blistering heat scalded our feet, making it harder to walk, and the desert winds blew sand into our eyes, making it difficult to see. Already struggling to ration what little water we had for drinking, there was none left for washing the gritty grains from our eyes. The irritation caused painful infections, and many children's bloodshot eyes oozed sticky green discharge.

The farther we walked into the desert, the harder it became to find water sources. The lions and wild dogs that had stalked us for months were replaced by dangerous desert inhabitants, like rattlesnakes and scorpions, which struck at our bare feet when we wandered too close to their hiding spots. There was little help for those who suffered poisonous bites or stings.

The number of people who gave up increased with every day spent walking across the desert sands. Exhaustion, hunger, and thirst drained many of the will to live. And despite my desire to get to Kenya and find Mama, I was not immune to death's pull. The desert sands stretched on forever. It took so much effort to keep moving forward. And for what? After every painful step, came another, and another. I was so tired and just wanted to sleep. I started to envy those who chose to stop. It would be easy to sit down and never move again. Death would find me eventually. I knew it would, just as it had found the others. All I had to do was stop, but Adual would not allow me to give up.

"There is purpose in life," she would tell me as she lifted me into her arms. "Look at me, Rachel. I got married, and my husband died a year later. I have no children of my own, but here I am, with you. Everything that has happened, all the loss and pain, we have survived. We will survive this, too."

At six years of age, I did not understand what Adual meant by "purpose," but I understood she believed it, and I believed in her, so on the days I could not find the strength to carry myself, Adual carried us both. And during the nights, when my small, flickering flame of hope that we would survive the walk to Kenya and find Mama again began to die, Adual's hope lit our way, over hundreds of kilometers and unforgiving terrain. I drew strength from her strength, and she drew strength from her unwavering faith. It carried us across the desert, all the way to the town of Nadapal, where SPLA and Kenyan soldiers stood guard at a border checkpoint.

Adual held me while the SPLA soldiers searched the refugees, confiscating any weapons they found. The men and boys were split into two groups. Those with registration cards from the refugee camp in Pinyudo were allowed passage through the checkpoint. Those without, whom the SPLA soldiers deemed healthy and strong, were pulled from the line, armed, and sent back to fight in the war.

The women and children were directed to a second checkpoint manned by Kenyan soldiers. Adual hugged me as the SPLA soldiers waved us through.

"With every step," she whispered through tears as we crossed the border into Kenya, "we are one step closer."

CHAPTER 18

Kakuma Refugee Camp, Kenya—August 1992

Although we had made it to Kenya, our walk was not over. The refugees who were not stopped at the border were forced to travel by foot over twenty-six kilometers to the United Nations High Commissioner for Refugees (UNHCR) processing center in the town of Lokichogio (Loki). It took us five and a half hours to make the journey, but the knowledge that we no longer had to worry about being captured or killed by GOS soldiers or Machar's rebels made the walk more bearable, and the hope that we might find missing loved ones in Kakuma hastened our steps.

Kenyans working for the UNHCR greeted us as we entered Loki. They led us to the UNHCR offices, where they took down our names and loaded us onto trucks for transport to Kakuma Refugee Camp. I was relieved not to have to walk the ninety-three kilometers to Kakuma, but the ride in the crowded, flatbed truck was not easy. People were sitting on top of one another, and there was no room to move. The desert sun beat down on us as the open-backed truck bounced and jostled over the rough roads. Adual held me tight so I did not fall from her lap.

Two hours after we were packed onto the crowded truck, we arrived at the Kakuma Refugee Camp. The camp had been constructed by the UNHCR and Kenyan government months earlier to contain the influx of over ten thousand boys from southern Sudan crossing the border to flee the civil war. The boys, most of whom were between the ages of eight and eighteen, had lost their homes and families to the war and were running to avoid death or forced conscription into the GOS or SPLA Armies. They had originally fled to Pinyudo Refugee Camp in Ethiopia, but the evacuation of Pinyudo forced them to cross Sudan again in search of sanctuary. As their numbers swelled and spilled over the Kenyan border and news of their plight spread, they became known throughout the world as the Lost Boys of Sudan. Within months of the Lost Boys' escape to Kenya, thousands of refugees from all over southern Sudan became residents of Kakuma Refugee Camp, including Adual and me.

Kakuma means "nowhere" in Swahili. It is located in Turkana County, the desolate, northwest corner of Kenya, bordering Uganda to the west and Sudan to the north. To create a camp for the refugees, the Kenyan government displaced many Turkana. Like the Dinka and Nuer, the Turkana people had been cattle herders for centuries. They depended on the desert land to raise and graze their herds. As we traveled down the dirt roads, they stood with their cattle in the arid fields, watching the trucks packed with refugees headed to Kakuma Refugee Camp. Their faces, hard with anger, offered no welcoming smiles.

Despite the bumpy ride, scorching temperatures, and unfriendly faces we met along the road to Kakuma, I could not help but feel excited. Adual and I had escaped the war, just as she'd promised. We could sleep at night without fearing attack from Machar's rebels or GOS soldiers. After two arduous months of walking, we had reached our destination. We could finally stop and rest. And above all, I could look for Mama. She, Uncle Abraham, and Aunt Monica had to be in Kakuma. No matter how long it took, I would find them.

"It's noted here that Rachel Achut Lual Deng will be in your care," a UNHCR worker stated as Adual and I waited outside Kakuma to receive supplies and instructions. "Is that correct?"

"Yes," Adual said.

"We conduct a head count once a year. It is mandatory both of you attend the annual count. If there is a change in Rachel's guardianship during the year, you will report it then."

Adual squeezed my hand and smiled at me. "There won't be."

"Rations of beans, oil, corn, and flour will be distributed on the first and fifteenth day of each month." The UNHCR worker handed Adual a ration punch card. The card had a barcode. Numbered and lettered squares outlined the perimeter of the card. Rows of punch squares and the UNHCR and World Food Programme (WFP) logos crowded the framework of small boxes.

"Do not lose this card. When you show up twice a month for your rations, you will be given the rations for you and the child in your care." The worker glanced at me. "Nothing more. Do you understand?"

Adual took the card. "Yes."

The worker then handed her a jerrican for collecting and transporting water and a few basic cooking pots and utensils. Adual gave me the jerrican to carry.

"You are both from Wernyol?"

"Yes."

"I'm assigning you to the settlement area Kakuma One, Zone One, Group Nine-A," the man said, looking over our paperwork. "Group Nine is comprised of Dinka refugees from Wernyol and Pawel."

Hope swelled in my chest. Mama, Abraham, and Monica were waiting for me in Kakuma. I just knew it. I pulled on Adual's hand. After nine months, I was finally going to be reunited with my family.

"Kakuma One, Zone One, Group Nine-A," Adual repeated to memorize the name.

"Do you have any questions?"

"I don't know—" Adual started to say.

"If you do, file them with the UNHCR offices." The man handed Adual and me each a gray blanket with the white UNHCR logo. "Welcome to Kakuma." Before we could respond or thank him, he waved forward the elderly man standing behind us. "Next!"

Unlike the GOS-run camp in Bor, the camp in Kakuma housed more than Dinka refugees. Men, women, and children from ethnic groups throughout southern Sudan also crowded the area, including Nuer. The war had driven them from their homes as well. The UN authorities and Kenyan government assigned the Nuer refugees to a zone separate from the Dinka refugees to ease tensions and decrease fighting between the warring groups.

When we reached Kakuma One, Zone One, Group Nine, I scoured each face, hoping to find Mama staring back at me. I wondered if she would recognize me after two years of being apart. When she'd left Wernyol to care for Baba, I was barely five years old. Now I was seven. I had grown taller in her absence, but over the last nine months spent running from rebels, being held captive in Bor, and fleeing across the deserts of Sudan, I had also lost a frightening amount of weight. The milaya Auntie Martha had given me in Gakyuom hung in loose sags and droopy sways from my bony frame. Mama might not recognize me, but I knew I would recognize her. When I found her, I would tell her right away who I was, and then she would see me. I looked for her, Abraham, and Monica in every grouping of refugees we passed, but I found only strangers.

"There are eight other groups and three other zones we can search once we are settled," Adual said when she saw disappointment weighing down my head and shoulders. "And trucks are bringing in new refugees every day. We will find her."

There was no hut awaiting us in Group Nine-A. If we wanted shelter, we would have to build one ourselves. The existing huts, mud abodes, and tents crowding the territory had been constructed by the refugees with what scarce resources they could find within the camp's borders. Many of the huts did not have thatched roofs, like the ones we had in Wernyol. The parched desert land supported only a few dying trees, making it impossible to gather enough materials to build the traditional roofs. The roofs in Kakuma were constructed from sheet metal provided by the UNHCR or cobbled together from empty metal oilcans that the refugees hammered flat.

I held my blanket over my head to shade myself from the blistering sun as we walked the dusty paths to an unoccupied patch of ground in Group Nine-A. We settled among other Dinka refugees from the area of Wernyol. The population consisted of mainly women and children. We asked everyone we met if they had seen Rebecca Agau or knew what had happened to my uncle Abraham and aunt Monica, but we received only sympathetic shakes of the head and questions about the lost loved ones of other refugees. Everyone in Kakuma was searching for someone.

I missed my family and grew increasingly frustrated

not learning any information about their whereabouts from the other refugees, but I also knew I was lucky to have Adual. Large groups of orphaned children had been taken in by other women, who were strangers to them. Adual had known me in Wernyol, cared for me in Bor, and protected me during our two months of walking to Kenya. She always placed my well-being before her own, making sure I ate or drank before she did and comforting me during the hot days and cold nights in Kakuma.

It would take months to construct a rudimentary shelter. While we worked day after day to collect branches from the dead trees spotting Kakuma One to create support posts for our hut, our UNHCR-issued blankets were the only protection we had from the elements. They were our shields against the harsh weather of Kakuma. At night, we wrapped our bodies in them to insulate ourselves from the cold as we slept beneath a tree. During the days, we draped them over the tree's bare branches to create some shade from the sun. We covered our heads with our blankets to shield ourselves from the sting of blowing sands carried on desert winds and hid under them when the rains finally fell. Beneath my thin, cloth shield, I'd listen to the weather rage.

Frequent dust storms and desert winds rattled the tin roofs of nearby huts in Group Nine, and the relentless sun and sweltering temperatures baked the metal until it burned to the touch. On the rare occasions it did rain, the first drops sizzled on the hot metal roofs, quickly evaporating in tendrils of steam, like wispy spirits hovering over the camp. The *plink-plink-plink* of rain falling on the roofs kept me awake on the nights it rained in Kakuma, but it was a beautiful sound. It was the sound of water, a resource we sorely lacked and desperately needed in the Kenyan desert. Rain was our only source of water in those first months in Kakuma. Adual and I would set out our pots, pans, and jerrican to capture the rain to use for drinking and cooking.

The hardened earth struggled to absorb the sudden rain showers. The water pooled on the ground. We attempted to scoop up the water in a losing battle to clear a dry area upon which we could sleep, but we did not complain. Rain meant water, and water meant life.

The lack of shelter and water were not the only dangers we faced in Kakuma. The desert that had become our temporary home was also the home of poisonous snakes and scorpions. Pained cries and startled screams often pierced the dark of night when someone was bit or stung. The refugees did what they could to help the victims, but there were no medical supplies or emergency services in Kakuma. The only treatments available were strips of cloth used as tourniquets and the painful pressing of the area around the bite or sting marks to squeeze the venom from the victim's body before it spread. If whoever treated the wound knew what they were doing and worked fast, by God's grace, the victim might live to see the next morning. But even the best efforts and most fervent prayers were not enough to save everyone. Before we lay down to sleep each night, Adual checked the area under our tree for any snakes or scorpions hidden in the dirt or brush. I slept better knowing Adual was with me, watching for danger and keeping me safe.

Every two weeks, Adual and I would walk through Kakuma One to the distribution area with her ration punch card to collect our oil, corn, flour, and beans. As we stood in line, I'd search the faces of those waiting with us, hoping to find Mama, Uncle Abraham, or Aunt Monica, but they were never there. Despite my disappointment, I refused to stop looking. Of the hundreds of refugees we'd asked about Mama, not one person had ever told me that she or Abraham and Monica were dead. Until someone did, I vowed to never stop searching for my family.

Two months after our arrival in Kakuma, however, my family found me. Adual and I were resting under our blankets beneath our tree to escape the sweltering sun, when a boy who looked to be around nine or ten years old approached us. Clutched in his hands was a tiny, ragged blanket.

"I am looking for Rachel Achut Lual Deng," he told Adual.

I peeked out from beneath my blanket. The tall, lanky boy studying my face looked vaguely familiar, but I was not sure who he was. After months of wandering southern

Sudan with little food and even less water, the refugees of Kakuma were walking skeletons, with tight, thin skin stretching over protruding bones and hollowed cheeks. If I had known the boy before, I did not recognize him now.

The boy squatted before me. "Are you Rachel?"

I looked to Adual for help, uncertain if I could trust this stranger.

Adual craned her neck to peer behind the boy. I looked, too, hoping to find Mama, but the boy was alone.

"Who's asking?" Adual asked.

"I am." The boy smiled. "I'm her uncle Andrew."

CHAPTER 19

Kakuma Refugee Camp, Kenya—October 1992

I did not know the boy, who claimed to be my uncle, but I knew his name. I had heard it repeated in Koko's prayers for over a year after her youngest stepson had been taken by the SPLA when he was seven. Andrew's eyes shone with the same kindness as my aunt Monica's, and his smile held the same confidence as my uncle Abraham's. If there had been more weight on his bones, he would have been a smaller version of his older brother, but starvation had stolen any remnants of childhood from Andrew's face. I knew I looked no different. No child in Kakuma did.

After Adual introduced herself and verified I was indeed Rachel Achut Lual Deng, Andrew's smile widened.

"I couldn't believe it when I heard you were here," he said. "I've been coming to Group Nine every weekend for six months looking for any news about our family. And today, one of the women told me a little girl named Rachel from Wernyol arrived two months ago. I had to come right away to see if it was you."

"You've been here for six months?" Adual asked.

Andrew nodded. "Closer to eight now. I was in one of

the first groups of Lost Boys to arrive. We were in Ethiopia at Pinyudo Camp, but they forced us to leave . . ." His voice trailed off.

"We heard about what happened in Pinyudo from a soldier," Adual said. "It is fortunate you survived."

Andrew's smile faltered. He rubbed the worn, threadbare blanket he clutched between his thumbs and forefingers. "Many of my friends didn't."

"I'm sorry," Adual said.

Andrew took a deep breath. "But I'm here now, and so is Rachel." He looked at me, and his smile reappeared. "Where's your mama?"

"I don't know," I said.

Andrew glanced around at the clusters of refugees huddled beneath blankets under nearby trees. "But she's here with you, right?"

Adual stood and draped her blanket across two branches to better shield me from the unrelenting sun. "Rebecca was in Torit caring for Michael when Wernyol was attacked."

Andrew's attention snapped back to her. "What happened to Michael? Is my brother all right?"

It was strange to think of Andrew and Baba as brothers. Andrew was far closer to my age than to Baba's. Despite their age difference, they had both been taken by the SPLA. And though Andrew was no older than ten, he had firsthand knowledge of the dangers his older brother had faced on the battlefields of the Second Sudanese Civil War.

"He was wounded in a battle with the GOS almost two years ago," Adual explained. "Rebecca left to be with him as soon as she heard the news."

"But he was alive?" Andrew asked.

Adual nodded. "Last we heard."

Andrew anxiously rubbed the blanket again between his fingers until I thought he'd wear a hole through the thin material. "Are they still in Torit?"

"We don't know," Adual admitted.

Staring at Andrew, I remembered he was not the only one of my uncles taken by the SPLA to fight in the war. "Is Uncle Ater with you?" I asked.

Confusion furrowed Andrew's brow. "Ater was killed in battle over a year ago. Didn't the SPLA send word to Wernyol about his death?"

"No," Adual said.

Andrew's nervous fingers continued to work the blanket as he searched the faces of the refugees sitting beneath the trees around us. "Then your koko doesn't know." His worried gaze finally settled on me. "Is she with you, Rachel?"

I shook my head.

Andrew's fingers stilled. I looked down at my lap, unable to bear the pain in his eyes, but I could not hide from the fear and anguish in his voice.

"Where is she?"

With Adual's help, I began to tell Andrew about Koko

and the hut in Pawel. He sank to the ground. I tried to continue, but tears choked off my voice.

Andrew reached over and patted my leg. "It's okay, Rachel. You don't have to say any more." As hard as it was for me to speak of that night in the hut with Koko, it must have been harder for Andrew to hear it. It had been over two years since he had seen his stepmother, and now he knew he would never see her again. I remembered Adual assuring me Mama was still alive because no one had told us she was dead. Any hope Andrew had held that he would see Koko again had been destroyed the second I told him about the hut in Pawel. I didn't blame him for not wanting to talk about it more. He had heard enough.

We sat in silence.

After several minutes, Andrew took a deep breath and then slowly released it, but his grip on the blanket did not relax. A glimmer of hope returned to his eyes as he looked at me. "Are Abraham and Monica here?"

"After the rebels attacked our home, Koko told them to run ahead without us," I said. The memory of Abraham promising his mama they'd find us again when it was safe and the desperate cries of Monica as her brother took her hand and fled into the night echoed through my trauma-tized mind. "We didn't see them after that."

Adual and I waited while Andrew processed the news that I was the only immediate member of the Deng fam-ily to make it to Kakuma. Suddenly, this young boy, who had been ripped from his family at age seven and forced to become a child soldier in a war he did not understand, found himself as the "man" of his family.

A family of two.

A ten-year-old boy and his seven-year-old niece.

Andrew wrapped a skinny arm around my shoulder. "It's just you and me, here, Rachel."

I glanced at Adual. Though she didn't comment on Andrew ignoring her presence under the tree and in my life, I could tell by her pinched brow and downcast eyes that his words had wounded her. I wanted to correct Andrew. I wanted to explain that I also had Adual, and even though she wasn't a Deng, she was my family, too.

But I had just met Andrew. He was my uncle, and I didn't want to hurt him any more than I already had, so I said nothing.

"Don't worry, Rachel. I'll take care of you." He handed me the small blanket. "I thought you could use something to keep you warm at night." Without the blanket to hold, he reached back and rubbed the base of his neck. "I'm sorry it isn't bigger. It's all I could find."

"Thank you." I placed the blanket on my lap. "Will I have to live with you now?"

Adual tensed beside me.

"You can't," he said. "I'm not in Group Nine. I live in an area just for the Lost Boys."

I had heard others in Group Nine-A speak of the Lost Boys of Kakuma. Everyone had a theory about why they were not housed with the rest of the refugees. Some thought it was because the young soldiers were too dangerous to be with civilians. Others assumed the SPLA wanted the Lost Boys kept together so they could easily transport them back to fight in the war. A few even believed in a more sinister conspiracy, in which the Kenyan government planned to sell the child soldiers to other countries as mercenaries. Whatever the real reason, no refugees were permitted to live within the area of Kakuma reserved for the Lost Boys.

"So you'll have to stay in Group Nine-A," Andrew told me.

The tension in Adual's body released at the news. "How many Lost Boys are there?"

"Almost ten thousand when we got here." Andrew shrugged. "I don't know how many there are now."

Adual shook her head. "So many destroyed families. So many orphaned children. And for what? Does anyone even remember why we are at war anymore?"

"I don't know why it started," Andrew admitted. "But you should hear the other soldiers talk. Everyone wants revenge. After the rebel attacks on Wernyol and the other Dinka towns and villages, a bunch of the Dinka survivors began attacking Nuer villages. All of southern Sudan is a war zone now."

"We saw that on our walk here," Adual said. "There is nowhere safe in Sudan anymore."

"For anyone," Andrew agreed. "Dinka, Nuer. Everyone

is coming here. I heard they plan to expand the camp, so there will be a Kakuma Two to handle all the new refugees. I just hope the camp doesn't get so big Kenya does to the refugees what Ethiopia did. There'd be nowhere else for us to go."

Andrew stayed for a while longer, talking to Adual about the war and Kakuma and telling me about the other distant family members and neighbors from Wernyol he had found in Group Nine. He promised to introduce me to them soon.

As the sun sank lower, painting the desert sky in African tulip tree blossom hues of reddish-orange and golden yellow, Andrew stood to leave.

"I have to go, but I'll visit again next weekend." He bent down and wrapped his little blanket around my shoulders. "It's you and me here, Rachel," he repeated. "We are family. I promise to take care of you and keep you safe."

A week later, Andrew returned to Group Nine-A, but this time, he was not alone.

He found Adual and me sitting beneath our tree, where Adual was tending to my sore feet.

"Who did you bring with you today, Andrew?" Adual asked, smiling up at the strange man and woman standing beside him.

"This is James and Mara. They're from Wernyol and live in Group Nine, too. They are my cousins," Andrew said. "They are *our* cousins, Rachel. When I told them about finding you, they wanted to meet you."

Mara smiled down at me. "Hello, Rachel." Her smile looked strained and unnatural, as though it had been so long since life had given her reason to smile that she'd forgotten how.

I pressed closer to Adual. "Hello," I said in a small voice.

"They also wanted to speak with you," Andrew told Adual.

Adual set aside the sharpened stick she was using to root out any guinea worms from my feet and shifted me on her lap. "With me? What about?"

"About Rachel coming to live with us," Mara said.

I pressed closer to Adual. Hers arms tightened around me. I did not want to go live with this strange man and woman. I didn't need them to take care of me. I had Adual.

"You'll like living with James and Mara," Andrew said. "They have a daughter your age, and they've taken in six other children who don't have any family here. The other girls are around your age, too, so you'll have friends to play with. Doesn't that sound fun, Rachel?"

Adual looked up at Mara standing beside Andrew. Mara was eyeing the few pots and rations Adual and I had tucked beneath our tree.

"It sounds like you have your hands full with so many children," Adual said to Mara. "I'd be happy to bring Rachel over anytime to play with them."

"She is coming to live with us," Mara stated.

Adual pulled me closer. "I want to know why," she said. "I have been caring for Rachel for almost a year now. I have kept her safe and alive. Why does she have to go with you?"

"Because we are her family," James said, speaking for the first time since they'd arrived. "*We* are Rachel's family. She belongs with us."

I wanted to yell at James and tell him he was wrong. They were not my family. Adual was. She had cared for me like I was her own. She had saved me. If it hadn't been for her, I would have died in Bor. They had no right to take me from her now. I belonged with her, and she belonged with me. If they took me away, I might have other kids to play with, but Adual would have no one. She'd be all alone, just like I was when she'd found me, sitting on the road in Gakyuom. She had taken me into her arms that day and had not let go since.

But as I sat in her lap, beneath our tree, while James, Mara, and Andrew told Adual how they had a right to care for me because we were related by blood, Adual's hold on me weakened.

"I don't want to go with them," I cried when she gathered my blankets and an aduɔk of rainwater for me to take to my new home in Kakuma.

She knelt before me and wiped away my tears. "I know. I don't want you to go either, but we will still both be in

172

Group Nine-A, and I promise, I will come visit you every day."

"Every day?"

Adual pulled me into one last hug. "As soon as you wake, I will be there, and you can come visit me anytime you want."

"Come on," Andrew said, putting his arm around my shoulder and steering me away from Adual. "I'll introduce you to the other girls. Our cousins even have a hut, so you won't have to sleep outside under a tree anymore."

James took my blankets and aduɔk from Adual. "We expect you to bring us Rachel's rations every two weeks until we can claim her at the next head count."

"Of course," Adual said.

I stopped and glanced back at Adual crying alone beneath our tree.

"Please take good care of Rachel," she begged Mara. "She's suffered so much already."

Mara grabbed hold of my hand and dragged me away from Adual and her tears. "We all have."

CHAPTER 20

Kakuma Refugee Camp, Kenya—November 1992

Adual kept her promise. Every morning when I woke, she walked the ten minutes to my cousin's hut with a bowl of porridge for me. The porridge came out of her rations, but she insisted I eat it all.

Andrew had not lied about my cousin's hut or the other children my age under their care. What he either failed to mention, or perhaps did not realize about our cousins, was they didn't allow any of the children in their care to sleep in their hut, except for their daughter. They claimed there was not enough room and promised to build another shelter for the rest of us. Their claims and promises did little to protect us from the weather or deadly desert creatures, a fact I learned one night as I slept on the ground outside their hut with only my UNHCR blanket and the blanket Andrew had given me as protection.

A sudden, sharp, stinging pain ripped me from sleep, deepened from an exhausting day completing chores for my cousins. I cried out and clutched my left foot. In the muted moonlight, a long black shadow slithered away in the darkness.

"Snake!" I screamed. "A snake bit me!"

My cries awoke the other children sleeping near me and pulled my cousins and their daughter from their hut. Adults and children from neighboring huts rushed outside to see what was wrong and who was causing the commotion.

While the men searched the area for the snake, Mara knelt beside me. "Where did it bite you?"

"My foot." My breaths came fast and short as a strange numbness spread through my left foot and crept up my leg like an invisible snake slithering inside my body.

Mara's trembling hands hovered over me. She glanced around for help, but the other adults were searching for the snake.

"I can't feel my leg!" I wailed.

"Stay calm and control your breathing," Mara snapped, grabbing the small blanket Andrew had given me. She tore a strip of cloth from the material and wrapped it around my lower leg, just above my ankle. "It will slow the spread of the venom." A flash of memory seared through my mind as she pulled it tight.

Koko and me, hiding in the hut in Pawel on the night of the attack. Koko, tearing a strip of cloth from her milaya and calmly telling me how to tie it around her leg to stop the bleeding from the bullet wound. Her pushing away her own fear and pain to ease mine with encouraging smiles and reassuring words.

You can do this, Achut. I know you can.

I held on to the memory of Koko as the numbing venom spread into my hip and toward my chest.

"I want Adual!" I cried.

"Stay calm and stop talking! I'm trying to remember what to do." Mara positioned her fingers around the puncture marks left by the snake's fangs and pressed down hard.

The numbness receded from the intense pressure, and hot pain burned through my foot. I pulled back from her grip.

"Stop it!" She slapped my foot and grabbed hold again.

I cried out as she pinched, harder and harder, squeezing all the venom she could from the two holes. Pinpricks of white light burst before my eyes, and my body went rigid. My chest heaved in panicked sobs.

"Control your breathing!" Mara ordered as she continued to milk the venom from the snakebite with her strong hands.

I tried to, but as the paralyzing numbness crept back and slithered into my shoulder and down my arm, my breaths came faster and shallow.

"Am I dying?" I asked.

Mara didn't answer. She kept squeezing venom from the holes until my foot bled. She wiped the blood away with the rest of Andrew's blanket. The other children huddled close, their eyes wide with fear.

"We killed the snake!" James announced, holding the decapitated body of a long black snake up for all to see. Several of the children screamed and scrambled away from him.

After the men had checked the area again for more snakes, spiders, and scorpions, Mara ordered the children to go back to sleep.

"How is Rachel?" James asked his wife.

"I squeezed as much of the venom out as I could. All we can do now is wait and pray it was enough." She draped the remains of Andrew's blanket over my legs. "Get some sleep," she told me before she and James returned to their hut.

As I lay there in the dark, not knowing if I would survive the night, I wished I were with Adual, safe beneath our tree. She'd know how to help. No matter how bad things had been in Bor and the desert, Adual always knew how to calm my fears. She'd hold me close and dry my tears.

It's all right. I'm here, Rachel. You're not alone.

I was surrounded by people in my cousins' crowded corner of Group Nine-A. Six other children slept in the darkness next to me, and I could hear the whispered voices and rumbling snores of dozens of other adults and children in the huts nearby, but I was alone. Alone in my pain, and alone in my fear. Tears ran down the sides of my face as I stared up at the full moon. I wanted Adual. I wanted Koko. I wanted Mama. I wanted someone who loved me to tell me everything would be all right. Someone to remind me I was not alone.

Half my body was paralyzed when Adual arrived the next morning with a bowl of porridge and my portion of the bimonthly rations she'd collected the previous day. James and Mara met her outside the hut to claim the bag of supplies and tell Adual about the snakebite.

Adual dropped the sack of beans and hurried over to where I lay.

Mara followed her. "I did my best. I'd never treated a snakebite before."

"Why isn't she moving?" Adual asked when I didn't sit up to greet her.

"Her left side is paralyzed," James said, picking up the rations.

"She will regain movement again eventually," Mara added, "if she survives. I've heard it happen with others. But if she doesn't—"

Adual shot her a warning glare.

"We still expect you to bring us her rations until the next head count," James said. "We have many children to feed." Then he and Mara took my rations inside their hut.

Adual removed Andrew's blanket from my legs. Her eyes widened, and a sharp intake of breath slipped through her lips.

"What's wrong?" Unable to move my left leg or sit upright on my own, I lifted my head and propped myself up on my right elbow to angle my body enough so that I could see my foot. My leg was swollen from my toes to below my left kneecap. I started to cry. "Am I going to die?"

"No." Adual covered my legs with the blanket. "I know

what to do." She pressed a kiss to my forehead. "I have to go get something. Don't worry. I'll be right back."

She must have run to her tree because she returned sooner than I'd expected. She knelt at my side, removed the blanket, and held up the thin wooden needle she had used to remove guinea worms from my feet during our long walk across southern Sudan. "I have to lance the wound, or the infection will spread."

"Will it hurt?" I asked.

"Your foot is numb, so you should not feel much pain."

With a steady hand, she slowly pressed the needle into the tight, swollen skin around the snakebite. Creamy yellow pus seeped from the cut. Then, just as Mara had the night before, Adual pressed on all sides of the wound with her fingers. Cloudy pink fluid oozed from the small incision. She wiped it away and pressed again. As she worked at cleansing the infection from my foot, she spoke to me with reassuring words and gentle tones. She repeated the process until bright red blood flowed from the cut. Then she pulled me into her arms and helped feed me the porridge she'd brought. When the bowl was scraped clean, she placed it on the ground and started to stroke my head.

"It's all right, Rachel. I'm here." She wiped tears from her face with the back of her hand. "You will survive this. I will make sure of it."

Calmed by her voice and words, I closed my eyes. She continued to stroke my head until I drifted to sleep in her arms. I don't remember when she left, but I know she returned the next morning, just as she'd promised.

For weeks, Adual tended to my wound several times a day to stave off any infection, and she brought a bowl of porridge for me each morning to keep my body strong and help me heal, but she could never stay long. No matter how much she pleaded with my cousins, Mara and James would not allow Adual to take me with her so that she could care for me day and night. So, every day, when the shadows stretched toward evening, I watched Adual walk alone back to our tree, and every night, when fear and doubt pressed in around me, I waited in the darkness for the sun to rise and Adual to return.

CHAPTER 21

Kakuma Refugee Camp, Kenya—December 1992

Under Adual's care, I eventually regained feeling on the left side of my body. As soon as I was able to move and walk again, my cousins put me back to work with the other girls fetching water from the lake when enough rainwater had fallen and collecting sticks for the new hut the men were building. Chores were not optional. Children who did not complete their chores to my cousins' satisfaction were punished with sound beatings.

I had been spared such harsh discipline when in the care of Mama, Koko, and Adual, who believed in correcting unwanted behaviors with gentle guidance and clear expectations, so the first time my cousins beat me, I was terrified. I ran off and hid beneath a bush all night. When they found me the next morning, my punishment for running away was another beating.

On the first and fifteenth of every month, Adual would bring my half of the rations, which my cousins immediately took inside their hut. It was obvious to the other children and me that as our daily portions of food decreased, my cousins' daughter continued to gain weight. Hungry and angry, we started to shun her, which earned us more beatings.

When I finished my work each day, I would sneak over to see Adual. She always fed me and cared for my feet, removing any guinea worms she found. I'd ask if she'd heard any news about Mama being alive. Her answer was always the same.

"Not yet, but I also haven't heard she isn't, so we must keep looking and hoping."

Andrew visited me every weekend, just as he'd promised. After the first several visits, he started bringing two other Lost Boys with him. Pabior was one of Andrew's hut mates. He was a few years older than Andrew. Andrew also introduced me to his best friend, Philip. Andrew and Philip had been at SPLA military school together before fleeing to the Pinyudo Refugee Camp in Ethiopia and then on to Kakuma.

Philip was Nuer. This did not seem to be an issue in the Lost Boys' section of Kakuma. There were as many Nuer Lost Boys as there were Dinka. They had trained and fought alongside one another and fled the war together. They had been brothers-in-arms, a fact that had not changed when they'd reached Kakuma.

This was not a sentiment shared by the refugees in the other sections of Kakuma, especially Group Nine-A. The sight of a Nuer boy or man elicited anger and resentment from the Dinka refugees, who had survived the massacres at Wernyol and Pawel and had lost many loved ones to the Nuer rebels. The Nuer refugees were equally angry at the Dinka, and except for the Lost Boys' section of Kakuma, the camp remained segregated based on the two opposing sides. Dinka and Nuer who wandered alone into their enemy's territory did not always escape alive. The attacks often happened at night. Like snakes, the attackers would strike and then slither off into the darkness. Sometimes, their victims' bodies were found. Many times, they were not. There were no police in Kakuma to investigate disappearances or deaths, and officials did not learn a person was missing or dead until the annual head count, so revenge killings were common in the camp. Dinka and Nuer were locked in a vicious cycle of revenge and death, where no one won and everyone lost.

The Dinkas' distrust of the Nuer followed Philip in angry glares and vile words as Andrew, Pabior, and Philip walked through Group Nine-A every weekend to visit me.

"Ignore them," Andrew would tell Philip. "Nuer or not, you are my brother. If anyone has an issue with that, they can take it up with me."

If anyone started a fight with Philip, Andrew would let Philip handle it, but as soon as other boys joined in the attack, Andrew stepped in to help his friend.

I admired my uncle Andrew. At ten years old, he had more wisdom, kindness, and courage than most of the adults in Kakuma. He recognized right from wrong and would not hesitate to call out others on their hypocrisy. Whether he'd known them for several years or a couple days, Andrew fought for the people he considered family, despite the risk to his own safety.

In addition to having Andrew's loyalty and protection, Philip also had the option to escape the discrimination he faced in Group Nine-A by returning to the Lost Boys' section of Kakuma, where he was welcomed and accepted. Three of my cousins, who arrived in Kakuma six months after Adual and me, were not so fortunate.

Matthew, Julia, and Thomas were cousins on my baba's side of the family. Their mama was Dinka, but their baba was Nuer. In his late twenties, Matthew was the oldest, but having been raised by the Dinka side of his family in Wernyol, he did not bear the Nuer markings on his forehead. Matthew had served in the SPLA with my baba, but he had been discharged from the military when guinea worms damaged his right leg to the extent his knee was always locked and he could no longer fulfill his duties as a soldier. At nine years old, Julia was two years older than me. Thomas was a year younger at age six. Like me, Matthew, Julia, and Thomas had escaped the massacre in Wernyol. Unlike me, they knew what had happened to their mama. She had been killed by the rebels during the attack.

Prior to the massacres, it was not uncommon for men and women from the two largest ethnic groups in southern Sudan to marry. Many children in the area were both Dinka and Nuer. After the fighting between the Nuer and

Dinka began, the children faced anger from both sides. They were children with no people to call their own. In the eyes of the Dinka and Nuer, they bore the sins of their enemies, and Kakuma proved to be more dangerous for them than for the rest of us.

When Matthew, Julia, and Thomas arrived in Kakuma, despite the UNHCR workers' recommendation that they be placed in a Nuer section, Matthew insisted they be housed with their mama's family and friends from Wernyol. They settled next to Mara and James's hut. Andrew was excited to meet more relatives and immediately welcomed them into our broken family.

A few months after Adual and I arrived at Kakuma, the UNHCR built water systems in each of the camp's groups. The Kenyans controlled the systems, which they opened three times a day, at 6:00 A.M., noon, and 4:00 P.M., for refugees to fill their jerricans and containers. You could only get water once a day. The lines were always long, and if you missed the three scheduled times, you had to wait until the next day to get water for you and your family. Fearful there would be no water left later in the day, people would start lining up at midnight for the 6:00 A.M. distribution. Mara was adamant that we not miss our opportunity to fetch water at the 6:00 A.M. time and would send us girls to stand in line all night with our jerricans. We were not the only children waiting in line until morning. Most families sent their children to hold their spots, and the line became the perfect place for kids to talk and play.

On the first night Julia accompanied us to the Group Nine-A water distribution station, a group of boys and girls started a game of keep-away with a ball they'd made by tying strips of cloth together. We often played games in line to help pass the time.

"Rachel, you're in the middle," an older girl announced.

"Come on, Rachel!" the other girls from my cousins' hut cheered as I took my place in the center of the circle. As the shortest in our group, I was often chosen to go first.

Everyone laughed, including me, as I jumped for the ball arcing high above my head. I missed and spun around to face whoever caught the ball, determined to snatch it out of the air on the next throw. It was during those rare moments of friendly competition and playful teasing, we could forget about the hunger, loss, and war, even if for just a brief time.

A tall boy with a long, skinny neck threw the ball across the circle to his friend. I jumped up, and my fingertips grazed the ball.

"So close!" the boy with the long neck said with a laugh. "You just need to grow taller, Rachel."

The boy's friend tried to throw the ball back to him, but the throw curved to the right, and the ball rolled outside the circle. I sprinted after it, scooping up the ball before anyone else could.

"Who needs height when I have speed?" I said, strutting past the boy. I craned my neck up as high as I could. "I'd rather be a cheetah than a giraffe."

Everyone laughed, including the boy.

"Rachel, you get to pick who goes in the middle next," he said.

Several kids waved their arms in the air, begging to be selected. I spotted Julia, off to the side, watching our game. Like the rest of the girls in Kakuma, Julia's hair was cut short, and she wore a shirt, long skirt, and no shoes. Boys were allowed to wear shorts, but girls were restricted to skirts or dresses. We had little choice in the colors or designs of our clothes. We wore what articles of clothing were distributed to us by a Catholic nun named Sister Elizabeth, who periodically visited Kakuma with donated clothing from Europe.

The long skirt Julia wore as she watched us play barely covered her knees. The same skirt on me would have hung halfway down my shins. My cousin stood several inches taller than me, as well as most of the girls her age. I envied her height, but as the new girl in our group, Julia just wanted to fit in. Standing outside the circle, she curled her shoulders forward and bowed her head to make herself smaller, but I knew it didn't matter how small Julia made herself, if she wanted to be accepted by the other kids in Group Nine-A, she couldn't stand back and wait.

"I choose Julia!" I waved for my cousin to join the game. "Come on, Julia! It will be fun."

Julia's head and shoulders dipped lower as she made her way into the center of the circle.

"Let's see them get the ball past you," I said.

A timid smile wavered on Julia's lips. She raised her long arms in the air, preparing to block or catch the first throw.

I took my spot between two other girls in the circle, but an older girl snatched the ball from my hands. "We're not playing with *her*."

"Why not? She's my cousin."

"She's Nuer," another girl said, spitting on the ground at Julia's feet.

Like a pack of hyenas, the girls surrounded Julia, throwing vile words and names at her.

"Leave her alone!" I tried to grab my cousin's hand to pull her away, but the girls closed their ranks.

"Why are you in Group Nine anyway?" one of the girls asked Julia.

Julia's eyes darted from one angry face to the next. "My family is here," she said in a small voice.

"Mine's not," a girl yelled, shoving Julia, "because of Nuer like you!"

I didn't see who threw the first punch, but I threw the second. I had learned from Andrew not to interfere with a fight if it was a fair match, but this was far from a fair match, and I wasn't going to leave Julia to fight it alone.

"Let go of her!" I screamed, punching my way through the group of girls attacking my cousin.

The girls landed some hits, but so did Julia and I.

Finally, a few of the older boys in line for water pulled us apart, but no one escaped the fight unscathed. Bruises, swelling, and scratch marks marred our faces and arms.

"Why are you defending her, Rachel?" one of the girls asked as I took Julia's hand. "She's Nuer. They destroyed our homes and killed our families!"

"Her home was Wernyol, just like ours!" I yelled. "Her mama was killed in the attack, just like your families, just like my koko! You talk about Nuer. You talk about Dinka. We have all lost! She is not the enemy!"

After that first fight, Julia stood a bit taller around the other girls in Group Nine-A. She and I often left the 6:00 A.M. water collection with fresh cuts and bruises following run-ins with bullies, but we never let them scare us away. Julia returned each night, prepared to face their anger. And I returned each night, prepared to defend her.

CHAPTER 22

Kakuma Refugee Camp, Kenya—1993–95

With all we lacked in Kakuma, there was one thing we had in abundance. Time.

We spent our days and nights waiting.

Waiting for water.

Waiting for food.

Waiting for shelter.

Waiting for news of lost loved ones.

Waiting for the sun to rise and drive away the darkness.

Waiting for the sun to set and drive away the heat.

Waiting for peace in Sudan.

Waiting to return to our homes.

And, for too many, waiting for death.

To pass the hours we had to wait in line for water, we played games, like soccer and keep-away, shared stories and gossip we'd overheard around the camp, and met the new refugees who'd arrived in Kakuma.

I'd been in Kakuma for a year when I met Deborah one night while waiting for water. Deborah had been separated from her mama when they'd fled their home, and, like me, did not know if her mama was alive or dead. When Deborah had arrived in Kakuma, she discovered her two older brothers at the refugee camp. As was the case with thousands of Sudanese Lost Boys, Deborah's brothers had been taken from her family years before to fight for the SPLA. Like Andrew, they had escaped the brutal evacuation of Pinyudo and walked to Kenya, seeking sanctuary from the war. Deborah had been happy to find her brothers, but she was not permitted to live with them in the Lost Boys' section of Kakuma. Instead, she was fostered by her uncle's family in Group Nine-A.

Deborah was a year younger than me and a bit shy. While the other kids in line were talking over one another, Deborah was content to listen, which was perfect for me because I liked to talk. I told her all about Kakuma. I told her when and where to go to bathe and how far we had to walk away from the huts to relieve ourselves. I explained to her the different sections in the camp and how her brothers would be allowed to visit her from the Lost Boys' section on weekends, like Andrew visited me. I warned her about the snakes, spiders, and scorpions and what to do if she was bit or stung. I even showed her the scar on my foot from the snakebite I'd survived. Deborah listened for hours while I talked about Mama, Koko, and Adual, and when Deborah told me that she feared her mama was dead, I shared Adual's words with her.

"Has anyone told you your mama is dead?"

"No," Deborah admitted.

"Then until someone does, you must believe she is alive and will find you someday."

"Do you really believe your mama will find you, Rachel?"

"I believe in Adual. She has never lied to me about anything. She would not lie to me about something as important as my mama."

"Then I will believe her, too," Deborah said. "And I will hope someday both our mamas will come to Kakuma to find us."

I smiled at my new friend. "We'll look for them together."

Deborah and I searched for our mamas in every new truck packed with refugees arriving in Kakuma. We did not find them among the sea of new faces, but we did meet some relatives who had also fled southern Sudan.

A few months after I met Deborah, Andrew introduced me to another family member. Although Jacob was only eighteen years old, he was my baba's uncle, making him my great-uncle. Jacob had been living with Andrew and the other Lost Boys in Kakuma. When he learned his late sister's children were living with us in Group Nine-A, he moved in with Matthew, his wife, Julia, and Thomas. Julia was not happy about the new addition to their family.

"I hate him," she told Deborah and me as we stood in line for water one night. "When he wants water or food, he wants it right away, and if I don't get it fast enough, he—"

"What?" I asked.

When his sister didn't answer, Thomas did. "He beats us."

I was not surprised by Thomas's admission. I had noticed bruises on Julia's back when we bathed at the lake. Beatings were not unusual in Kakuma. Many parents and adults believed the threat of physical harm motivated children to behave and complete their chores in a timely manner, but Julia and Thomas were also not used to such severe punishment. Matthew and his wife had never raised a hand to either of them.

I pulled Julia into a hug. "I'm sorry."

Julia sniffed back tears. "I know he's your great-uncle, Rachel, but stay away from him as much as you can. You too, Deborah."

Anger over Jacob's mistreatment of Julia burned in my stomach. I wanted to protect her from Jacob like I had defended her from those in Group Nine-A who bullied her about being half Nuer. But Jacob was ten years older than me, and he was family. I knew if I said or did anything to defend Julia, I would only make things worse for her and myself, so I stood in line and held Julia as she cried, and I took her advice and avoided Jacob when I could.

The friendships I formed with Deborah, Andrew, Julia, and Thomas strengthened during my first two years in

Kakuma. Like the women of Bor, we leaned on one another for support and formed an unbreakable bond through our shared suffering. Along with Adual, they helped fill the missing pieces of my heart torn away by the war, and in doing so, they became more than friends.

They became family.

We waited for time to pass in Kakuma together. And despite the insatiable hunger, unbearable hopelessness, and constant death that stalked our days and haunted our nights, we found opportunities to celebrate the lives we had while working toward the lives we hoped to someday rebuild.

In 1995, several Sudanese teachers who had taught the Lost Boys in Pinyudo collaborated with teachers from Kenya to create a school for the children in Kakuma. After Deborah, Julia, Thomas, and I finished fetching water each morning, we would hurry over to a grouping of trees that the teachers had established as our school. They did not organize classes by age, but rather by skill level. Five days a week, my friends and I gathered beneath the sparse canopy of the trees to learn with two hundred classmates, who ranged in age from five to twenty years old. Our school did not have pencils or paper. We practiced our letters and numbers by writing in the dirt with sticks.

"Education is the path to your future," one of the Sudanese teachers told us at the end of our first day of lessons. "To survive in Kakuma, you must feed not only your body, but your mind. You must consume knowledge and hope, just as you consume food and water. With an education, you nurture your mind, which opens you up to more opportunities in the world and feeds your hope for a better tomorrow. We all endured many hardships to come to Kakuma because we wanted a better tomorrow." He smiled at us. "You do want a better tomorrow, don't you?"

Two hundred voices answered in unison, "Yes, Teacher!"

"Then come back tomorrow and the next day and the day after that. Keep coming back to educate your minds and fight for your better tomorrow."

I learned my ABC's and numbers in the school under the trees at Kakuma. I came to school tired and hungry. Before instruction began, I had to check the area for poisonous snakes, scorpions, and spiders. Most days, I sat on the hard, sunbaked earth. When it rained, I sat in the mud, but I always came to school. The teachers had promised us a path to a better tomorrow, and no weather, hunger, or desert dangers were going to keep me from following it.

My favorite part of school was at seven o'clock every morning, when our class of two hundred students gathered in a large circle with the other classes of our school to sing together. It was a beautiful, unifying way to start the day with over two thousand voices joining together in song.

On the days when we did not have school, my friends and I often spent our hours after chores at cultural celebrations and church. People gathered to play music from their villages and enjoy an afternoon of traditional Dinka dances. Adults and older children taught the younger children choreography and songs, assuring our cherished traditions were not also lost to the war. In those moments of music and movement, as I danced and sang with my friends, we were transported back to a happier time when village dances marked milestones in people's lives and celebrated the transition from childhood to adulthood. Like a balm, they soothed the constant rub of life in Kakuma and briefly numbed the unending pain of loss.

I also passed many hours in Kakuma at church. The refugees in Group Nine-A would gather every Sunday evening in a cleared-out area. People sat on large stones or the ground for Bible Study and to practice new hymns for two hours, followed by an hour of communal prayer. In addition to church, my friends and I attended religion classes during the week. The classes were called Sunday school even though we met every Monday, Wednesday, and Friday. Our teacher, Joseph, taught the children under the age of fourteen new hymns, which we practiced for our Sunday mass performances scheduled for the beginning and end of each month while the older teenagers practiced for their performances scheduled for the middle of each month.

School and church were welcome distractions in Kakuma, but despite how hard I tried to forget, nothing, not even the best of distractions or intentions, could keep the pain and loss away for long. Like scorpions burrowed beneath the shifting desert sands, the memories struck when I was least prepared for their deadly sting.

One such painful memory struck without warning three years after Adual and I had arrived in Kakuma. My friends and I had finished our chores and joined the other children in our class for Sunday school. Everyone was talking and playing while we waited for class to begin. When our teacher, Joseph, arrived, he checked his watch.

Teachers were among the few people who owned watches in Kakuma. The rest of us estimated the time of day or night based on the length and position of the shadows cast by our bodies when we stood in the sun or moonlight. It wasn't as precise a time-telling method as a watch, but it was fun, and we would compete to see whose estimate came closest to the times on our teachers' watches. Deborah, Julia, and I quickly checked our shadows and exchanged guesses of the time.

"What time is it?" I asked our teacher, hoping my shadow estimate was closer than my friends'.

"It's time to prepare for our next performance." Joseph clapped his hands loudly to get the class's attention and then waited patiently as his students gathered in the weak shade of a small grouping of leafless, brittle trees.

Deborah, Julia, and I hurried over to sit on the ground directly in front of Joseph. We all loved singing. All of us, except Thomas. My younger cousin broke out in a cold sweat at the mere thought of singing in front of others.

His aversion to singing had nothing to do with him disliking music. Thomas loved music, but unfortunately for him, and anyone standing near him, Thomas couldn't carry a tune if we attached a handle to it.

He plopped down next to me and groaned. "Not more singing."

"Hush," his sister said, shooting him a stern glare.

When everyone was seated and quiet, Joseph addressed the class. "Many in our congregation are struggling, so for our next performance, I have chosen a hymn I hope will give people the strength to carry on through their pain and grief. If you recognize it, please sing along with me now." He took a deep breath and lifted his chin. His deep, baritone voice filled the small clearing where we sat.

"Let us be strong."

The melody and words struck like a viper, fast and hard. A small gasp escaped my lips.

Deborah leaned over and whispered in my ear. "What's wrong, Rachel?"

I ignored her, focusing all my attention on our teacher's voice and the familiar hymn.

"We are fighting with the devil. Push away the fear."

The memory of Koko and me working in the garden on our family compound in Wernyol sharpened into focus.

This is your baba's favorite hymn, Koko had said as she worked her hand hoe into the soil. *He sings it before every battle to strengthen his heart. The words give him the courage*

*to keep fighting and the will to survive, so he can someday
come home to his family.*

As I listened to Joseph sing, I wondered if Baba was
still fighting with the devil on the battlefields of southern
Sudan or if the rebels had found him and Mama in Torit,
like they'd found Koko and me inside the hut in Pawel.

Thoughts of Pawel, which I'd buried deep in my mind,
clawed their way to the surface. Koko holding me in her
lap, humming Baba's favorite song softly against my ear.
A loud banging at the door. Koko's milaya swept over my
head. The scent of cloves and thin leaves. The warmth of
her skin pressed against mine. Voices begging for mercy.
Three whispered words, spoken in equal measures of love,
fear, and heartbreak.

You are strong.

"Rachel?" Deborah nudged me with her elbow. "Are
you all right?"

"What?" I said, shaking free of the memory. I looked
around and found Deborah, Julia, and Thomas staring at
me. "Yes. I'm fine."

"Then why are you crying?" Deborah asked.

I reached up and felt my cheeks. They were slick with
tears.

When we were not practicing our songs, Joseph led our
Sunday school class in prayers and read us Bible stories.

I'd sit with my friends and listen to stories of the many hardships and trials people in the Bible faced and survived, from wandering the desert for forty years to suffering betrayal and persecution at the hands of those once considered friends and neighbors. Their stories gave me strength and hope. I recalled their suffering and perseverance on days when my own suffering became too great and on nights when my despair grew too heavy.

School and church offered an escape for me in Kakuma. A way to forget for a while. I looked for more opportunities to spend time there, like volunteering to help clear the area before everyone gathered for mass and leading songs in Sunday school. But not everyone found the respite in church and school that I had. Some looked for other ways to forget.

Around the time Andrew turned thirteen, he stopped joining us for mass on Sundays. I asked him why the next weekend when he, Pabior, and Philip came to visit.

"What's the point?" he said. "We have been here for three years, Rachel. It is obvious, God spends none of his time thinking about us. Why should I spend any of my time thinking about him? Why should we sing songs of praise to him when he has abandoned us in Kakuma? Why should we pray when he either is not listening or does not care?"

His answer frightened me. I had heard others talk like that in Kakuma. Once they had given up hope, death soon followed.

"But Adual says we find hope and comfort in prayer."

"Then she can look for it there, and so can you. I have found it somewhere else."

Despite my persistent questions, Andrew and the others refused to explain what he'd meant.

In the weeks that followed, he started missing his weekend visits. On the rare occasion he did stop by, he was often late and smelled of alcohol.

When I brought my concerns to Adual in the hut where she lived with six orphaned children she had taken into her care, she shook her head in sadness.

"I fear Andrew, like many of the Lost Boys, have turned to alcohol to numb their pain and forget the trauma they have suffered. It is a temporary fix that only brings more suffering to them and their loved ones."

My concern for my uncle turned to fear. Too many refugees drank alcohol to get them through the long days and nights of waiting in Kakuma. The demand for alcohol was met by women in the camp, who knew a basic recipe for corn whiskey. After soaking the corn for days in water, they'd dry out the swollen kernels to make yeast, which was essential in the fermentation process for producing the alcohol they then bartered or sold to desperate customers. Drunk men, women, and even some children staggered down the dirt paths of Group Nine-A. They started drinking before dawn and were passed out before dusk. I had witnessed the destructive effects of alcohol on people and their families. Chores went undone. Money and belongings were squandered. Children were neglected. Judgment eroded. Anger erupted. And fights turned deadly. This was not the path I wanted for my uncle.

"What can we do to help him?" I asked Adual.

"We can remind him that he is not alone and there are people here who care about him."

"What if that doesn't help?"

Adual took my hands in hers. "Then we pray for him."

That night, I followed Adual's advice. Lying on the floor of the hut James had built for the girls he and Mara had taken into their care, I prayed Andrew would stop drinking and find the hope that he, like so many of the orphaned children in Kakuma, had lost.

In the years that followed, I spent my abundance of time in Kakuma praying for my friends, family, and lost loved ones, including Andrew.

And waiting for God to answer.

CHAPTER 23

Kakuma Refugee Camp, Kenya—1995–96

We fled from the war in Sudan, but we could not outrun death. It followed us to Kakuma.

Every morning when we woke, another body was discovered.

Every night when we waited in line for water, another person was missing.

Some deaths came as a surprise. Most did not. All were mourned.

There were no coroners in Kakuma. For some, the cause of death was evident: a poisonous bite, illness, suicide, or killing by the warring factions in the camp. For others, the cause of death remained a mystery. There were no experts to tell us if someone had suffered a heart attack or stroke, or if they had been consumed by cancer.

Whether the cause was known or not, the removal of the body was always left to those with whom the person had lived. Family members or friends of the dead would place the body in a blanket secured between two long wooden poles. Then four people, two in the front and two in the back, would position themselves at the ends of the poles and lift the makeshift stretcher and body to begin the arduous walk to the camp cemetery. The walk was long, and the refugees were weak from lack of food and water. A group of people always walked behind the stretcher in a solemn processional to take turns carrying the body until they finally reached the cemetery, where they would dig a grave and bury the deceased.

Despite the constant deaths in Kakuma, the number of refugees in the camp continued to grow. By the time I was eleven, the camp had tripled in size with the additions of Kakuma Two and Kakuma Three. Even with the two new areas, the camp could not support the hundreds of thousands of refugees who now called it home, but with each new refugee came the hope that one day it would be Mama walking into Group Nine-A.

In early 1996, one of the thousands of new refugees arriving in Kakuma renewed our fading hope. Julia and I were playing a game of keep-away from Thomas while waiting in line for water when Deborah joined us. She stood there, staring off into the distance.

"What's wrong?" I asked, tossing the ball to Julia.

Deborah's gaze remained fixed on a point beyond the boundaries of Kakuma. "My aunt told me something this morning I can't believe. Something I am afraid to believe."

"What did she say?" Julia asked, throwing the ball back to me.

Deborah blinked once, breaking her hold on the horizon. Her warm brown eyes met mine. "She said my mama arrived in Narus yesterday and is on her way here."

I dropped the ball. "What?"

We hurried over to our friend.

"Is she sure?" Thomas asked.

"Yes." When Deborah spoke, her words held no emotion, no belief, no hope. "So are my brothers."

"But you're not?" I asked.

Deborah's vacant stare returned to the world outside Kakuma. "Since I arrived here, so many people have told me my mama was here. I've gotten my hopes up every time, only to learn they were lying or playing a mean joke on me."

"But what if this time it's not a lie or joke?" Thomas asked.

"What if it is?" Deborah snapped, her voice rising in panic. "I don't want to get my hopes up again, just to be disappointed." Her shoulders rose and fell in an exhausted sigh, and her head bowed. She looked at us with tears in her eyes. "It hurts too much, and I'm so very tired of hurting."

I wrapped my arm around her shoulder and pulled her close. "I know."

"You don't believe even a little bit that your aunt and brothers could be right this time," Julia asked, "and your mama is on her way here to Kakuma?"

"I'll believe it when I see her with my own eyes."

The next morning, we gathered near the entrance of Kakuma One to wait with our friend. Deborah's brothers and aunt joined us. Dozens of other refugees also waited to see who would arrive. Everyone was excited and talking, except Deborah. She stood away from the people and noise, silently staring down the dirt path. Any new refugees being admitted into Kakuma One would walk down that path, including Deborah's mama.

As the first group of refugees made their way toward us, I stood by my best friend. "Do you see her?"

"No."

I asked her the same question with each group that walked past, and she responded with the same answer. I started to worry Deborah had been right not to get her hopes up when a woman's voice cried out from the fourth group of new refugees entering Kakuma One.

"Deborah!"

A tall, emaciated woman broke free from the crowd and ran toward us. Deborah's eyes widened in shock, but she did not move. Weeping with joy, the woman threw her arms around Deborah and kissed her face.

"My daughter! My beautiful daughter!"

Deborah's arms hung limp at her sides as the woman hugged her.

"Mama!" Deborah's two older brothers ran over.

Their mama embraced both of them and kissed their faces. "My boys!"

I stood with Julia and Thomas and cried. My heart

swelled with joy for my friend and hope for myself. If Deborah's mama was still alive after all this time, my mama could be out there, too. She could be looking for me. I couldn't wait to tell Adual the good news.

Everyone was jumping around in excitement, hugging, and crying, except Deborah. She stood there watching the jubilation erupting all around her, but she did not join the celebration.

I did not understand her reaction. We had prayed for four years that our mamas were alive and would someday find us, and that day had come for Deborah and her brothers. Her mama was alive and in Kakuma. She was holding Deborah, and yet Deborah's face and body were as unexpressive and rigid as if she were being hugged by a stranger. It was only later in life that I understood after so many years of hoping to find her mama, only to be disappointed again and again, Deborah's shocked mind could not process or trust the miracle of her reality in that moment of reunion. It would be two days before Deborah believed God had finally answered her prayers and her mama had found her.

After Deborah's mama arrived in Kakuma, I studied the face of every new refugee, convinced I would find my mama, too, but as days stretched into weeks and weeks piled into months, my hope of finding Mama faded again and I stopped looking.

"There's always tomorrow," Adual would remind me, "so there's always hope."

Although my guardianship had been officially transferred from Adual to my cousins at my first Group Nine-A head count when I was seven, Adual remained a constant and important person in my life. She was my home in Kakuma, a safe haven when life became unrecognizable and unbearable. I saw her every day. Some days she'd visit me. Some days I'd visit her. In the shade beneath our tree, we'd sit and talk for hours.

While I told her what I'd learned in school and showed her the new letters I'd mastered by etching them in the sand, Adual would tend to my sore, cracked feet. While I sang her the songs my Sunday school class was preparing for the next mass, she'd strip me of my lice-infested clothes and lay them in the sun, spreading hot sand over them to kill the small, itchy parasites. She'd get quiet when she noticed new bruises on my back, punishments for not performing my chores to my cousins' satisfaction. She'd wrap me in a gentle embrace and tell me she was sorry. Then I'd rest my head in her lap and give her the play-by-plays of that morning's games at the water collection line while she picked any lice from my hair. If there were too many to remove by hand, she would shave my head with an old straight razor while telling me all about her day and the children she had taken into her care.

By the end of our conversations, my feet were cleaned, my hair and clothes were free of lice, and my heart was full of the kindness and love Adual shared so generously with me and others. Every Sunday, Adual would sit in the front of the gathered crowd for mass so she had an unobstructed view of my Sunday school class's performance. She'd watch me sing and dance with the smile of a proud mama, and she'd wait for me after mass so she could tell me what a good job I had done. We'd pray and sing together. And she reminded me to never give up hope.

We had been in Kakuma for four years, and of all the refugees who had come into the camp not one had any information about my mama and baba. No one knew if they were alive, but no one could tell us they were dead. My hope of ever seeing Mama again was left suspended in a cruel purgatory with no closure to my grief and no promise of an answer to what had become of my parents.

"Never give up hope," Adual would tell me. "Your mama would never give up on you, so don't you give up on her."

I wanted to believe Adual. I wished I had her unwavering faith in God and my mama, but it had been six years since I'd watched Mama walk away from me in our garden. Six years since I'd seen her face and heard her promise that she would come back for me. Six years, more than half my short life, I had waited for her, but the more time that passed, the more difficult it became to believe Mama was alive. It hurt less to think she might be dead and couldn't come for me, than to believe she was alive and chose not to.

209

I was not the only child in Kakuma left wondering if they'd ever see their parents again. There were children, who like Deborah and her brothers, had found their mamas, but for many, like me, the search for missing loved ones only produced disappointment and frustration. There was a whole generation of lost children in Kakuma. During the day, they wandered the camp searching for their parents. At night, they prayed God would send their parents back to them. I, too, prayed each night to be reunited with my mama, but as I drifted to sleep, I always ended my prayers with words of thanks, grateful God had sent Adual to watch over me when Mama couldn't.

There were no telephones in Kakuma. News traveled by word of mouth. Joyous news, like the birth of a child, a new marriage, or families reuniting with lost relatives traveled through the camp on excited voices lifted in songs and cheers. Rumors and secrets slithered from hut to hut on whispers behind cupped hands. Bad news, such as a death, was announced in mournful cries. At night, the pained wails echoed across the camp. The screams pulled us from our sleep and huts. We'd follow the cries until we arrived at the origin of the screaming and saw who had died. There was hardly a night in Kakuma when I wasn't awakened by death screams, but there is one night, a few days before Christmas 1996, that will be seared in my memory forever.

I was asleep in my hut with the other girls after an enjoyable evening at church, praying and singing with Adual, when a child's scream tore through the night. We ran from our hut to see what was wrong and who had died. Mara, still half-asleep, came out from the hut she shared with her husband and daughter. Julia, Thomas, Matthew, his wife, and Jacob were already standing outside their hut.

"What direction is it coming from?" Mara asked.

Matthew shook his head. "I'm not sure."

We stood in silence, listening. It wasn't long before the voice cried out again. We looked toward the east side of Group Nine-A. Julia, Thomas, and I hurried ahead of everyone as we made our way toward the scream. The pained cry continued, pulling more refugees from their huts. As we followed the screams through the darkness, my heart raced and my steps quickened until I was running down the dirt path I had walked every day since my cousins had claimed me. By the time we reached the outskirts of the compound of huts where Adual lived, I sprinted ahead of the others.

"Please, God, no," I prayed as the silhouette of her hut became visible.

A crowd had gathered outside.

I ran up to five of the children who lived with Adual. They were all crying.

"Who is it?" I asked.

When no one answered, I rushed to the door of the hut, but a man stopped me from entering.

"Let me in!"

"I can't," he said.

"Why not? What happened? Who is in there?" I demanded.

Mara and the others caught up to me. The man stepped aside to let Mara enter the hut. I moved to follow, but the man blocked my path again. "I'm sorry."

Another anguished scream tore through the night. I turned to see the sixth child whom Adual had taken into her care crying on her knees.

"No." My heart and mind broke, one with grief and one with disbelief. "Not Adual."

For the briefest second, I considered running away so no one could tell me she was dead. But I did not run. I sank to the ground in front of Adual's hut and wept. It did not matter how far I ran. It did not matter if I never heard the words "Adual is dead." I knew. I knew she was gone by the devastated tears of the children she'd cared for in Kakuma. I knew she was gone in the inability of every adult to look me in the eyes as they exited her hut. And I knew Adual was gone because she did not rush to me with open arms to pull me into her embrace at the sound of my cries.

Julia and Thomas sat next to me and wept. We did not speak. There were no words.

Minutes later, Deborah, her mama, and her aunt arrived. They, too, had heard the death scream. Her mama and aunt spoke with Mara.

Deborah knelt before me and took my hands in hers. "Does anyone know how she died?"

I shook my head. "I don't know." Shards of a memory sliced through the fog of shock.

A dirt road.

A sea of strangers.

Despair driving me to my knees.

The pull to let go.

The numbing surrender.

A gentle touch.

A kind voice.

A name.

My name.

Spoken with hope.

A face.

Her face.

Pulling me back.

I'm here, Rachel. You're not alone.

I scrambled to my feet. "I need to see her."

The man at the door would not let me pass.

"Please," I begged.

Deborah took my hand. "Come on," she said, her voice weak with sadness. "We'll walk you back to your hut."

I pulled away. "No. I'm not leaving her."

Tears glistened in Thomas's eyes. "She's gone, Rachel."

"We should go," Julia said, her head bowed as if in prayer. "There's nothing we can do for her now."

"I said I'm not leaving." I sat down on the ground outside

the hut. "She needs to know I am here." My voice broke as I stared at the closed door. Adual was on the other side. "She needs to know she is not alone."

I sat all night outside her hut, staring at the closed door. Time passed in short bursts and long stretches while I waited. People flocked around Adual's hut like hungry vultures, desperate to pick through the mystery of her death.

"She was always giving her rations to children," they whispered. "She was skin and bones. She wouldn't be the first in Kakuma to die of starvation."

"She could have had a heart attack or stroke. They kill with no warning."

"I heard she had walked to the lake to bathe earlier in the evening. I bet she was bit by a snake or stung by a scorpion."

"Most likely she was sick. The old man in the hut next to hers died of malaria yesterday, and a child four huts over died of dysentery just last week."

Each theory was possible and upsetting, but as the night reached for morning, logical theories twisted into cruel conspiracies.

"The attacks on women found alone are getting worse. She could have been killed by Nuer refugees or assaulted by a group of Turkana."

"You know she had no family or children of her own. She probably took her own life."

I wanted to scream and chase them all away. They didn't know Adual. She would never kill herself, not when she knew so many young lives depended on her, not when she knew I depended on her.

They did not remove her body until morning. When the first hints of dawn etched the horizon in the night sky, four men carried her from the hut on a makeshift stretcher.

"It's time to go home, Rachel," Mara said.

I watched the men walk away with Adual's body. "Not yet."

"You need to be in line for water before six," she said.

"I know."

With the body gone, Mara and the other vultures left. I waited until they disappeared into their huts, and then I stood and followed Adual to the cemetery.

I kept my distance. I knew if the men carrying her saw me, they'd send me back, but I had to follow her. I had to see that she was given a proper burial. I had to see where her life ended so I was not left wondering what had become of her, this woman who had never abandoned me. I would not abandon her. Not even in death.

It took an hour to walk to the cemetery. By the time we arrived on the clearing of land situated on the outskirts of

Kakuma, morning bathed the sky and desert in golden light. I watched from a distance as the men dug a shallow grave and placed Adual's body inside. I cried as they buried her beneath the unforgiving earth of Kakuma. And I waited until I was alone before approaching her grave.

I sat beside her small plot long into the morning. I did not go to the water distribution. I did not attend school. I knew a beating awaited me when I eventually returned to my cousins' huts in Group Nine-A, but I did not care.

I took a handful of dirt from Adual's grave and squeezed it until my fingers ached. I did not know what had taken her from me. I did not know whose theory was right. Had it been starvation or illness? Had she died from a venomous bite or sting? Had she been attacked? But as I sat there, alone, by her burial plot, I decided I did not need to know which devil had taken Adual's life. There was just one question festering in my mind that demanded an answer.

Lifting my tear-streaked face to the brightening sky above the rising sun, I screamed.

It was not a death scream, sagging with sorrow and grief, like those echoing from every corner of Kakuma at night. After six years of loss and death, my heart had been scraped hollow of grief. The scream I lifted to the heavens that morning shook through my body and tore through my throat. It sliced into the morning sky like a panga, sharp and unforgiving.

There were no whispers of sadness dulling its edge.
There were no remnants of faith weakening its cut.
There was only rage.
"Where were you, God?"

CHAPTER 24

Kakuma Refugee Camp, Kenya—1996–98

I did not attend Christmas mass. I stopped going to church at all. My friends tried to convince me to come back, but I refused. Andrew had been right. God had abandoned us. As I thought back on the last six years of my life, I wondered if God had ever been there at all. He'd not been with us when the Nuer rebels attacked Wernyol and Pawel. He'd turned a blind eye to our suffering in Bor and allowed death to stalk us as we crossed the deserts of Sudan. And he'd certainly not shown up for Adual or any of us in Kakuma, so I no longer felt the need or desire to show up for him.

After Adual's death, the children who had been under her care were taken in by other families. Everyone returned to their lives, but I could not go back, and I refused to move forward. While the other children attended school and church each day, I walked to Adual's hut and sat beneath our tree. She was not there to feed me, heal my feet, or clean my clothes and hair. She was no longer there to listen to my stories and calm my fears, but the memory of her lingered there, so I returned to our tree every day, determined that Adual not be forgotten.

When I did not return to church, my Sunday school teacher, Joseph, and my friends found me sitting beneath the tree.

Joseph sat beside me. "I know you are hurting, Rachel."

"I'm not hurting," I said. "I'm angry."

"That is a natural emotion when you lose someone you love."

"I didn't lose Adual," I said in a calm, measured voice. "She was taken from me. God took her from me."

Joseph nodded, as though he understood. "It is not for us to understand God's plan. It is just for us to have faith in it. Please, come back to church so we can help you through your grief."

"I told you," I said, my voice rising in frustration. "I'm not grieving. I'm angry. And if this is God's plan, it is cruel. He is cruel, and I will not follow him."

"God is testing you, Rachel," Joseph said.

"Then I failed," I yelled. "If this is God's way of testing me, he wins. I'm done." I stood and left before Joseph or the others could stop me.

I walked to the cemetery and wandered around the unmarked plots, trying to remember where they'd buried Adual. I could not find her. I returned the next day and the day after that, but every mound of earth looked the same, so I decided to ask for help.

I found one of the men in Group Nine-A, who had buried Adual, working on the construction of a hut for a new batch of refugees. His name was Tong.

"Will you bring me to Adual's grave?" I asked.

Tong paused in hammering out an empty oilcan to be used for roofing and looked up at me. "I'm sorry. I can't."

"You can't or you won't?"

He raised his hammer and brought it down on the curved piece of metal. "I won't."

I waited until he stopped hammering. "Why not?"

"Because it is not good for you," he said, placing the flattened piece onto a pile of scrap metal. "I know how close you two were, Rachel. It is not healthy for you to spend your time with the dead. Too much time with the dead, and you will want to join them. I won't have your death on my hands." He picked up another can and prepared to hammer it, but I snatched the can away.

"Please," I begged, holding the can out of reach. "I have to go. She was my family."

Tong sighed. "Fine, but if I show you where she is buried, you must promise that you will never go back there again."

I tossed him the can. "If you show me where she is buried, I will say my goodbyes and never go back."

His eyes narrowed, as though he were searching for any hint of deception or hesitancy in my vow.

Lifting my chin, I stared back at him. "I promise."

"I still don't think this is a good idea," he said with a shake of his head. He dropped the can on the pile and pocketed his hammer. "But follow me."

As I trailed after Tong, I rubbed a worn scrap of cloth I'd torn from the blanket Andrew had given me between my thumb and fingers and remembered the day when he had found me with Adual beneath our tree. After four years of use, the faded, threadbare material no longer provided warmth or protection, but the small square of cloth would now serve a greater purpose.

Tong led me to Adual's burial plot and waited as I knelt and pretended to pray.

"You know," he said, turning away from me to gesture to the thousands of burial plots in Kakuma's cemetery, "if you come to the cemetery by yourself, the dead will rise from their graves and attack you, even your Adual."

I knew he was trying to scare me into never returning to the cemetery alone by spinning a frightening tale of zombies clawing out of their graves. I pretended to listen and look afraid, but while he wasn't watching, I picked up a rock and placed it in the middle of the scrap of Andrew's blanket. I wrapped the blanket around the rock and worked it into the ground beside Adual's grave. Just as Andrew had given me the blanket when he'd found me four years earlier, I left a remnant of it with Adual so I could find her again.

When Tong turned to see if his stories had adequately terrified me, I covered the corner of the blanket, peeking out of the ground, with my foot before he noticed.

"Are you ready to go back?" he asked.

"Yes."

"And you promise never to return?"

As I followed him out of the cemetery, I remembered the vow I'd made the night Adual died. She needed to know I was there. She needed to know she was not alone. I glanced back at the piece of blanket poking out from the dusty earth of her grave. "I promise."

Every day after school, I made the hour-long walk to the cemetery and looked for my scrap of blanket marking Adual's grave. Mara grew suspicious of my long absences from Group Nine-A, but I took the beatings, and the next day, I would walk again to the cemetery to sit with Adual.

By April, I had still not returned to church, and as the congregation prepared for our Easter celebration, I recalled Adual's devotion to God and the lessons she'd taught me. She not only preached God's word; she'd lived it. She'd fed the poor, even when she had little food for herself. She'd cared for orphaned children as though they were her own. She'd never lifted her voice or hand in anger. She'd shown me kindness and faith and forgiveness and never asked for anything in return. She'd sacrificed her life to save others, including me.

As I sat beside her grave the day before Easter, I spoke to the woman who had been the closest thing I'd had to a mother for the last six years.

"If you came back today, you'd be so disappointed in me," I said, hanging my head in shame. "You taught me to believe in God, but I am too angry to believe."

Tears fell from my face onto her grave. They darkened the sand for a second before disappearing. "Tomorrow's Easter. I remember how much you loved Easter mass." I smiled. "So did Koko." I rubbed the bit of Andrew's blanket between my fingers as I recalled the Easter masses I'd attended with both women. "They say Jesus died for us." I thought about the stories of his sacrifice, and then I thought about the sacrifices Koko and Adual had made. "I know Koko died for me." I pulled on the blanket until more of the frayed cloth was visible, and I thought of Koko and Adual and the hopes they'd had for my life. "I don't know if I can believe in God, Adual, but I believed in you, and you believed in God, so for you and for Koko, I will return to church tomorrow."

I placed my hand on the hot sand covering Adual's grave. "I wish you were here to go with me. I wish you were here to teach me more. I miss you so much, but I have not forgotten the lessons you did teach me, and I promise, if I survive Kakuma, as long as I live and no matter where I go, I will carry your lessons with me. I will carry you with me, Adual. Always."

I kept my promise to Adual and attended Easter mass. Over the next two years, I continued to visit her grave, but my trips became less frequent as I realized I did not need to go to the cemetery to be close to her. I carried her in my heart. On the days her absence consumed my thoughts, I returned to our tree, closed my eyes, and imagined her sitting next to me. I still didn't know if I felt God's presence, but I felt Adual's. My faith in her love guided me through my darkest days and endless nights.

CHAPTER 25

Kakuma Refugee Camp, Kenya—1998

Seven years after I escaped death in Wernyol, it found me in Kakuma. I don't remember being bitten by the mosquito that infected me with malaria, but the virus quickly ravaged my malnourished body. When Deborah and Julia came to get me for school one morning, a year after I'd returned to church and life beyond Kakuma's cemetery, they found me on the floor of my hut, burning with fever, shaking with chills, and lying in my own sick. I was too weak from vomiting and diarrhea to walk. They tried to get me to drink some water so I didn't dehydrate, but my stomach sent even the smallest sips back up in violent retching. Painful dry heaving brought up yellow bile that burned my throat. I became delirious from fevers and dehydration and cried out for Adual, Koko, and Mama.

After two days of me not being able to hold down any food or water, Mara fetched Andrew and three other men to carry me to the hospital the UNHCR had built in Kakuma. I hadn't seen Andrew in weeks. Over the years, his visits to Group Nine-A had become less frequent, and he'd stopped attending church and school altogether.

But he was there now, and even if it would be the last time I would see him before I died, I was grateful he was with me.

They carefully lifted me from the ground and placed me in a makeshift stretcher, just like the one they'd used to carry Adual and so many other refugees to the cemetery.

"Is she even breathing?" a woman whispered to Mara as Andrew and the men carried me from the hut.

"Barely. She'll be dead before they get her to the hospital," another woman said.

My limp body swayed to the men's synchronized steps, and I slipped in and out of consciousness during the walk. In the few moments I had any clarity about where I was and what was happening, I remembered Bor and the piles of bones. Fear-laced adrenaline spiked through my veins.

I don't want to become a pile of bones! my incoherent mind screamed, but all that escaped my chapped, cracked lips was a pained moan.

The memory of the bones pulled my thoughts to Adual. Fragments of her burial drifted through my muddied thoughts. I wanted to ask Andrew to bury me beside her, but I couldn't find the strength to speak.

I don't remember how long it took Andrew and the others to carry me to the hospital. All I remember was the pain and fear. The hospital was full when we arrived. There were too many sick and dying people in Kakuma. The staff instructed Andrew and the men to place me beneath a grouping of trees, where dozens of other patients awaited treatment. Andrew ran back to his hut to fetch a couple blankets so I wouldn't have to lie directly on the ground. While he was gone, a kind Kenyan nurse quickly placed an IV in my arm to help stave off dehydration.

"I'll be back to check on you as soon as I can," she said before hurrying to treat the dozens of other refugees crying out for help beneath the trees.

Andrew returned and spread two blankets he'd found onto a small patch of unoccupied ground under the shade of some branches. As the other men lifted me onto the blankets, I once again lost consciousness. When I woke later with another bout of vomiting, Andrew, the men, and their stretcher were gone, and night had fallen. I stared up at the stars and cried.

I was thirteen. I was dying. And I was alone.

As I lay on the ground outside the hospital, my thoughts wandered back to Adual dying in her hut, with no one to help or comfort her. I wondered if she, too, had sensed death coming for her. I hoped not. I hoped death had slipped in silently and stolen Adual's last breath while she'd peacefully slept, surrounded by the children she'd taken under her care. As my muscles seized in another bout of dry heaving, I prayed for death to be merciful. Of all the deaths I had witnessed over my life, dying in one's sleep seemed the gentlest way to go. All I had to do was close my eyes.

I wondered if Adual and Koko were waiting for me. I pictured Adual's beautiful smile and eyes glistening with tears of joy and love when she saw me. I imagined melting into Koko's warm embrace, inhaling her scent of cloves and thin leaves, and drifting to sleep to the steady beat of her heart.

In those last moments of consciousness, my thoughts reached out for Mama. I imagined her standing with Adual and Koko, her arms outstretched and open. Perhaps that was why she'd never come for me. Perhaps, after seven years of running from death, death is where I would find her.

I was so tired. I had struggled to survive for so long. I just wanted to rest. As I closed my eyes, I wondered if death would hurt.

It couldn't hurt as much as life, I thought.

And then I let go.

I woke to singing. The familiar words, distant and garbled, as though I were hearing them from beneath the waters of a deep lake, guided me to the surface. I gasped for air when I emerged. At first, I thought I had died in my sleep and Koko was singing me Baba's favorite hymn, but as the fog of sleep slowly lifted, I realized there were multiple voices singing.

I tried to open my eyes, but they squeezed shut again against the glare of sunlight.

"She's awake!"

I knew that voice. "Deborah?"

Someone grabbed my hand. "Yes, Rachel. I'm here. We all are."

Blinking against the light, I opened my eyes. Deborah, Julia, Thomas, Joseph, and Andrew were seated around me on the ground.

My mouth was dry, and my throat was raw. "How long have I been here?" I asked, looking around the clearing outside the hospital.

Julia took my other hand in hers. "Seven days."

"We thought we were going to lose you," Thomas said.

"But I told the doctors it would take more than a mosquito bite to take down a Deng," Andrew added.

I tried to smile, but it was taking all my strength just to keep my eyes open.

"Joseph has been coming to lead us in prayer and song to help you heal and grow stronger," Julia said.

"I knew you'd pull through." My Sunday school teacher smiled at me. "There is too much good for you to still do in the world for God to take you now."

"Maybe he was just testing me," I said.

Joseph's smile widened. "Then I'd say you've passed."

"We've been coming here to sit with you." Deborah squeezed my hand. "And we will continue to be here until you can come back to Group Nine-A with us."

"Now get some more rest," Andrew ordered, "so we can get you out of here soon."

"Don't worry," Thomas said. "We'll be here when you wake up."

Tears welled in my eyes. Despite all the people in my life I had lost, I was not alone. There were still people who cared about me in the world. People willing to fight to save me from unbearable grief, all-consuming anger, sudden sickness, and even death.

"Thank you," I told my friends.

Deborah and Julia kept hold of my hands as Joseph led them in Baba's hymn. I even heard Thomas's off-key singing join with the others.

Too weak to raise my voice with theirs, I repeated the comforting words and melody in my mind until exhaustion overwhelmed me.

"Thank you," I whispered again. Then I closed my eyes and let their voices and Baba's song guide me back to sleep.

CHAPTER 26

Kakuma Refugee Camp, Kenya—1998–2000

After my recovery from malaria, I spent less time alone with the dead and more time together with the living. I returned to school and church every day with Julia, Deborah, and Thomas. I carried Adual's caring spirit with me, shared her hope and faith with others, and volunteered to teach the younger children in camp. Andrew and Philip started visiting regularly again. They introduced me to other Lost Boys, including their friend Simon. Having Andrew back in my life gave me a connection to my family I'd been missing since Adual's death.

Andrew, however, did not return to school or church, but he did begin accompanying Deborah and me to fetch water and rations. I welcomed his presence. I had missed him during the years he'd stayed away, but I was surprised by his sudden interest in joining us whenever we ventured far from our section of Group Nine-A.

"It's not safe for you to be walking around alone," he explained while Philip and he trailed us on their bikes as we began our bimonthly 4:00 A.M. walk to the ration distribution center.

"We've been walking around alone for years," I said.

Andrew pedaled a loop around Deborah and me. "You were girls then."

"Aren't we girls now?" Deborah asked with a laugh.

"Yes, but soon you will be *older* girls, and it's not safe for older girls to walk around Kakuma unaccompanied." Andrew braked in front of me, forcing me to stop. "And you must never walk anywhere alone, especially after sunset. I heard you went to the lake alone last night, Rachel."

"Who told you that?" I asked, but I already knew the answer. After I'd been released from the hospital, Julia had overheard Andrew asking Jacob to keep an eye on me when he was not around.

"It doesn't matter," Andrew said, waving off my question. "What matters is you should never be out at night by yourself."

"I had to go pee." To avoid illnesses and infections brought on by human waste, we had to walk two kilometers, away from the huts of Kakuma and into an uninhabited part of the desert outside the camp, to relieve ourselves. "Do you expect me to hold it until morning?"

"Yes, or ask Thomas or Jacob to go with you, but never go alone."

"I'm not a baby anymore, Andrew," I said, stepping around his bike. I knew the line for rations would be growing by the minute. If we didn't hurry, we'd be forced to wait hours to get our rations and then we'd be late for school. I had no desire to take a beating from Mara because Andrew slowed us down with his lectures.

"I know," Andrew said, pedaling after me. "That's the problem."

"This is serious, Rachel," Philip said, riding alongside Deborah. "There are men outside and inside this camp who attack women and older girls they find alone."

"I can protect myself." I had been pulled into several fights in Kakuma, usually in defense of my friends. I didn't win them all, but I won enough to have gained the confidence that I could handle myself.

"Not against these kinds of attacks," Andrew said.

"My mama and brothers gave me the same lecture last night," Deborah admitted.

"That's because everyone heard about a group of men who attacked a girl on her way to collect dried wood two evenings ago," Andrew said.

"Did they find who attacked her?" I asked.

"She didn't get a good look at them," Philip said. "She thought they might be Turkana. They were wearing tunics with the cloth knotted on one shoulder, but there are rumors of men from the camp wearing their clothes the same way to disguise themselves as Turkana when they assault girls and women."

"So, there's nowhere safe for me?" I asked. "Not inside or outside Kakuma?"

Andrew braked in front of us again. "You will be safe if

you listen to me." He lowered his gaze, forcing me to look him in the eye. "Rachel, I need you to promise you will never again put yourself in a situation where you could be caught alone with a man."

"Fine. I promise, but if you and Philip insist on following us on our chores, you have to promise me something, too."

"What's that?"

"That you will carry our rations back to camp. Those bags of beans are heavy."

Andrew smiled. "Fine. I promise."

Andrew's presence during my chores protected me from the threat of assault, but he could not shield me from the other dangers lurking in every cramped corner of Kakuma. No one could. There were too many people, too little food, and too much time. The monotony of daily life in the camp wore on the people trapped within its invisible walls. When I was not at school or church, time slowed to a stop. When it did, I'd try to remember Adual's words of hope.

There's always tomorrow, Rachel.

Shielding my eyes from its glare, I'd peer up at the relentless sun, stuck in the endless sky, just as I was stuck in Kakuma. Neither of us moving forward. Neither of us moving on.

"But how will tomorrow ever come," I'd ask during

my one-sided conversations with Adual, "if today will not end?"

As I neared my sixth year in Kakuma, however, two things in my life did change: I reached puberty and my cousins started discussing my future.

In Wernyol, marriages were made to form strong alliances between families. Had the war not driven us from our home, my parents and Koko would have taken the time and care to find me a good match for a husband. When I started menstruating, between the ages of thirteen and fifteen, they would have celebrated me reaching my childbearing years by announcing to the village I was ready for marriage. Eligible men would then have offered my father cows in exchange for my hand. By the time I had turned sixteen, I would have been a wife and mother, living with my husband on his family's land just as Dinka women had done for generations.

In Kakuma, marriages were a matter of survival, and young women were a commodity. Most girls had little say in the matter. A marriage was their contribution to supporting their families. Not only did parents and guardians receive dowries for the girls, they also were no longer burdened with having to feed and support them.

While marriages for most girls in their adolescence were determined and negotiated by their families in Kakuma, some chose to marry on their own. When their living circumstances proved unbearable, they would find a man to marry them so they could escape the abuse or neglect of their situations. It was a future the girls of Kakuma were fated to endure. It was a future I did not want, but in Kakuma, a young girl's future was not her own.

In late 1998, a rumor had reached the camp that offered the boys and girls of Kakuma a new hope for their futures, including mine. A refugee relocation program was being established. Leaders from Europe, North America, and Australia had promised to create a pathway for the younger refugees of Kakuma to come to their countries. It was the first time in more than six years we could dream of building a life outside the refugee camp. Any morsel of information about the pending relocation program was gobbled up by the hundreds of thousands of men, women, and children in Kakuma. I was not immune to the excitement over the rumored relocation program or the hope it stirred among the young refugees.

By early 2000, applications to be considered for the program were announced, and by April, the first interviews were scheduled. Lost Boys ages eighteen and younger were given priority in the selection process. Some older Lost Boys were permitted to apply if they were grouped with younger applicants who did not have parents or guardians. Girls under eighteen were also allowed to apply if their application was submitted with Lost Boys to whom they were related. Adults were not permitted to apply, even if their children were selected.

Every Friday night, someone from the UNHCR would tack a new list of names on the bulletin boards situated in each zone in Kakuma. Refugees would gather around the board, searching for their names. Those lucky individuals, whose names were on the lists, reported to their first interview the next Monday. After their initial interview, if their names appeared on the list a second time, they knew they'd been chosen to move forward in the selection process. If their name was not on the list after they'd completed their first interview, they knew they would not be moving on, not in the selection process, and not from Kakuma.

Andrew, Thomas, and I applied immediately. After many tears and at their mama's insistence, Deborah and her brothers also applied. Julia did not. Her older brother had refused to allow her to apply for the refugee relocation program. His plan for his sister's future did not include her leaving Kakuma. Thomas tried to talk to Matthew and his wife, pleading that Julia be allowed to apply, but Matthew would not listen. They needed the money and security Julia's betrothal would bring their family.

Unlike Julia's brother, Andrew was determined to get me out of Kakuma despite my cousins' insistence that I stay.

"Rachel should remain in Kakuma with us," James told my uncle.

"If you take her away, Andrew," Mara argued, "Rachel will lose her culture. She will lose her language. Is that what you want for her?"

"Rachel has already lost everything," Andrew told

them. "She has nothing left to lose. The only people who will gain anything from her staying in Kakuma is you. She is coming with me."

Andrew refused to discuss the topic with them further. He was my closest living relative in the camp, and at eighteen years of age, he would now determine my future, not my cousins. When it was announced the relocation program's initial focus was to settle younger Lost Boys in new communities around the world, Andrew made sure my application was included with his.

"I am not leaving you here, Rachel," he told me. "When I found you under that tree, I promised to keep you safe. I will not break that promise."

Philip, Thomas, Pabior, Simon, Jacob, and another Lost Boy named Mark completed our group of applicants. Julia had warned Deborah and me on more than one occasion to avoid Jacob. His cruel, bullying behavior toward her had not improved over the years. I was not happy Andrew had included him in our group application, but Andrew reminded me Jacob was family and we had to keep the few members we had left in our family together.

We met at the board every Friday, waiting for the new list to be posted and hoping our names would be included. For five months, we left disappointed, but we always returned the next week.

Not everyone did.

Many refugees who had completed their first interviews but not found their names on the next list never returned.

There were no second chances in the selection process. Applicants could not contest the committee's decision. If they were not chosen to move past the first round of interviews, that was the end of their application and, for many, the end of their hope.

Applying as a group did not better our chances of being selected. Often one or two applicants in a group were rejected, while the rest of their group was chosen for relocation, separating friends and families and damning individuals to lives alone in Kakuma. As more applicants were denied, alcoholism and suicides in the camp increased.

As excited as I was about the prospect of being chosen for the program, I was terrified of the possibility I'd be rejected while Andrew, Thomas, Deborah, and the others were selected. Following Adual's passing, their friendship and support had pulled me back from the brink of death. I could not survive Kakuma without them.

In September 2000, Deborah, Thomas, and I met Andrew and the other Lost Boys at the bulletin board, just as we had every Friday at midnight for five months. Mara had demanded I finish my chores before going, so we were late. Andrew and the other boys were already at the board. Deborah and I waited our turn with the rest of the girls behind the large crowd of boys.

"Oh my God!" Andrew exclaimed, pushing his way through the crowd. "You guys aren't going to believe this! Our names are there!"

"You're joking," I said.

"No." Andrew shrugged. "Why would I do that?" He grabbed my hand. "This is it, Rachel. I promise you. I'm taking you away from this place."

"Whose names are up there?" Deborah asked.

"All of ours!" Andrew exclaimed. "We all are scheduled for interviews on Monday!"

Despite Andrew and the other boys' enthusiasm and their promise they were not playing a trick on me, I struggled to believe my name was on the list. I waited until the crowd dispersed before approaching the board. I had to see my name for myself.

I stared at the list. After nine years of unfulfilled hopes and crushing disappointments, I could not believe my eyes. Baba's favorite hymn floated to the surface of my shocked thoughts.

Let your heart be strong.

I whispered the lyrics as I reached up and touched the name to make sure it was real.

Rachel Achut Lual Deng.

CHAPTER 27

Kakuma Refugee Camp, Kenya—September 2000

Deborah, her brothers, Andrew, Thomas, and I spent the weekend before our interviews carefully scripting and revising our answers. We had spoken to enough refugees who had been through the interview process to know what questions would be asked.

Where were you born?

Where are your parents?

Why did you leave Sudan?

How did you get to Kakuma?

Who came with you?

Were you a soldier in the SPLA or the GOS Army?

Were you involved in fighting in the war?

What are your goals?

Why do you want to come to Canada? To Australia? To Europe? To the US?

"We can't be too prepared," Andrew told us when Thomas and I complained about having to practice our responses again. "We only get one shot at this."

"What if they don't take all of us?" Thomas asked.

"They will," Andrew answered.

"What if they don't?" I asked.

"They will," Andrew repeated with more force. Then his voice fell. "They have to."

When the day of my interview finally arrived, I could recite my answers in my sleep. I walked with Deborah, Thomas, and Jacob to the building where the interviews would be conducted. No one talked. We were too excited and too nervous to speak. Andrew and Deborah's brothers were waiting for us with Simon, Mark, and Pabior. We sat outside the closed gate with dozens of other refugees rehearsing their answers, praying, and listening for their names to be called.

After a short wait, a young Dinka woman and a Kenyan man opened the gate. The woman explained in Dinka the process to the waiting crowd of anxious refugees. Family members and individuals who had requested on their applications to be considered for the relocation program together would be called into the building as a group. Once inside, they would be separated and interviewed individually. The Dinka woman would accompany each person into his or her interview to serve as an interpreter. Decisions made after the interview were final. She then asked if there were any questions. No one raised their hand. We all knew what to expect in the interview, and we all knew what was at stake.

The man with the interpreter then called out the names

for the first groupings. Deborah and her brothers were among them.

"Good luck," I told her as she walked through the gate.

"Thanks." She tried to smile, but nervousness stretched her attempt into more of a grimace.

"Let's go over our answers again," Andrew told Thomas and me as soon as the door closed behind Deborah.

Andrew pretended to be the interviewer, asking us questions and scrutinizing the speed and quality of our responses. I tried to focus, but my thoughts kept straying to my friend and how she was doing in her interview. I remembered how relieved we'd felt when Andrew told us both our names were on the interview schedule board. I couldn't imagine interviewing without Deborah. It was hard enough applying to the program without Julia.

Deborah and I had spent every day together for the last eight years. Aside from Andrew, Julia, and Thomas, she was the closest thing I had to family, not only in Kakuma, but in the world. Deborah had to be selected for the program. If I was chosen for relocation, I didn't know if I could leave Kakuma without her. I started to pace.

"Rachel, sit down," Thomas said. "You're making me nervous."

"I can't."

I wore a path in the ground with my pacing as my mind ran through every possible outcome and horrible scenario. I didn't stop moving until the door opened and Deborah and her brothers exited the building. A wave of relief washed over me when I saw the smile on my friend's face. Her interview must have gone well. Now I just had to *not* mess up mine. I resumed my pacing and mentally reviewed my answers for the millionth time.

Several minutes later, the gate opened, and the Kenyan man called out my name, along with Andrew's and the others boys' in our group. As we followed the interpreter and man past Deborah, she grabbed my hand and gave it a quick squeeze.

"Good luck."

"Thanks."

While Andrew, the others, and I waited in a hallway to be called for our interviews, I stared at the closed door to the room where my interviewer sat, asking questions and determining fates, like some all-powerful judge. My entire future depended on how I answered his questions.

The door opened, and the interpreter stepped into the hallway.

"Rachel Achut Lual Deng."

I glanced at Andrew.

He smiled. "Remember what we practiced."

I nodded, hoping to gain an ounce of confidence from the strength in his voice, and then I followed the interpreter into the room.

The room was sparse. Two empty chairs were positioned before a desk. An older man, with white hair and a white beard, sat in a third chair behind the desk. He greeted me with a friendly smile and introduced himself, but I didn't hear his name. All I heard were the answers Andrew had drilled into my brain, repeating over and over again. The man motioned to one of the empty chairs. I sat down and tried to quiet my thoughts enough to focus on the interview. The interpreter sat beside me.

I shifted in the wooden chair, uncertain what to do with my hands or where to look as the interviewer stared at me. Assuming his scrutinizing gaze lingered because of how gaunt I was, I tugged at the hem of the school uniform skirt the UNHCR had given me, trying to cover my bony knees.

After a moment, the man began the interview. He spoke English. I only knew a few basic words of English, so when he paused, I looked to the interpreter for help.

"I am going to ask you a few questions, Rachel," she said, translating the man's words into Dinka. "I want you to relax and be honest."

The word "honest" shook me from my insecurities and fear. I looked at the man, wondering if he assumed I would lie to him. He held my gaze and smiled.

"First question." He picked up a pen and positioned it at the top of a sheet of paper on the desk. "Tell me, Rachel, why do you want to come to the US?"

All the responses Andrew and I had practiced for when the interviewer inevitably asked me "why" raced through my mind. Answers about how I wanted to become an American citizen and contribute to their great country. Answers about getting a good education and finding a steady job. Answers about living in a democracy, where if I worked hard, I could fulfill all my dreams. Answers about helping make the world a better place. Answers that would give me my best shot at passing the interview and escaping Kakuma.

All those responses would be truthful, but as I sat there, thinking about the man's question and his request for honesty, I had only one answer.

"I want life."

The translator's eyes widened in surprise. She waited for me to expand on my response. When I didn't, she cleared her throat and conveyed my answer in English to the interviewer.

He sat back in his chair. "You don't have life here?"

My eyes stung with nine years of grief and pain, but I had no more tears to give Kakuma. I did not know if my honesty would earn me a chance in the US or trap me forever in this purgatory. There was a risk my answer might offend the man. It could be seen as an insult to the work the US did with the UNHCR in Kenya, but the interviewer needed to hear the truth. Someone needed to hear it, and for someone to hear it, someone first had to speak it.

I lifted my chin and fought the urge to look away from the man's perplexed gaze. "We don't have life here. All we have is hope. Hope it will rain so we have enough water. Hope our small rations will last the month. Hope we will wake in the morning. Hope we will see our friends again at the well. Hope death will spare us for one more day.

We have hope here, but hope is not life. *This* is not life."
Emotion broke my voice, but I would not let it silence
me. "I want life."

I waited as the interpreter conveyed my answer to the
man. When she'd finished, the interviewer put down his
pen. His eyes shone with tears as he stared at me.

He did not ask another question.

CHAPTER 28

*Kakuma Refugee Camp, Kenya, to New York City,
United States—September–December 2000*

I was not called back for a second interview.

The interviewer pushed my application through without one. Two weeks later, my name appeared on the board with the names of all the refugees who had been selected as part of the first group in the program to be relocated. I experienced a storm of emotions as I stood before the board, staring at my name. My initial relief and excitement over being selected to leave Kakuma after nine years of suffering was washed away by currents of doubt and fear.

I had never received word of my parents' fate in Sudan. How could I leave Kakuma and start a new life on another continent, an ocean away, without knowing if my parents had survived the war or if they'd suffered the same fate as Koko? As desperate as I was to escape Kakuma and find life beyond the confines of the refugee camp, I questioned if I could leave everyone, those still alive and those gone, behind. A few weeks later, I learned I would not have to face the decision alone.

Andrew had been right. We would all be leaving Kakuma together. After successfully completing two more interviews, Deborah, her brothers, Andrew, Thomas, Jacob, and the other Lost Boys in our application group had also been chosen as part of the relocation program to the United States. Philip had also been selected, but he was placed with a group of Lost Boys who would be brought to the United States two months later.

The three months between our interviews and our scheduled departure from Kakuma were spent passing a series of medical exams. During the examinations, my height and weight were measured for the first time in my life. At fifteen years of age, I was five feet eight inches tall and weighed barely ninety-five pounds. The UN workers also assigned each candidate for relocation a new official birth year. We did not have birth certificates in Wernyol and could not prove our ages. We could estimate the time of year we were born based on family members recalling whether it occurred during the rainy or dry season, or if our birth coincided with a significant event, holiday, celebration, or date of historical importance, such as the start of the war, but we did not know the actual date of our births, nor did we celebrate birthdays. Our US visas, however, required specific birth dates, so we were ushered into a room, where an older man, like a carnival worker at a Guess Your Age booth, stared at us for several minutes before declaring our birth years.

"1985," the old man said after looking me up and down.

A woman then wrote January 1, 1985, as my birth date on my official paperwork.

All the children in Kakuma who went through the relocation program process ended up sharing the same birth month and day, January 1. Only our birth years differed, depending on the old man's less-than-scientific assessments.

In the whirlwind of excitement and preparations before leaving Kakuma, there were also many tears shed. Deborah's mama had insisted she and her brothers apply to the program so they could have a chance at a better life, but leaving Kakuma behind meant leaving her behind, at least until Deborah and her brothers were settled in the United States and could start the process of bringing their mama over, too.

Fourteen-year-old Thomas also had mixed feelings about leaving. Julia and he had survived the war and refugee camp together. He was devastated at the thought of leaving his sister behind.

"When I get there," he told her, "I will do my best to support you any way I can, and someday, I promise I will bring you to the US."

But Thomas and Julia knew the truth. Julia would never join us in the United States. The reality of her situation, as was the reality for too many young girls in Kakuma, caused much despair as the date of our departure drew near. For Julia, it also fostered another emotion, anger. She resented being tethered to a future she did not want and a life that would never be her own.

Thomas, Deborah, and I tried our best to comfort her. We spent the day before we left Kakuma hugging and crying, and even though no one said the word "goodbye," the finality of the moment was felt in every tearful embrace.

I didn't sleep that night. Every doubt and fear I'd experienced three months earlier, when I'd read my name on the list of refugees chosen for relocation, resurfaced with an urgency I could no longer ignore. The memory of Adual saying until someone told us otherwise, my mama was alive repeated in my mind on an endless loop. My imagination conjured images of Mama arriving in Kakuma after I'd left for America. I pictured her looking for me, only to learn I was gone, that I had not waited for her. But then I thought of what my future would be if I stayed in Kakuma. I would face the same future as Julia. My doubts and fears twisted into frustration. I had been holding on to a dream that may never be, clinging to the hope that Mama was still alive when the guarantee of a life beyond survival was finally within my reach. As I tossed and turned on my mat, Koko's warning as we'd fled through the forest the night of the rebel attack whispered from the recesses of my memory.

Don't look back, Achut.

Koko was right. I could not reach out for my future while holding on to the past. I could not move forward

251

while looking back. I had to stop wondering "what if" and let go of the hope that my parents had lived so that I could live. As I lay there, wrestling with my doubts and fears and waiting for morning, I once again let Koko's words guide me through the darkness.

Her advice had saved me then.

I trusted it would save me now.

Nine years after Adual and I had stepped across the border into Kenya, I left Kakuma.

Mara, James, and I exchanged goodbyes outside their hut.

"We'll miss you," Mara said, giving me a brief, final hug.

"We wish you well, Rachel," James added. "Don't forget our Dinka culture when you start your new life in America."

"I won't," I said, and then I joined Deborah, Thomas, and Jacob on our final walk through Group Nine-A.

Friends and family accompanied us as we made our way to the Kakuma runway, where a plane waited to transport us and a hundred other young refugees to Nairobi. It was our first experience on an airplane, and the plane waiting to take us from Kakuma to Nairobi did not help ease my fears about flying. The exterior of the plane was yellowed and rusty. The interior held threadbare seats and not much more. There were not even sick bags available, which would have been useful and appreciated with so many new flyers on such a turbulent flight.

I sat next to Deborah. She and I had been excited to learn we'd been selected to go to the US together. Many of the other refugees on our plane were headed to other countries in Europe or being relocated to Australia after we landed in Nairobi, so we were relieved to know we would not only be on the same continent, but in the same country. Our excitement diminished, however, when we received the final destinations we'd been assigned in America.

"My brothers and I are going to Lansing, Michigan," Deborah had said, reading her paperwork. "What about you?"

Disappointment weighed down my words. "I'm going to some place called Houston, Texas."

"Oh," Deborah said. "Maybe it's close to Michigan."

"Maybe."

"Don't be sad. We are going to the United States! And you will have Andrew, Thomas, and the others with you, right?"

"Right." I was relieved I would be living with Andrew and Thomas in Houston. Thanks to Julia, I knew to avoid Jacob, but I didn't really know the other boys in our group. Andrew had lived with Simon, Mark, and Pabior in Kakuma. He'd brought them over to visit me in Group Nine-A on a couple occasions, and they seemed nice enough, but they all looked to Jacob as their unofficial leader. At twenty-seven years old and six feet six inches tall, Jacob was the oldest of the group and towered over the others, a fact he reminded us of often. I had been able to steer clear of him in Group Nine-A, but it would be harder to avoid Jacob when we were all living together in Houston. I was happy Andrew and Thomas would have the reassurance of friends from Kakuma with them in our new home. I just wished I would, too.

"Besides," Deborah said, "you and I will talk all the time and make plans to visit one another as soon as we can. It won't be like Kakuma in America. We will be free to go where we want." She wrapped me in a hug. "We will be able to visit one another all the time." Unaware of the great distance and cost involved in traveling from Texas to Michigan, Deborah's hopeful promises eased my growing anxiety over being separated from her.

As we waited for the plane to depart, we stared out the window. Hundreds of refugees had gathered outside the fencing beside the runway to say goodbye. I recognized many faces in the crowd. People from Group Nine-A, including friends from church and Sunday school, cried and waved. Julia stood among them. Through tears, I waved back and wondered what would become of them. Sadness and guilt pressed on my chest, making it difficult to breathe. I thought of all the times over the last nine years when I'd dreamed of escaping Kakuma. Now I was.

Beside me, Deborah wept. Her mama stood alone in the crowd, her face wet with tears as she waved to her children. I had waited nearly a decade for my mama to find me in Kakuma, but she never came. As I watched Deborah's mama, doubts from the night before crept back into my thoughts. What if she came looking for me after I left? It was the same question that had plagued my thoughts when Koko and I fled Wernyol and when Adual and I escaped Bor. Mama would never find me if I kept leaving. But then I realized, I'd had no choice. Not in Wernyol and not in Bor. I'd had to leave those places to survive, just as I had to leave Kakuma now to survive.

Koko's words echoed in my memory. *Don't look back. It will slow your steps.*

Her advice had been right when we'd run through the forests that night when I was six. And it was right, nearly ten years later, as I sat on that plane waiting to leave Kakuma. I could not move forward to my future if I remained stuck in my past, and neither could Deborah.

I squeezed her hand. "It will be all right."

"I am leaving my mama," she said. "How is this all right?"

"You are leaving Kakuma. Your mama wants this for you and your brothers, and you are blessed to have someone there, someone who loves you, watching you go to a better place. So, let us go to this new country, where if you work hard, you can help take care of your family, including your mama."

Deborah scrubbed her tears away with the back of her hand. "You're right. This is what we have prayed for all these years." Pressing a kiss to her fingertips, she placed her hand against the window. Her mama covered her mouth with one trembling hand and reached out the other. She was still reaching for her children as the plane taxied down the runway and she disappeared from view.

After a short, bumpy flight spent praying and holding our feet above the growing puddles of vomit spreading across the floor, we landed in Nairobi. I couldn't get off that plane fast enough and hoped the plane we would be boarding the next day was better than the one I'd just escaped.

We were housed over night at Gold, a temporary compound built as a holding area for the Lost Boys and Girls from Kakuma awaiting flights for relocation to Europe, Australia, and North America. The large, one-story building was divided into two spacious, open rooms packed with dozens of bunk beds so the refugees could rest while they waited for the vans that would transport them to the airport. The boys, who outnumbered the girls ten to one, were assigned the larger of the two rooms. The girls were placed in the other. As Deborah and I sat and talked about what life would be like in the United States, an older girl approached us.

"Where are you headed?" she asked.

"Lansing, Michigan," Deborah answered.

The girl jutted her chin at me. "What about you?"

I showed her my paperwork.

"Oh my God!" she exclaimed. "We're going to the same place!"

"Really?"

She showed me her papers. "See! Houston, Texas. What's your name?"

"Rachel."

"I'm Sarah. Looks like we're going to be neighbors, Rachel." She sat down beside Deborah and me and told us all about herself and how long she had been in Kakuma. Sarah was funny and outgoing. I immediately liked her.

As she ran down a list of all the things she wanted to do in Houston, she began including me in her plans. Her enthusiasm was contagious. Suddenly her exciting plans were *our* exciting plans. I smiled. Maybe by the time we reached Houston, I would have a friend there after all.

The planes that took us to Amsterdam and then to New York City were far sturdier than the one we'd flown on from Kakuma. Not only did they have sick bags tucked in the backs of every seat, they also had bathrooms, TVs, and food and drinks. Hungry as I was, I was hesitant to eat the new foods the flight attendants placed on the trays before us. The chicken was cold, so I worried it was not cooked, and I had never seen broccoli before and was convinced they were trying to poison us with the strange, small, tree-like vegetables. Wary of the food, I chanced a sip from the green-canned beverage labeled Sprite, which the airline had provided. It was my first experience with soda. I liked the sweet, citrus taste of the clear drink, but I did not anticipate the carbonated bubbles. Surprised by the odd sensation, I snorted and choked, sending the fizzy liquid spilling from my nostrils. It burned my nose and made my eyes water. I did not dare a second sip.

Our fellow passengers were friendly and quite curious about the large group of Sudanese children wearing matching uniforms. The boys in our group wore pants, plain gray sweatshirts with the letters UNHCR on the front, and whatever pair of shoes they'd worn in Kakuma. Most of them had sneakers. The girls, including Sarah, Deborah, and me, wore the same gray UNHCR sweatshirts, but instead of pants, we wore navy-blue skirts. We also each wore a pair of underwear, but no bras, and our shoes from Kakuma, though my shoes were a pair of open-toed slippers. Throughout the flights, several passengers inquired where we were from and where we were headed. When we told them, they wished us luck and said they would keep us in their prayers. The flights were long, but I tried to sleep when the other passengers and my mind would allow me.

After two days of travel, including a short layover in Amsterdam, where we said goodbye to the refugees headed to countries in Europe, we landed at JFK airport in the United States. We waited in our seats as the other passengers collected their belongings. We had no bags to collect from the overhead bins. We were wearing everything we owned. When the rest of the passengers disembarked, three flight attendants led us off the plane. They each held a sign with our names written on them.

The airport was huge, and there were so many people of all shapes, sizes, and skin tones. I don't know where they were going, but everyone was in a hurry. I tried to stick close to Deborah and her brothers, afraid I'd get lost in the rush of people, but the flight attendants separated us by our destination groupings.

After our guides read down the lists of names on their boards to assure that we were all accounted for, one of the flight attendants stepped forward and addressed the group, using hand signals to aid in our understanding of English.

"Those going on to Lansing, Michigan, please follow me to the gate for your connecting flight," she said, waving for the refugees in her group to follow her into the throngs of people headed toward the main terminal.

Jacob, who spoke the most English in our group, translated the attendant's instructions for the rest of us.

"I guess this is it," Deborah said, grabbing her brothers' hands and hurrying to keep up with her group.

My heart raced. "Wait!"

This was all happening too fast. We didn't even have a chance to hug one last time or wish one another good luck. I still didn't even know how far Lansing was from Houston or how to contact Deborah once we were settled in our new homes.

Before she disappeared into the river of people flowing past, she looked back and waved. "Bye, Rachel."

I waved back. "Bye, Deborah," I whispered, and then, like everyone else I'd cared about in my life, my best friend was gone.

I didn't have time to cry. I had to focus all my attention on not losing my group as we navigated our way through the crowds, struggling to keep up with the remaining flight attendant. She led us to a moving staircase and strode onto the top step. As she stood on the metal step, it carried her down the staircase to the next level. I had never seen an escalator before, much less ridden on one. None of us had. After a few worried glances and shrugged shoulders, the boys in our group, one by one, followed the flight attendant onto the escalator. I waited toward the back, afraid I would fall down the moving stairs with its metal teeth. When it was my turn to step on, I hesitated.

Angry voices and groans of frustration swelled behind me.

I glanced back at the gathering crowd. I could not understand the English words they spat at me, but the hard tone they used, accompanied by impatient, annoyed glares, left no need for translation. I had two choices. Get on the escalator or get out of the crowd's way.

I looked at the escalator. Andrew and the others were getting farther away. If they reached the bottom before I got on, I would lose sight of them and be lost in a strange airport in a strange city where I didn't speak the language.

Summoning what fragile courage I had left, I took hold of the moving railings and slid one foot onto the top step.

"God help me!" I screamed in Dinka as my front foot and body were pulled forward, down the escalator, while my back foot remained firmly planted on the platform above. When my legs could not stretch apart any farther, the moving stairs dragged my back foot from the platform. I rode the whole way down, straddling three steps and screaming for God's help in my native language, much to the shock of the people behind me and the amusement of Andrew and the others waiting for me at the bottom of the escalator.

When I made it safely to the lower floor, the flight attendant escorted us to a man holding a sign that read LOST BOYS. The man quickly took attendance to make sure he had the right group and the flight attendant hadn't lost one of the Lost Boys he'd been tasked with collecting. Once everyone was accounted for, he explained we would not be continuing on to Houston that night. All connecting flights had been canceled, and we would be staying in a hotel for the night due to a blizzard.

"What's a blizzard?" Thomas whispered to me.

I shrugged.

The man led us past the baggage claim areas to the large glass doors leading outside. The moment we looked out the windows, we stopped short, and our mouths fell open.

"I think that's a blizzard," I said to Thomas.

The entire night sky swirled in a frenzied flurry of white.

"That's snow," Thomas said, his voice rising with excitement. "It's snowing!"

We had heard about snow, but none of us had ever seen it before. Everyone in our group was laughing, and Thomas and I jumped up and down.

The man escorting us smiled. "That's not normally how people react to getting snowed in by a blizzard." He then noticed my feet. "You can't be traipsing through the snow in slippers. You'll freeze. Everyone wait inside. I'll go get the van and pull it around."

When he parked the van in the loading area, we climbed inside, and he drove us to a nearby hotel. Thomas and I couldn't wait to get out of the van and touch the snow.

It was beautiful but much colder than I expected. My sweatshirt, skirt, and slippers were not exactly winter wear, but that didn't stop me from dancing in the snow with Thomas and scooping up handfuls to throw at one another until my feet and hands went numb.

They put us in rooms based on our destinations and groupings. Because we were the youngest in our group of seven headed to Houston, Thomas and I shared a room with two beds, a bathroom, and a TV, but we never turned it on. We sat in front of our hotel room window, watching the snow. The wind howled, rattling the windowpanes. We watched it carry the snow on ever-changing gusts in sweeps and swirls. It covered the world in an endless blanket of white. At times, the snowflakes were so numerous and the wind so strong, we couldn't see the buildings across the street.

It was magical.

Thomas and I stayed up all night watching the snow fall and wondering what other wonderful, new experiences awaited us in Houston.

CHAPTER 29

Houston, Texas—December 2000

There was no snow in Texas, only rain. I missed the mesmerizing dance of the falling snowflakes outside the plane window when we landed in Houston, but I did not miss the bitter cold.

I did miss Deborah. It had been difficult to see her walk away at the airport in New York. This was the first time we had not been together in almost eight years. I wondered if she had landed in Michigan yet and if they had snow there. I hoped not. Deborah did not like the cold.

There were fifteen of us from Kakuma on the flight to Houston. Our group consisted of Sarah, her brother, her cousin, another group of five Lost Boys, the six boys in my group, and me. I was grateful Sarah was there so I wasn't the only girl.

We did not follow the other passengers to the baggage claim area after disembarking. We had nothing to claim. A young Black woman in her early twenties met us outside the gate. She held a sign labeled UNHCR with the words LOST BOYS written in bold letters. It was not the first time Sarah and I were referred to as Lost Boys with the others, and it would not be the last.

As soon as the woman spotted the fifteen of us in our matching sweatshirts, she smiled and waved her arms in wide arcs above her head. "Hello! My name is Veronica. I am your YMCA case worker. Welcome to Houston!"

Jacob once again served as our translator. After he'd conveyed her introduction to us in Dinka, she ran down a list of names, checking each off with a pen when one of us raised our hand.

"You all must be exhausted," she said. "I remember how long the trip from Kenya was when my family came here. The jet lag was brutal. It can take a few days to acclimate to the time difference. Why don't we get you settled in your apartments for the night so you can rest?"

She waited patiently as Jacob translated, and then she led us out of the airport.

It was still raining when we stepped outside. By the time we reached the bus Veronica had waiting in the parking lot, my clothes were drenched, and my slippers were soaked through. The temperatures were still colder than the constant heat of Kakuma, but I was relieved I could not see my breath every time I exhaled like when we'd landed in New York City.

Jacob sat up front with Veronica, answering her many questions about our trip. I sat in the back with Sarah. It was only the third vehicle I had ever ridden in, and I stared out the window the entire drive.

"There are so many cars," I said to Sarah.

"There must be more cars in Houston than all of Sudan," she replied in awe.

The ride was surprisingly comfortable. Veronica's bus did not bump and lurch over the roads like the truck that had taken Adual and me from Loki to Kakuma.

"The roads are so smooth," I said, watching in wonder as the city blurred by the windows. "And I have never seen so many buildings."

Some stretched higher than trees into the night sky. I marveled at their great heights, wondering how anyone could make a building so tall. And the lights! They were everywhere, in a rainbow of colors. Soft white and yellow lights glowed from tall poles lining the streets, and bright red, yellow, and green lights dangled from wires strung above intersections. Brilliant, multicolored signs glowed on storefronts and at the entrances of huge parking lots surrounded by clusters of stores and restaurants.

As we drove through neighborhoods, there were even strings of lights outlining many of the homes and strung around small trees and bushes. Lines of white lights. Assortments of reds, blues, and greens. Steadily shining lights. Flashing and twinkling lights.

Throughout the drive, a cacophony of new sounds assaulted my ears. Strange music and voices emanated from speakers inside the bus. Outside the vehicle, horns honked, loud and abrupt, and sirens wailed, undulating and shrill.

Overwhelmed by the sights and sounds, a throbbing ache grew behind my eyes.

"The houses aren't usually decorated like this," Veronica explained, and Jacob translated, "but it's almost Christmas. Most of those lights will come down after New Year's. I love this time of year. Everything looks so festive, even in the rain."

The raindrops streaming down the bus window captured the glowing colors of the lights as we drove through another neighborhood. The colors bled and ran down the glass in meandering paths. I gazed above the city, looking for any glimpse of the night sky I knew in Sudan and Kenya, but Houston had so many lights blazing into the darkness, they outshone the moon and stars.

Veronica dropped Sarah, her brother, and cousin off at their apartment first. I was sad to see Sarah go, but Veronica assured us we would see one another when she picked us up for our first orientation class in the morning. She then took the other five Lost Boys to an apartment building a few blocks from where she left Sarah before driving us to our apartment.

"We have a fully furnished apartment ready for you," Veronica said, parking in front of a two-story building.

As she led us inside, she explained that the YMCA would be providing us with monthly stipends as well as food stamps to cover the cost of rent, food, and other necessities. Because they were eighteen and older, Jacob, Andrew, Simon, Mark, and Pabior would receive their share of the monthly allowance. Thomas's and my shares would be given to Jacob, who, as the oldest in our group, was considered our guardian. The YMCA would continue to provide the older boys with money each month until they'd completed their vocational training programs and secured jobs.

While Jacob translated for us, we followed Veronica upstairs to the second floor, where she unlocked a door and ushered us inside. The apartment had a small kitchen and an attached living room with a couch, television, chairs, and a table for meals.

Veronica gave us a quick tour of the kitchen. "I bought a few things to get you through the night." She opened the refrigerator door. "Make sure to leave the milk in here when you're not drinking it. The refrigerator will keep it cold so it won't spoil."

I had never seen a refrigerator before. I slipped my hand inside before she closed the door.

"It's cold in there," I told Thomas.

He put his hand inside the refrigerator too and shivered. "It's like New York City."

Veronica smiled. "Tomorrow, I'll take you to buy some more food." She motioned to the other electronic appliances in the kitchen. "And we'll show you how to use these in our orientation classes at the YMCA. I'll give you a schedule tomorrow for when I will be picking you up for those classes."

We followed her down a short hallway off the living room. "There are three bedrooms, so you will have to share, and one of you will have to sleep on the couch until we can find more homes to foster you." She referred to a piece of paper she carried with our names. "Rachel and Thomas will be in one room because they are the youngest. The rest of you can double up however you like."

Pabior volunteered to sleep on the couch. Andrew and Simon chose the room across from Thomas's and my room. Jacob and Mark took the room down the hall, across from the bathroom. Each bedroom had two single beds with blankets and pillows, two small dressers, a nightstand, and a closet.

"Do you have any questions?" Veronica asked.

I had many questions but didn't know where to begin or how to ask them in English, so I shook my head.

Veronica handed Jacob seven copies of a key, one for each of us, for our new apartment. Our new home.

"Try to get some sleep. I will be back in the morning."

And then she was gone.

As emotionally and physically drained as I was from our long journey to Houston, I could not sleep. I missed Deborah and everyone from home. I tossed and turned, wondering what they were all doing and if they missed me, too. Thomas was just as restless, so we stayed up all night talking. We discussed the war and all the years we'd spent in Kakuma. We cried over the loved ones we'd lost and those we'd had to leave behind. We marveled about how we'd been chosen to come to the United States and pondered what came next.

We were exhausted from our sleepless night when Veronica picked us up for our first YMCA orientation class at 10:00 A.M. the next morning, but I was excited to see Sarah again and hear all about her apartment. At the YMCA, we were introduced to several other refugees who had been brought to the Houston area by the organization. Many were Sudanese Lost Boys. Veronica led the class on how to operate electric ovens, stoves, and microwaves. She also explained how to prepare the foods she'd stocked in our refrigerator and freezer.

I liked Veronica. She was friendly and outgoing. She tried engaging me in conversation throughout the orientation. Though I knew a little English, I was embarrassed by my pronunciation of English words and my Dinka accent, so I kept my responses to shy smiles and shakes and nods of my head.

After orientation, Veronica drove us to a large store that sold everything from clothes to food. Sarah and I couldn't believe the amount of clothing crammed onto racks and stacked in folded piles on tables. They had clothes for people of all ages, in every size and color. We were excited to pick out something new to wear but struggled to choose with so many options.

"You could have clothed all of Group Nine-A with what's in this one store," I said to Sarah as Veronica led us over to look for new shoes.

There were rows upon rows of shelves packed with boxes of shoes. I glanced down at the open-toed slippers I'd worn from Kakuma. I had received them when I was fourteen years old. Standing among such great abundance, in the only footwear I'd ever owned, I thought of Julia and the hundreds of thousands of refugees we'd left behind in Kakuma. Tears welled in my eyes. They had so little and needed so much.

Sarah sniffed back her own tears and took my hand in hers. "I know," she said, giving my hand a gentle squeeze. "I know."

After measuring our feet and helping us find the correct size shoes, Veronica took Sarah and me to another aisle. Without Jacob there to translate, she used hand gestures and acted out movements to help us comprehend any English words we had not learned in Kakuma.

"We need to get you both bras." She studied us for a moment, pulled two bras from a rack, and led us into a changing room. "Try these on. I'm guessing they are your sizes."

Holding the bras between our fingers, Sarah and I looked at one another. We had never worn bras before, and I wasn't thrilled about the idea of starting now. They looked strange and uncomfortable, but I didn't want to offend Veronica, so I tried one on. I was right. It was uncomfortable. I later learned bras were a required part of the dress code for girls attending school in America. Veronica said it was so boys weren't distracted from their lessons, which struck Sarah and me as odd. The boys' lessons in Kakuma had never suffered for the lack of girls wearing bras.

After we'd found our distraction-preventing bras, Veronica also helped us select personal and feminine hygiene products like deodorant and sanitary pads and explained how and why they were necessary. Her kind heart and patience reminded me of Adual. She spoke slowly and repeated her hand gestures as many times as we needed, and she never laughed or rolled her eyes when we did not understand.

Once Sarah and I had picked out a couple of new outfits, shoes, bras, and hygiene products, we rejoined the boys, and Jacob began translating for us again.

Veronica walked us over to the grocery area of the store, where we once again broke into small groups. "The food is organized by aisles," she explained, giving each group a shopping cart. "With fruits and vegetables in one section, meats in another, rice and bread in a separate area, and so on. I'll be walking around checking in with each group in case you have any questions."

Sarah and I grabbed a cart and started down the first aisle. I had never seen so much food in my entire life. It could have fed the refugees in Kakuma for months. So much of it came in boxes and bags, with colorful pictures and lots of words. I didn't know what most of the food was. We wandered up and down the aisles, searching for anything that looked familiar and appetizing.

In one of the last aisles, Sarah found a package of dried meat. "This doesn't look too bad," she said, placing two packages in our cart, one for her apartment and one for mine.

Veronica found us as we were leaving the aisle. "No, no, no," she said, taking the packages from our cart.

"No?" Sarah asked.

"Do you know what this is?" Veronica asked, holding up the bags.

We shook our heads.

"You're in the pet food aisle," she explained.

Sarah and I looked each other and shrugged.

"This is for dogs."

When we still looked confused, Veronica's brow furrowed in thought. Then her eyebrows shot up. "I know!" She pointed to a picture of a dog on the package. "Woof. Woof." Then she mimed bringing food to her mouth and chewing.

Sarah's and my eyes grew wide with understanding. We burst into laughter.

America sure is a strange place, I thought as we ran from the aisle, *with its moving staircases, food for dogs, and bras.*

CHAPTER 30

Houston, Texas—January 2001

Our first week in Houston was spent attending orientation classes at the YMCA and trying to apply what we'd learned in class to life in our apartment. It took us a while to figure out what foods we needed to keep in the refrigerator and which we could put in the cupboards, and it took us several attempts before we successfully managed to operate the oven and microwave.

The Sudanese community in Houston rallied together to cook us food. The meals they prepared were plentiful and delicious. The familiar smells and tastes of the spices pulled my thoughts back to Wernynol and eating around the fire with Mama, Abraham, Monica, and Koko. The boys and I were grateful for the food and the Sudanese community's generosity, but guilt accompanied every meal.

I couldn't remember the last time my stomach had ached from being too full, rather than too empty. I'd lie in bed at night, cradling my sore stomach, and thinking of those we left back in Kakuma. I knew their stomachs were keeping them awake, too. They were going to bed hungry, while we had more food than we could eat. The thought of them starving while we ate our fill haunted me. During our first week in Houston, I lost weight because my belly could not manage the food and my conscience could not stomach the guilt.

Veronica and another YMCA counselor named Lisa took us shopping a couple more times for clothes, shoes, and food. I was always happy when they picked us up for orientation classes and shopping trips because it meant I would see Sarah. The apartment building where she lived with her brother and cousin was located far from our building, and Jacob forbade me from walking there by myself. Jacob had wasted no time in setting down strict rules for everyone, especially me, and I found no allies with the other boys when I questioned Jacob's rules.

"It's too dangerous for you to go outside, Rachel," Andrew explained one afternoon as we tried to figure out how to cook rice on the stovetop for dinner. "You need to stay here, in the apartment, where you are safe."

"If it's so dangerous, why do you and the other boys get to go outside?"

"Because we're older," he said, turning the knobs, trying to get the front burner to heat. The last knob he tried clicked, and the front metal coil began to warm from cold black to hot red.

"Thomas is a year younger than me," I argued, handing him a pot of water, which he placed on the burner.

"That's different."

"How?"

"Thomas is a boy," Andrew said. "We don't have to worry about him. You're a girl. We need to protect you. *I* need to protect you."

"From what?"

"Do you remember in Kakuma, how I warned you not to walk around by yourself, especially at night?"

"Yes."

"Why did I warn you then?" Andrew asked.

I released a heavy sigh. "Because there were dangerous men there who would hurt me."

"Yes, and there are men like that in America, too, so you need to stay in the apartment."

"So, I'm a prisoner here."

Andrew ripped open the bag of rice and poured it in the pot of boiling water. "You're not a prisoner. You're protected."

The water calmed for a few seconds with the addition of the rice, but it was soon boiling again.

"I'm sixteen years old, Andrew! How long are you going to treat me like I'm still six?"

He placed a lid on the pot. "For as long as it takes to keep you safe." He turned down the heat on the burner and led me over to the table. He sat down and motioned for me to join him. "I know you're disappointed, Rachel, but this is how things are for girls." He pointed toward the door leading to the hallway outside our apartment. "We've only been in this country for a week. We don't know what dangers are out there yet. Until we do, you must stay here, where I know you will be safe, so please, no more arguing, especially with Jacob. It will just make him angry. There will be plenty of time to explore our new home and meet new people later, but for now, try to be a little patient. Veronica said school starts back up in a week, after the holiday. When it does, you'll get to leave the apartment for several hours, five days a week." He smiled at me. "And Thomas and I are enrolled at the same school, so we'll be able to keep an eye on you."

"Of course."

"Until then, you have to stay here."

"It's not fair, Andrew."

"I know." He wrapped an arm around my shoulder. "But I made a promise when I found you in Kakuma nine years ago that I would keep you safe. And I intend to keep that promise, whether you hate me for it or not."

The day after New Year's Day and my UNHCR-assigned sixteenth birthday, Andrew, Thomas, and I entered Bellaire High for our first day of school. I was disappointed Sarah would not be joining me there. It would have been nice to have a girl I knew with me, but at nineteen years old, Sarah was too old to attend Bellaire. The only high school in the area accepting refugees over eighteen years old was Lee High School, so Sarah had to enroll there with Simon and Pabior, while Mark and Jacob attended job training courses at the YMCA.

Bellaire was two stories high and had so many hallways and rooms, the guidance counselor we met gave us each a map to help with navigating the sprawling building. The counselor also gave us tape recorders, audiotapes, and books to take home.

"Listen to these every day, Rachel," the counselor said, showing me how to put one of the tapes in the recorder. "And then follow along in the book." She turned to the first page. It had pictures with English words underneath. A voice on the tape said the word "face," and the counselor pointed to the picture of the face and the word printed beneath it in the book. "This will help you practice your English at home."

"Thank you," I said, putting the recorder, tapes, and book in the backpack Veronica had purchased for me.

The counselor then escorted me to my first class. I arrived before the other students, and after being introduced to the teacher, I was assigned a desk at the front of the room, near the teacher's desk.

"This way if you have any questions," the teacher said, "it will be easier for you to ask."

I smiled.

The teacher and counselor glanced at one another as

though they were not sure I understood anything they were telling me. I did, at least most of it. Their hand motions helped, but I did not want to attempt my limited English, especially after a loud bell buzzed and students began to enter the classroom.

As they took their seats, a few students shot me curious looks while whispering and laughing behind cupped hands to one another. The rest were too engrossed in gossip and conversations about what they did over break to notice me. My palms began to sweat. I wiped them on the long red skirt I'd selected during my shopping trip with Veronica the day after we'd arrived in Houston. I'd thought the skirt was pretty when I'd picked it out, along with a white top and brown pair of open-toed sandals, but I'd lost more weight since we'd left Kakuma, and the clothes sagged on my bony frame. My face burned with embarrassment. Keeping my head low, I snuck a few furtive glances at the other girls as they entered the classroom and took their seats. It became glaringly evident my choice of clothing did not blend in with the more stylish, form-fitting outfits they wore with such confidence. I wanted to shrink down inside my oversized clothes and hide for the rest of the day. I wished Sarah were there, or even Andrew or Thomas, but they were alone in other classrooms, surrounded by strange people, sweating through their own first day of school in America.

I flinched at the buzz of another loud bell. The students

took their time settling in their seats, and then the teacher ran through her attendance list.

"We have a new student today, class. She just came to the United States. Her name is Rachel Lual." I was confused as to why she hadn't used my full name, but later learned in America, people didn't introduce themselves by using all their names, just two. The last name they'd chosen to use for me was my baba's name, Lual, so after that day, I became Rachel Lual.

Every pair of eyes in the room turned to look at me.

"I thought she was white," a boy in the back of the room said. "You don't look like a Rachel. Rachel is a white girl's name."

There were a few startled gasps, followed by several giggles. The teacher's eyes narrowed on the boy. Everyone turned and looked at him, except me. I kept my gaze fixed firmly on my desktop. I knew enough English to understand the boy's words and their meaning.

"Jessie," the teacher snapped, "that is not right. A name is a name. There are no 'white' names." She then told the boy to follow her into the hallway. She slammed the door behind them.

The prying stares of my classmates burrowed into me. I didn't feel sorry for that boy. What he'd said was cruel, but I also didn't completely disagree with him. The truth was, I'd never felt like a Rachel, but Rachel was the name I'd been given at my baptism, and Rachel was the name

I'd been called ever since, so he'd have to learn to live with it, just as I had.

Not speaking English further isolated me from my new peers in Houston. In the apartment with Andrew and the others, I spoke Dinka, but my inability to communicate with anyone at school made my world increasingly small and painfully lonely. I worked hard to learn the language of my new home. Every afternoon after school, I listened to the audiotapes my counselor had given me and practiced saying the words in the privacy of the room I shared with Thomas. I also watched shows on PBS, one of the few stations we received on our apartment's small TV. I'd listen carefully and repeat the English I heard on the entertaining programs. My favorite show was *Barney & Friends*.

Even with the help of the tutorial tapes and PBS's big purple dinosaur, my English was still limited. I was hesitant to attempt pronouncing the new words I'd learned in front of my peers at Bellaire High. My silence made it difficult to meet people and make friends at my new school. Thankfully, Sarah introduced me to friends she'd made at her school, many of whom were also Sudanese refugees. One boy named AJ was the older brother of two girls Sarah had met at Lee High School. AJ had come to the United States in 1992. He spoke Dinka but also spoke English and knew all the American slang and lingo. One day after school, AJ, his sisters, and Sarah picked me up to go shopping. Jacob was not happy.

"You said it was important for us to remain connected to our culture and roots," I argued. "Sarah and her friends are Dinka. I'll just be gone for a couple hours and will be back in time to help with dinner."

I slipped out the door before Jacob could stop me.

"You better be!" he yelled after me as I followed Sarah down the stairs and outside to the waiting car. If Jacob was angry, I decided I'd deal with that later. I was tired of him controlling every aspect of my new life in Houston. I was done asking for his permission to live.

Sarah introduced me to everyone before I climbed in the car.

"Hey, Rachel," AJ said in Dinka from the driver's seat. "What's up?"

I had never been asked that before and didn't understand why anyone would greet someone with such a strange question. I craned my neck up and looked around, hoping to answer the question correctly and not humiliate myself in front of Sarah and her new friends. "The sky?"

AJ doubled over laughing and slapped the steering wheel. My face burned with embarrassment. Clearly, my answer had not been right. I looked to Sarah for help.

She smiled, not at all ashamed of my answer. "Don't mind, AJ," she said, bumping my shoulder with hers. "I got it wrong the first time he asked me, too. I said 'birds.'"

AJ shook his head and laughed harder. "'What's up?' is like asking someone what they are doing."

"Oh. Then 'what's up' is I am waiting for you to take us shopping."

"Then climb in," AJ said, motioning to the back seat. "Let's go."

The shopping trip was the most fun I had had since arriving in the United States. I wasn't embarrassed to try my English around Sarah, AJ, and his sisters, and no one teased me about my Dinka accent. AJ even bought me my first CD.

"Do you like music?" he asked as we walked through the entertainment section of a store.

"Yes. Very much."

"Then you'll love this." He handed me a compact disc. On the cover, a Black man stood sideways, his eyes closed, and his face lifted. A blue guitar was tucked upside down under his arm. "The singer is Brian McKnight," AJ explained. "His songs are amazing, and his lyrics and singing are super clear." He handed me a small compact disc player. "You'll also need one of these. My sisters learned English from listening to McKnight's album. It'll help you, too, and it's a lot more fun than listening to those boring school tutorial tapes all the time."

"Thank you."

I hurried over to show Sarah what AJ had bought me. I told her I'd share them with her so she could learn English with me. I couldn't wait to return to the apartment and listen to every song on the CD. I smiled as I sat in AJ's car, listening to Sarah and the others talking and laughing. It was the first time since I'd arrived in Houston that I felt like I belonged, and my world had grown a little bigger.

When I got back to the apartment, Jacob was waiting at the door. "You're late," he said the second I entered the room.

Andrew was at the stove, preparing dinner. He tossed me a concerned glance. Thomas sat at the table. He kept his head bowed and his eyes locked on his English tutorial book and tape player.

"I'm only a few minutes late," I explained. "Sarah had to stop at the grocery store before they could drop me off."

"Sarah does not drive. Who drove you?"

"Her friends' brother, AJ."

Jacob snatched the bag from my hand and took out the CD and player. He studied the cover. "And did AJ buy you this?"

"Yes, but—"

"You are not to be accepting gifts from boys, Rachel."

"But he said it would help me learn English."

"The school gave you books and tapes to teach you English."

I looked to Andrew for help. "AJ said his sisters listened to this CD when they came here. It helped them learn English faster." But Andrew did not intervene. He always deferred to Jacob's judgment.

Jacob tossed the CD and player in the garbage can. "I

don't want to hear any more about AJ. You are to come home directly after school with Andrew and Thomas."

"I can't see Sarah at all?"

"You can see Sarah at church or the YMCA. That will be enough."

"I'm going to talk to Veronica about this," I threatened. "This isn't fair."

"You will *not* bring your petty complaints to Veronica or anyone else. They do not want to hear them. No one wants to hear them, Rachel. They have worked hard to bring us to America and provide us with a place to live, clothes to wear, and food to eat. It is selfish of you to ask for more."

Jacob walked around the room to address the other boys he'd gathered for his sermon. "We cannot risk doing or saying anything that will make them think we are too much trouble. There are plenty of other refugees dying to be in our place. If we become a problem for them . . ." He turned and stared at me. "If *you* cause trouble, they will deport us back to Kakuma. Is that what you want, Rachel? To be sent back? Are you so selfish you will risk everyone else's freedom and futures so you can get your way? Do you want Thomas and Andrew sent back to Kakuma?"

"No, I was just—"

"Then you will say nothing and do nothing except what is expected of you. You will go to school, you will come home, and you will do your schoolwork. That is what you will do."

"But—"

"This conversation is over," Jacob announced. "Now, go to your room and do your homework."

Later that night, when everyone else was asleep, I snuck into the kitchen and retrieved the CD and player from the trash. I hid them in my room and listened to them when Jacob was not home.

Jacob's control over all of us worsened over the next weeks. He dictated where I could go and who I could see. He put himself in charge of any money we received from the YMCA, including the money allocated for the older boys. If any of us needed even a few dollars for lunch or school supplies, we had to go to Jacob and plead our case. Jacob said he had to control our money because he was the most responsible one of our group, but Jacob just liked being in control of all of us, especially me.

One afternoon, a few weeks after we'd arrived in Houston, Jacob took more than just control. I had come home directly after school, as ordered, and was listening to my English tapes, while the other boys were allowed to go outside to hang out with friends they'd made in the neighborhood.

I was lying on my stomach on my bed, listening to the voice on the audiotape drone on, and repeating each word she said. I thought I was alone in the apartment. I was wrong.

My attention was completely focused on the English

tutorial. I did not hear anyone enter the room. Suddenly a heavy weight plopped down on my back, crushing me onto the mattress.

Startled, I turned and found Jacob sitting on me. "What are you doing? Get off me."

At first, I thought he was joking around, but then I noticed the hard look in his eyes.

"What are you going to do about it?" he asked in a cold, taunting voice.

I tried to push him off, but he was bigger and stronger than me and he had me pinned on my stomach to the bed.

Jacob didn't ask again or say another word as his hands groped my body. He didn't have to. He knew the answer. He had worked for weeks, manipulating the others and isolating me, to assure the answer to his question.

I squeezed my eyes shut. This could not be happening. I had obeyed all of Jacob's rules. I had followed Andrew's advice. I had avoided anyone or anywhere they warned would put me in danger. They said I'd be safe here.

They lied.

I could not move. I could not think. My face buried in my pillow, I listened for any approaching footsteps or voices, hoping someone, anyone would come inside the apartment and pull Jacob off me, but no one came.

As I lay there, under Jacob's suffocating weight, paralyzed with fear and desperately praying for the pain of his revolting touch to stop, his question repeated in my panicked mind.

What are you going to do about it?

Remembering his threat about being deported back to Kakuma if I complained or caused trouble, I bit down on my trembling lip as silent tears bled into my pillow.

I would do nothing to stop Jacob because I *could* do nothing.

He knew it, and now I knew it.

CHAPTER 31

Houston, Texas—March 2001

I lost track of how many times Jacob assaulted me after that first day in my bedroom. I often thought back to Julia's warnings about him. I wished I could heed her advice and avoid him, but despite my best efforts, he always found ways to corner me alone. He'd send the others on errands or make excuses to duck into the apartment during games outside with the boys.

Jacob knew what he was doing was wrong. His abuse was premeditated and cunning. He made sure there were no witnesses and no consequences. Consequences would lead to questions. And questions would eventually lead to Jacob. He knew a pregnancy would expose his lies and crimes, so Jacob confined each cruel, angry touch to his hands. The same hands he raised in worship and folded in prayer.

In the first days of the abuse, I waited for the others to save me. Surely, Andrew and Thomas must have noticed how my entire body went rigid with fear any time Jacob entered the room. Pabior, Mark, and Simon had to have heard the desperation in my voice when I begged to visit

Sarah or argued to join them on their errands. But no one noticed, and no one stopped Jacob.

As winter warmed into spring, Jacob became bolder. He'd sneak into the bedroom I shared with Thomas at night and assault me while Thomas slept mere meters away. He'd molest me before church and then raise his voice with the congregation in prayerful hymns as I sat numb beside him. He played the role of devout Christian to perfection, preaching morality to Andrew and the others after every Sunday sermon and Bible study class while breaking God's word and shattering my innocence and faith with every uninvited touch.

So many nights, I lay awake, dreading the creak of my bedroom door. I desperately wanted to tell Andrew and Thomas what was happening but worried if they learned the truth, they might not believe me. Worse yet, if they did believe me, I feared Andrew would kill Jacob and be arrested and we would be sent back to Kakuma. I could not let that happen, no matter how painful life was living with Jacob. I could not endanger the others' safety and freedom, so I remained silent. I couldn't help but wonder how the others did not notice the life dimming in my eyes with every passing day. I saw it every time I stared into the mirror.

The emptiness.

The hopelessness.

The inevitability.

I started hiding in my bedroom closet after school.

From Jacob.

From the shame.

From my life.

One March day, three months after we'd arrived in Houston to begin our new lives, I sat on the floor of my closet, thinking of the life I'd left behind in Kenya. It would have been so easy to let death claim me in Kakuma. I closed my eyes and imagined myself there again. All I would have had to do is stop.

Stop moving forward.

Stop fighting.

Just stop—

and wait.

But I was not in Kakuma. I could not wait for death to arrive. I would have to seek it out. I would have to act.

The sound of muffled voices and laughter drawing closer outside our apartment building jolted me from my thoughts. I opened the closet door and peeked into my bedroom to check the clock. It was later than I'd thought. The others would be home soon.

He would be home soon.

I closed the closet door. I was running out of time. I had to choose.

I ran my fingers over the items I'd snuck into the closet with me. After ten years of running from death, life had left me with two options: a knife or a rope.

I'd taken the knife from the wooden holder in the kitchen the night before while doing the dinner dishes. I had pulled the length of rope from a hoodie Veronica had bought for me.

Staring down at the two objects lying on the floor of the closet where I hid, I carefully considered each option.

Their functionality.

Their strength.

Their durability.

Their effectiveness.

Could they do what was needed?

Could I?

I had to make the right choice. Once the decision was made, there was no room for error or doubt.

Tears ran down my cheeks and over my lips. Death had taken so much from me over my sixteen years, but life had taken more.

Bit by bit.

Piece by piece.

It had stolen everything until there was only one thing left to take. I picked up the knife and rope and thought back on every loss I had suffered.

My hope.

My faith.

My trust.

My innocence.

My friends.

My security.

My home.

My family.

Even my name.

All that was left was my life. A life I could no longer endure. A life I no longer wanted.

A life.

My thoughts drifted back to my interview in Kakuma seven months earlier.

Tell me, Rachel, why do you want to go to the US?

I want life.

I closed my eyes, sending fresh tears streaming down my face. I had suffered so much, but I had also survived so much. Everything life had thrown at me. Everything life had taken from me.

I had survived.

The rope and knife trembled in my hands as I remembered the people who had fought for my survival. So many had sacrificed so I could live. I had no right to dishonor their memories by ending the life they'd fought so hard to save. I had no right to discard all they had sacrificed and all I had survived.

My hands stopped shaking, and my grip loosened. The rope and knife fell to the floor.

Despite all the pain and loss, I still wanted life, and no matter how long it took or how much I would have to sacrifice and suffer, I would have it.

I would not let Jacob or anyone else, including myself, take it from me.

CHAPTER 32

Houston, Texas—March–May 2001

Hiding in the closet, I made a plan. According to my UNHCR-assigned birthday, in two years, I would be eighteen years old, legally an adult, and permitted by law to leave Jacob's guardianship. I focused on January 1, 2003, and plotted out the entire plan.

On my eighteenth birthday, I would move out and live with Sarah or maybe Veronica. I would get a part-time job and graduate from high school. Once I had my diploma, I would work full-time until I could afford a place of my own, and then I'd start saving money to afford college. I could picture my life free from Jacob. I would be able to do what I wanted, when I wanted, and with whomever I wanted, and he wouldn't be able to say a thing. I could leave Houston and Texas. I could travel to Lansing, Michigan, and live with Deborah and her brothers. Maybe Thomas would come with me. The dream of my future would become my lifeline.

I had survived greater threats and deadlier predators with no promise of an end in sight. I remembered the long nights hiding in the hut in Pawel with Koko. How she'd held me close and whispered in my ear words of strength and promise.

We just have to make it through the night.

We just need to survive until morning.

We must be patient and silent.

You are strong.

Koko was right. To survive the next two years, I would have to be patient. And despite how much I wished to scream my pain for all to hear, how desperately I wanted to tell Andrew and Thomas what Jacob was doing to me, I knew to survive, I had to be silent. If I spoke the truth, Andrew would kill Jacob and be arrested, and Thomas, Mark, Pabior, Simon, and I would be deported. My truth would be a death sentence for all of us. I had to protect the others, even if it meant not protecting myself.

I closed my eyes and pulled forward the memory of waking in Koko's arms after our first night hiding in the hut in Pawel. I remembered seeing that shaft of soft hibiscus-red sunlight reach toward us from beneath the barricaded door. Tears fell from my eyes onto the rope and knife on the closet floor as Koko's words whispered in my memory.

We survived until morning, Achut.

The next two years would be difficult, but I had survived war and loss and death for sixteen years. I would survive Jacob, too.

* * *

It can be hard to remember the light when you've lived in darkness. I needed someone to remind me it still existed, so the next day, I approached Veronica at the YMCA. She was cleaning up after teaching a group of new refugees how to operate common household appliances.

"Veronica, can you help me?" I asked.

"Sure," she said, wiping off the countertop. "What do you need?"

I handed her a slip of paper with the name *Deborah Ding* and *Lansing, Michigan* written on it. "Please find my friend." Despite the promises we had made one another in Kakuma, Deborah and I hadn't spoken since we'd disembarked the plane in New York City. Though I'd desperately wanted to speak with her, I had no idea how to reach her.

"Is this all the information you have?" Veronica asked.

"Yes."

"It will be hard with so little to go on, but I'll try."

I thanked her and hurried from the room before Veronica noticed the tears in my eyes.

A week later, she pulled me out of a workshop on how to budget money and brought me into a small office at the YMCA. She smiled at me as she closed the door.

"Good news!" she said, clapping her hands together. "It wasn't easy, but I found your friend."

I felt hope for the first time in months.

"She and her brothers were placed with a family through foster care."

"Can I walk to see Deborah?"

"I'm afraid it is too far to walk," Veronica said.

"Will you drive me?" I asked.

"Even by car, the trip would take several days."

Disappointment dampened my excitement. "So, I can't see Deborah?"

"Not today." Veronica held up a piece of paper. "But I have her foster family's phone number. Would you like to call her?" She pointed to the phone.

"Yes!" I threw my arms around Veronica. "Thank you!"

She dialed the number. It rang several times before someone answered.

Veronica smiled at me. "Hello. This is Veronica from the YMCA in Houston. We spoke earlier. I have Rachel with me. She was hoping to speak with Deborah."

Veronica handed me the phone. There was silence on the other line, and then I heard her voice.

"Rachel?"

I started to cry.

"Rachel, are you all right?" Deborah asked in Dinka.

"Yes," I said, sniffing back tears. "I'm just happy to hear your voice. I've missed you."

"I've missed you, too. How is everyone in Houston?"

"Fine. We're all fine." Afraid if Deborah asked the wrong questions, I would be too tempted to tell her everything, I quickly changed the subject. I could not risk her brothers finding out about Jacob's abuse. I knew they would track down Andrew and tell him. "Tell me about Michigan. Are you happy there?"

"Yes, but I miss my mama."

"I'm sure she misses you, too."

Deborah told me all about the nice family who had taken in her brothers and her and the school she was attending.

"How are you doing in Houston?" she asked.

"I'm surviving," I said.

We talked for twenty minutes, and before we got off the phone, Veronica gave Deborah's foster family the phone number Deborah could use to reach me at our apartment. Every weekend after that, Deborah would call. I never told her about Jacob or the moment in my closet with the rope and knife. Just knowing she would be calling and I would be hearing her voice was enough to give me the strength to survive another week. In my darkest moments, those phone calls with Deborah reminded me there was still light on the horizon, even if I could not see it.

In the weeks that followed, the abuse continued, but a month after I made my plan to survive, I received news that my escape from Jacob could occur sooner than I'd expected. During our weekly classes at the YMCA, Veronica explained there had been concerns voiced over an underage girl being housed with six males. The YMCA had taken steps to find a foster family for me and possibly Thomas. Someone had finally recognized the issue with my living situation and were going to remove me from the apartment and Jacob's control. I hoped my foster care placement would be as good as Deborah's.

Veronica picked me up after school the next day and drove me to the local Kentucky Fried Chicken, where a middle-aged white couple waited to meet me.

"Hello, Rachel," the woman said when Veronica and I sat in the booth across from the husband and wife. They had ordered fried chicken, mashed potatoes, and biscuits for all of us.

"Hello," I said.

With Veronica's help and hand gestures, the couple explained they had one daughter, who was away in college. If they fostered me, I would be staying in her room. The thought of having a room to myself, away from Jacob, was almost too good to be true. As they talked, the plan I had created in my closet shifted. I would be able to finish high school in the safety of their home. I could focus on my studies without worrying about the next assault. I would be able to sleep at night without listening for the creak of my bedroom door. I could not only survive but live for the first time in ten years.

The couple and I talked for more than two hours. They asked me what classes I liked in school and if I played any sports or enjoyed any hobbies. Every minute I spent with them, my hope grew, and by the end of our meal, I wanted to move in with them right away. They even had room in their home and their lives for Thomas.

Our first meeting couldn't have gone any better. On

the car ride with Veronica back to the apartment, I closed my eyes and smiled. Morning was closer than I'd thought. I could almost feel its warm hibiscus light on my face. I ran up the stairs of our apartment building, excited to tell Thomas about the amazing opportunity the couple was offering us.

My smile faltered the second I opened the door and saw Jacob waiting for me. Andrew was standing next to him. He didn't say anything when I entered the apartment, but I could tell by his nervous fidgeting something was wrong. Thomas, Pabior, Simon, and Mark were seated at the table.

Jacob motioned for me to join them. "Close the door and sit down, Rachel."

"I've already eaten." Desperate to avoid the conversation he seemed determined to have, I started down the hallway to my room.

"I said sit down."

I pulled an empty chair next to Thomas and sat down, placing myself as far from Jacob as I could in the small room. Thomas's eyes darted to me for the briefest second before returning to the table. I didn't know what Jacob had called us all together to discuss, but I could tell by Thomas's slumped shoulders and bowed head that it was not good news. Dread sank in my stomach like a weighty stone.

Did they find out about Jacob? Did Andrew know?

I glanced up at Andrew, but he and the others would not look at me.

What had Jacob told them? Had he blamed everything on me?

My mind raced, trying to prepare a defense for whatever lies Jacob had fabricated to poison the others against me, but how was I to create an antidote when I didn't know what poison Jacob had used? I stared down at the table and waited.

"We've been talking," Jacob announced. "And we've decided it would be best for us to leave Houston."

My head snapped up. Of everything I'd thought Jacob might say, I had not anticipated this.

"What?" I looked to Andrew. "What is he talking about?"

"We know all about the YMCA's plan to take you away, Rachel," Jacob said. "We're not going to let that happen."

"But they are a nice family." I spoke directly to Andrew. "I met them today. They want to take Thomas, too." I glanced over at Thomas. "They said they would welcome us both in their home. We could even have our own rooms."

"No one is taking anyone," Jacob snapped.

"It's not up to you," I said.

"Yes. It is. I am the oldest. I am Thomas's and your guardian."

I look to Andrew for help. "But the YMCA and Veronica have already made plans for them to foster us."

"Let them make their plans," Jacob said. "We have plans of our own. I have a cousin in Oregon. A couple from his church has agreed to let us live with them in Portland."

I wasn't sure where Oregon was, but I knew if Jacob wanted to move us there, it was nowhere near Houston. "But—"

"We cannot let them take Rachel," Jacob said, ignoring me and addressing his speech to the five other boys. "We came here as a group, as a family. We are not going to let anyone separate us." His voice grew louder. He spoke with the passion of a fire-and-brimstone preacher delivering a Sunday sermon.

"If they take Rachel, they will teach her *their* ways, *their* lack of morals. They will not protect her like we do. They will let her start dating boys."

I watched Jacob's words manipulate the others' minds, bending their opinions to match his own. At the mention of dating, inside or outside the Sudanese community, Andrew's jaw clenched, and his eyes narrowed.

My breaths came short and shallow. Jacob would never let me go. I would be trapped with him until I was eighteen and he no longer had legal control over me. I would be his prisoner for two more years, during which time, he would continue to make my world smaller and smaller until no one else remained, not even me.

"We cannot let them raise her to forget her culture and her language," Jacob continued. "We cannot let them turn her into someone who thinks and acts like they do. Even if they mean well, they will turn her into someone she is not.

They will turn her into someone we no longer recognize. We cannot allow them to let Rachel forget who she is!"

Thomas kept his head bowed, but the others nodded in agreement, even Andrew.

I stared at Jacob. He glared back at me, his eyes hard with cruel confidence.

In that moment, I knew. No one was going to save me. Not the YMCA. Not Veronica. Not the family who'd offered to open their home to Thomas and me. Not even Andrew. Numb with shock, I pushed back from the table and stood.

"Where are you going?" Andrew asked.

"Do I have any say in this decision?"

"No," Jacob stated.

"Then there is no reason for me to listen to this." I walked down the hall to my room.

"Rachel, I know you're disappointed, but this is for the best!" Andrew called after me. "We are doing this to protect you. I—"

I closed the door before he could finish.

CHAPTER 33

Portland, Oregon—June–December 2001

We left Houston two weeks later, the day after the school year ended. Mark, Pabior, and Simon chose not to join us. I envied them. They were old enough to legally walk away from Jacob.

"Nineteen more months," I reminded myself as I followed Andrew, Thomas, and Jacob onto the bus headed to Oregon. "I just have to survive to my eighteenth birthday, and then I can leave. Nineteen more months, and I'll be free."

When we arrived in Portland, Jacob's cousin introduced us to David and Sue, an older white couple from his church. They had agreed to take Jacob, Andrew, Thomas, and me into their home until Jacob and Andrew found work and saved enough money to afford an apartment or house for the four of us. David and Sue had a lovely two-story home with two bedrooms downstairs for us to use. Thomas and I once again shared a room. Andrew and Jacob stayed in the room across from us while David and Sue slept in their bedroom upstairs.

David and Sue were a caring, generous couple and did

everything they could to make us feel welcome in their home and city. They enrolled Thomas and me in a private school, but we struggled to keep up with our classes due to our limited English, so after a week, they agreed to let us enroll at Roosevelt High, the local public school. The counselors, teachers, and students at Roosevelt welcomed Thomas and me into their school and made sure we had support in every class. I improved in my history and science courses with their help. Outside of school, David and Sue also introduced us to other Sudanese refugees from their church and community.

Andrew became friends with Atem and Chol Deng. The cousins were in their thirties and had come to America many years earlier. They occasionally came by the house to talk and play dominoes. One day, they brought a girl named Akoi with them. Akoi lived with her mama. She explained she and I were second or third cousins—she wasn't quite sure which—on my baba's side. It was nice to meet another relative, especially a girl my age. Akoi was kind to me. She gave me her phone number, and we spoke almost every day on Sue and David's cordless phone. I was grateful for her friendship when Thomas and I attended our first day at Roosevelt High. It was a comfort to find a friendly face in the sea of strangers staring at me as I entered the new school.

Akoi told me all about her family and spoke often of her older sister, Daruka, whom she missed. Daruka lived in Kansas City, Missouri, with her husband and their two young children. Akoi and I discussed visiting her some-day. On the long nights when my eighteenth birthday felt so far away, I would think of our plans and dream of escaping Portland and Jacob to go with Akoi to Kansas City, where I had some family, even if the family were strangers to me.

Nineteen more months, I'd remind myself each night, counting down the days until I would finally be free.

I had hoped the fact that we were living in someone's home and that our host family was sleeping a floor above us would dissuade Jacob from continuing his sexual abuse, but after our first week in Portland, he cornered me in the kitchen, when the couple was at work and Andrew and Thomas were outside playing basketball.

After that day, I did everything I could think of to make it harder for him to ever touch me again. I avoided being home alone with him whenever I could. I joined multiple after-school activities and clubs, including the tennis and cross-country teams. I stopped wearing skirts and dresses. When people asked why I was always wearing jeans and a belt, and not skirts like the other girls in the Sudanese community, I lied and told them I found pants more comfortable. I even wore jeans to bed, and I always slept on my stomach.

Every evening, when Thomas and I went to our room, I asked him to switch beds with me for the night.

"Again?" Thomas would whine.

"Please."

"Why? What's going on, Rachel?"

"Nothing," I lied. "I just can't figure out which one I like better."

Thomas would roll his eyes. "Fine." Then he'd toss his pillow onto the bed across the room, vacating his bed for me to use for the night.

I let him believe I was being fussy. I couldn't tell him the real reason I wanted to constantly switch beds was because I was hiding from Jacob, who snuck into our room each night, after everyone was asleep. I was afraid of what Thomas would think of me, and I was terrified of what Andrew would do if he found out.

It worked for a while. I'd lay awake, listening for Jacob's footsteps in the hallway and the creak of our door opening. I'd hold my breath as he crept into the room. In the darkness, he could not see who was in which bed, and often he chose wrong.

"What's going on?" Thomas would ask in a groggy voice when Jacob mistakenly woke him.

"Nothing," Jacob would mutter as he hurried for the door. "I was just checking to make sure you were both asleep."

"How are we supposed to get any rest if he keeps coming in here and waking us up?" Thomas would complain after Jacob left.

As Thomas drifted back to sleep, I would lie on my

stomach in my belted jeans trembling and I would remind myself of the promise I made in that closet in Houston.

"I just have to make it through the night," I would repeat, remembering Koko's words from the hut in Pawel. "I need to be patient and silent for a little longer. I just have to survive until morning."

It worked. Night after night, for months, until one winter night when my patience and silence shattered.

Thomas and I had retired to our room after a fun night of dominoes with Andrew, Chol, and Akoi. I had been successful at avoiding Jacob for several weeks and fell asleep that night on my stomach, with my jeans on and belt cinched. I didn't hear Jacob come in the room. I didn't know he was standing over my bed until he grabbed me. Frustrated by my successful attempts to avoid him and angry to find me asleep on my stomach again, he flipped me over. His hands tugged at my pants and yanked on my belt.

A desperate voice cried out in my mind. *Not again!*

My arms swung wildly in the darkness. One of my fists connected with the side of Jacob's head. He muttered a muffled vulgarity and let go of my belt. I scrambled away from him, trying to get off the bed to run for the door, but his hands found me and pushed me back down.

The screams in my mind erupted from my throat in a single word. "No!"

My cry woke Thomas.

"I knew it!" he yelled.

I froze and stared at him. "You knew?"

Before I could process the fact that while I'd suffered in silence for months to protect Thomas and the others, Thomas had suspected the abuse all along and done nothing to protect me, he launched himself across the room and jumped onto Jacob's back. "Get off her!"

I opened my mouth to scream again, but my voice was strangled by Jacob's hands wrapping around my neck. The harder I fought, the tighter he squeezed. I clawed at his arms, desperate for air. Small dots of white light burst before my eyes, and my vision blurred.

"Let her go!" Thomas roared. He clung to Jacob's back, striking him on the head and face.

Jacob released my throat to shield himself from Thomas's blows. I gasped for air, sucking in large breaths until the pinpricks of light dissolved from my sight and my vision cleared. I scrambled back from Jacob, but this time, I did not run for the door. Repressed rage from months of abuse and years of trauma surged through my veins with the intensity of desert lightning. As Jacob swung at Thomas, I lunged across the bed, kicking and hitting him with all my strength and fury.

Suddenly, the bedroom door swung open, and the lights flipped on. We stopped fighting and looked to the doorway, where Andrew stood. His shocked gaze darted from Thomas to me and then narrowed on Jacob.

"I'll kill you," he said, storming into the room.

"No, Andrew. Don't!" I yelled.

Thomas and I released Jacob and charged at Andrew. Our combined momentum drove him back through the doorway and into the hall, where we struggled to restrain him.

"I can't believe you did this!" Andrew screamed, his long arms stretching over our shoulders, his hands reaching for Jacob. "I'll kill you!"

Thomas and I pressed all our body weight against him.

"Andrew, stop," I begged. "You'll wake David and Sue."

But Andrew was beyond listening.

"Get out of here!" Thomas yelled at Jacob.

Jacob did not have to be told twice. Wiping the blood dripping from his nose on the back of his hand, he glared at me and then skirted past Andrew's reach. He ran into the room they shared and slammed the door.

"Let go of me!" Andrew yanked his arm free from my hold. When I tried to grab him again, he shoved me against the wall and pushed Thomas off him. Before we could stop Andrew, he rushed to the door and grabbed the knob, but Jacob had locked him out.

"Get out here, you coward!" Andrew screamed, pounding on the door. "Or do you only have courage when attacking young girls?"

The creak of a bed and thump of hurried footsteps drummed through the ceiling above us. Thomas and I glanced up and then looked at one another, our eyes wide with fear. When David and Sue saw what was happening, they would call the police. Andrew could be arrested.

They would kick us out of their house. They would make us leave America. We would be sent back to Kakuma, where we would die.

"Andrew, stop!" Thomas pleaded. He tried to pull him away from the door, but Andrew was too strong and too determined.

As he threw himself against the locked door, David and Sue appeared at the bottom of the stairs in their pajamas.

"What's going on?" David asked.

Thomas stepped in front of Andrew. "Nothing."

"That didn't sound like nothing," David said. "Where is Jacob?"

Andrew yelled at the locked door in Dinka, raising his voice to make sure Jacob heard every word. "He's hiding—like the coward he is!" We all flinched as he punched the door again.

"Where's the phone?" David asked his wife. "I'm calling the police."

As I watched Sue hand her husband the cordless phone from their kitchen, every fear my imagination had conjured over the last year if Andrew found out about Jacob manifested in a moment of sheer panic. I stood there trembling as David dialed 911 and stepped into the kitchen.

Andrew continued punching the hallway walls and yelling at Jacob, while Jacob hid.

My nightmare had come to life. It was all happening so fast. Andrew was going to be arrested, and we were all going to be sent back to Kakuma. Even if I wanted to explain to the police what had happened, what Jacob had done to me, I worried I didn't know enough English to make them understand. And I knew Jacob would say I was lying.

I glanced at Thomas. He was shaking, too. I had to stop this.

"Please," I begged Sue, "no police!" I ran over to Andrew and grabbed his arm. "Please stop," I told him in Dinka.

Andrew stared down at me, his eyes wild with rage. His knuckles were swollen and bloodied. "It was *our* responsibility to keep you safe, Rachel," he said in Dinka, pain pinching his words. He cocked back his fist and punched the locked door again. "It was *my* responsibility!"

"The police are on their way," David said, placing the phone on the charger.

It was too late. I pushed past Andrew, grabbed the cordless phone, and ran outside. I had no time for Andrew's rage. I had enough of my own. It burned so hot inside me, I did not feel the bitter bite of the winter night as I sank onto the front steps, dressed only in my jeans and a shirt. All I felt was anger.

I was angry at Jacob for everything he had done to me. I was angry at Thomas for suspecting I was being abused and saying nothing. And I was angry at Andrew and everyone else who had believed Jacob's lies. Everyone who'd praised his Christian ways and prayed next to him in Bible study mere hours after he'd violated me. Everyone who'd ignored the warning signs and never questioned his decisions. Everyone who'd left me alone with him, again and again, for over a year. How could the world be so blind? How could they not have seen Jacob for who he was, for who I knew him to be: a liar, a manipulator, a predator?

Maybe the world only cared when they were forced to see.

Maybe, if I allowed Jacob to maintain his lie, the world would eagerly believe it again.

As I sat outside, clutching the phone and waiting for the police to arrive, Sue joined me.

"You can talk to me, Rachel," she said, placing a coat around my shoulders. "You can trust us to help you, but you need to tell me what happened tonight. What did Jacob do to cause Andrew to lash out like he did?"

I knew Sue meant every word she said to me on the steps that night, and I wanted more than anything to trust that she could help, but I also knew Jacob. I knew how easily he would explain everything away. How he would twist my words and their minds.

I stared at Sue with tears in my eyes and desperately tried to find the English words to explain. I knew what to say in Dinka. I knew the precise words to use to explain Jacob's every sin against me, words that would leave no room for doubt about his guilt. But I did not possess those words in English, so I cobbled together the few words I did know and prayed Sue would understand.

"He wants to take my clothes off."

I watched the expression on Sue's face transform from concern to horror. Her eyes widened, and she covered her mouth with her hand. She took a deep breath and asked me, "Jacob?"

I nodded. "He wants to take my clothes off."

She pulled me into a hug. "I'm so sorry," she whispered. "I need to tell David. Promise me you'll wait right here."

I nodded and watched as she stood and marched into the house.

From the porch, I heard her telling David what I had said. She then asked Thomas if what I'd said was true. Thomas's English was no better than mine, but I heard his answer clearly.

"Yes. He wants to take her clothes off."

"I want him out of here!" Sue yelled. "I want Jacob gone now!"

"Just wait a minute," David said, trying to calm his wife. "Let's wait until the police arrive and let them handle this."

While Jacob hid behind the locked door of his room and the others waited inside for the police to arrive, I sat alone on the porch in the bitter darkness. My head dipped, and I stared down at my lap. The ends of my belt hung loose, resting on my legs. With trembling hands, I tried to fasten them together again, but the buckle was broken.

It was then I realized. No matter what promise I'd made to Sue or Koko or even myself, I could no longer wait. Not another year. Not another day. Not another minute.

I would no longer wait until the night ended. I would charge into its darkness, my fists and voice raised.

Dropping the ends of my broken belt, I turned on the phone I'd grabbed when I'd run out of the house, and dialed. It took several rings before Akoi answered. When she did, her voice was heavy with sleep.

"Rachel? What time is it?"

"I don't know. Late. I need to talk to you."

A yawn stretched her words long and thin. "It's the middle of the night. Can this wait until morning?

"No, it can't. *I* can't. Not anymore. Please, Akoi. I need you to come get me—now."

"Okay. I'll be there as soon as I can. Are you all right?"

"No." The dark abyss of night held no hint of the promise of morning's light from where I sat alone on those cold steps in Portland, but I knew it was there, just beyond the horizon. Waiting for me to take one more step. "But I will be."

CHAPTER 34

Kansas City, Missouri—February 2002

I had been living in Kansas City with Akoi's sister, Daruka, and her family for several weeks when I received an unexpected call from Portland.

At first, I was hesitant to answer. When the police had arrived that night and questioned me about what had happened with Jacob, I'd told them the same thing I'd told Sue. Jacob's lies must have been more convincing because they did not arrest him that night or follow up their investigation the next day as they'd promised. I'd refused to stay in that house with Jacob another second and left with Akoi and stayed with her and her mama for the night. Andrew and Thomas begged me to come back, but I never wanted to see Jacob again, and I was too angry and hurt over Andrew's blindness and Thomas's silence to Jacob's abuse to see them either. I wanted to get as far away from Jacob and Portland as possible.

The next day at school, I'd told my counselor what had happened and asked for her help. She had me placed in a group home until Akoi and her mama arranged for me to move to Kansas City with Daruka, who was family and could take over guardianship of me until I was eighteen. Two weeks later, I'd boarded a Greyhound bus with a ticket my counselor had purchased for me, and I left Jacob, the others, and Portland behind with no desire to ever look back.

It hadn't been easy moving to Kansas City. I knew no one in Missouri. Even the people in the Sudanese community that had blood relations to me were strangers. I had been sleeping on the floor in Daruka's kids' room, and when I was not attending school, I was babysitting and cleaning for her. Daruka was my baba's cousin, and I was grateful she had welcomed me into her home and provided me with food and shelter. But no matter how far I ran, I could not outrun what had happened in Houston and Portland.

Holding Daruka's house phone to my ear, I stepped into another room to get away from the noise of her toddlers playing.

"Hello."

"Rachel! I can't believe I finally found you."

Though I recognized the caller's Dinka words, I did not recognize his voice. "Who is this?"

"It's me, Atem."

When I did not respond, he kept talking. "Your uncle Andrew's friend from Portland. I used to visit you and your uncles at Sue and David's house with Akoi and my cousin Chol. Do you remember me?"

"Yes," I said. "How are you, Atem?"

"I am good. I am married now."

Five weeks before Jacob attacked me for the last time, Atem had flown to Kenya to visit his remaining family members and get married. He had stayed in Kenya for several months.

"Congratulations," I said.

"Thank you, but that is not why I am calling."

"Why *are* you calling?" I asked.

"I have been trying to find you since I got back from Kenya."

This surprised me. Atem had always been nice to me, but he had been Andrew's friend, not mine. I could not imagine what he needed to discuss with me.

"I've been here, in Kansas City, since March," I explained.

"Akoi told me."

My body tensed. I wondered what else Akoi had told him. I had not shared many details of that night with my friend, but she had understood enough to help me get out of Portland and away from Jacob. My leaving, however, did not end the story. News of my abrupt departure from Sue and David's house in the middle of the night had spread through the Dinka community. People clamored to hear every sordid detail, and Jacob had wasted no time filling in the holes left by my silence and absence with his lies. Even those in the community who questioned Jacob's claims of innocence insinuated I was not blameless. They argued that an innocent victim would not run away from the truth. They proclaimed an innocent victim would not protect her attacker with silence. The stories of what happened that night continued to grow long after I'd left Portland. When rumors of Jacob's abuse reached Kansas City, so did accusations and blame for what everyone assumed I had done to welcome his unwanted advances. I ignored their insinuations and focused on my schoolwork and chores. I told myself I didn't care what anyone else thought, but Atem's unexpected call made me wonder what stories about me Atem had heard when he'd returned to Portland, and worse yet, what stories he'd believed.

Gripping the phone, I braced myself for his judgment. "She did?"

Atem's voice quieted. "Yes. I am sorry to hear about what happened, Rachel. I know Andrew and Thomas feel terrible. Are you all right?"

"I am better now that I am several states away from him."

"Of course," Atem said, struggling to find the right words. "I'm glad you are okay."

"Thanks, but why were you trying to find me?"

"Right," Atem said "I have some news."

My stomach dropped as frightening scenarios tore through my mind. Were Thomas and Andrew in trouble? Had Jacob hurt Thomas for protecting me the night of the attack? Did Andrew's anger over Jacob's abuse worsen after I'd left? Had he retaliated against Jacob and been arrested?

As upset as I still was with Andrew and Thomas, I did not want anything bad to happen to either of them.

"What's wrong?" I asked. "Are Andrew and Thomas okay?"

"Yes, yes," Atem said. "They are fine. I have news from Kakuma."

"Kakuma?"

"Yes. I was visiting family in Group Nine-A at Kakuma and knew that was where you and Thomas had lived, so I asked if anyone there remembered you. A man recognized your name and said he knew your parents. He said they were at New Cush Refugee Camp in southern Sudan. Rachel, your parents are alive, and they are looking for you!"

Of everything Atem could have said, those were the words I was not prepared to hear.

"No," I said, and then I hung up the phone and returned to my homework.

It didn't matter if Atem believed what he'd said, I knew it was a lie. It had to be. My parents were dead. There was no other explanation. If they had survived the war, they would have searched for me. They would not have allowed me to live and nearly die in Kakuma for nine years. They would not have allowed me to come to America without them and face abuse at my great-uncle Jacob's hands. Atem was wrong. The man at Kakuma had lied. He was probably trying to get money from him or a way to America because there was no way my parents were alive.

Days later, I received another call from Portland. This time it was Andrew.

"Rachel, you are on a three-way call," he told me before I could say I didn't want to talk to him. I had still not forgiven him and the others for not seeing Jacob for who he was. For not stopping the abuse happening right under their noses. "There is someone who wants to speak with you."

"Who?" I asked.

"Baba du." *Your father.*

I hung up and dropped the phone. I didn't know who Andrew had on the other end of the call, but it was not my baba.

The phone rang again. The second I answered, Andrew began talking.

"Rachel, you have to listen. We only have a few minutes, or we'll have to wait another thirty days to schedule a phone call with New Cush Refugee Camp."

I did not respond, but I also did not hang up.

"Michael," Andrew said, using my baba's Christian name, "Rachel is on the line. Can you hear us?"

I listened to the scratchy connection, waiting for the stranger on the other end of the line to speak, curious about what his voice would sound like. I had only met my father once in my life, when I was barely a year old. I would not recognize his voice, and he would not recognize mine, so whoever the stranger was on our three-way call had to know his voice would be proof of nothing.

Anger stirred in my stomach at the thought of someone preying on Andrew's and my emotions, pretending to be someone we'd loved and lost.

After several seconds, an unfamiliar voice, hesitant and tight with emotion, crackled over the connection. "Majok? Is it really you?"

My breath seized. I had not been called that nickname in over eleven years.

"It's me," the man said, "baba du."

My grip on the phone tightened. This was not possible. It had to be a trick. Someone who had known my baba, a distant relative or fellow SPLA soldier, with whom he'd mentioned his nickname for me when talking about his home and family, was using the information to play a cruel trick on us. I started to pull the phone away from my ear, determined to hang up on the fraud and his lies.

"Your mama is here," the man said.

The word "mama" pulled me back to the phone, but there was only silence on the other end of the line.

"Hello?" I said.

A stifled sob and more silence followed. For a moment, I thought the connection had been lost, and then the strange man's voice returned.

"I'm sorry, Majok. Your mama is too emotional to talk right now."

His words tore open the scabbed, calloused scar of the hope I'd buried in Kakuma. It had festered beneath years of disappointment and resentment. *Liar!* I was furious with the stranger on the phone. I hated him for telling me Mama was there. I hated him for giving me any hope she was alive.

But I hated myself more. After everything I had endured and learned, how could I be so easily duped into believing again, even for the briefest of moments?

"I have to go, Andrew," I told my uncle.

"Rachel, please. If you'd just listen," Andrew begged, "I promise—"

"No. No more promises."

"Rachel."

"I'm sorry. I can't do this."

And then the stranger on the line did something unexpected. He started to sing.

The song began weak and uncertain but gradually gained strength. And though his voice was strange to my ears, the words and melody were hauntingly familiar.

"Let your heart be strong."

The song pulled me back to the hut in Pawel. It placed me once again into Koko's arms as she whispered the lyrics to me in the darkness. Older memories followed. Koko singing while I helped her in the gardens of our home in Wernyol, and as I drifted to sleep on my mat with my small hands burrowed in Panyliap's soft fur while he slept, curled up beside me. It was the song Koko sang to remember her oldest son. It had been his favorite hymn. Its message of strength when fighting the good fight had given him courage to face his enemies and death on the battlefields of Sudan. He'd sung it before every battle. He'd sung it to me when I was just a baby, and he was a proud father, holding his firstborn child for the first and last time.

I listened in shock and silence until the stranger on the phone sang the last note of the familiar hymn that had comforted me when I'd hid from the Nuer rebels in Pawel, when I'd raised my voice with the other refugees in a desperate search for hope in Group Nine-A, and when I'd fought to survive malaria and death in Kakuma.

When the stranger had finished and silence once again stretched, tight and tentative, between us, I said one word.

"Baba?"

CHAPTER 35

Kansas City, Missouri—February–March 2002

I called Atem the moment I hung up the phone on Andrew and the stranger.

"Did you see them?" I asked when he answered. "Did you actually see my parents?"

"Yes. When I heard they were alive, I traveled to New Cush Refugee Camp."

"And you're sure it was them? You're absolutely positive?"

"I have a picture, Rachel. I've just been waiting for you to ask. I can mail it to you tomorrow and schedule another call with New Cush Refugee Camp for a month from now if you want me to."

"You have a picture of them?"

"Yes. I will send it to you if you are ready. Are you sure you're ready for this, Rachel?"

"Yes."

It was a lie. I knew it, and I suspect Atem knew it.

I wasn't ready. I didn't know if I'd ever be ready, but I had to know. For years, I'd believed my parents were dead. It was the only explanation for why they never came for me. They couldn't. I had made peace with that fact. I had mourned their loss. Sitting in that plane on the runway in Kakuma, I'd had to convince myself Mama was gone, like Koko. To escape the endless suffering of life in the refugee camp, I'd had to believe I was leaving no one behind so I could move forward.

As I sat there, considering the possibility I had been wrong, a spark of hope warmed in my heart, but it quickly cooled and hardened with anger. If I had been wrong, it meant my parents didn't die in the war. It meant they had been alive and living in Sudan all along. It meant they could have come for me.

During the days when I'd sat, frightened and confused, in the hut in Pawel.

Over the weeks I'd walked, tired and hurt, across unforgiving terrain and through treacherous waters.

In the months I'd spent trapped under the watchful eyes of cruel soldiers, within a growing circle of bones.

Through the years when I'd prayed to God, begging for help.

For food.

For water.

For kindness.

For understanding.

For mercy.

For the hours I'd hid in a closet, debating between a rope and knife.

In all that time, they could have come for me, but they didn't.

If Atem was right and my parents were alive, it meant they had moved on without me. Just as I had moved on without them.

I didn't know if I could live with that truth. I didn't know how to make peace with them or with myself.

Two days later, a letter arrived from Portland. Daruka handed it to me as I walked in the door after school.

"This one is for you."

I took it into the bedroom I shared with Daruka's children and closed the door. Whatever truth the photo revealed, it was a truth I wanted to face alone. My hands trembled. I inhaled deep, holding the breath in my lungs for several heartbeats. I had never been ready to face the obstacles life had thrust in my way, but I had faced them anyway. Slowly releasing my breath, I opened the envelope.

There was no letter inside. Just a photo of a man and woman sitting in front of a garden of tomato plants.

I did not recognize the man. I knew I wouldn't, even if he was my baba, so I studied the image of the woman seated next to him. She was older than I remembered, and there was an aching sadness in her eyes that hadn't been there twelve years earlier, but I knew her face.

Mama.

For years, I had lain awake at night, trying to remember what she looked like and praying to God to bring her back to me. With each passing day, her image faded until all that remained when I tried to conjure her face in my mind was darkness and pain. On the long walks across Sudan, the thought of finding Mama in the next town or village had kept my tired, aching legs moving forward.

Each step is one step closer, Adual had promised.

And I'd believed her. I had whiled away the long hours imagining how I would feel in that moment if I were to ever see Mama's face again. Would I experience joy? Relief? Gratitude? Disbelief? Anger?

But as I stared at her face in the photo, I felt—

Nothing.

With steady hands, I turned over the photo, slid it in the envelope, and put it in my backpack.

When I returned to the kitchen, Daruka was waiting at the table.

"May I see it?" she asked.

I took out the envelope and handed it to her.

She looked up at me before opening it. "If I tell you this is them, will you believe me?"

Daruka had known both my parents in Wernyol. She would be able to recognize not only Mama, but also Baba, her cousin.

I shrugged. "Maybe. Maybe not."

She took out the photo and covered her mouth with

one hand. Tears streamed down her face, and her shoulders shook with sobs.

"These are your parents, Rachel."

I stared at her with a hollow sense of detachment, as though I was standing apart from my life, watching it happen to someone else. I left her at the kitchen table, holding the photo of my parents and crying, and I went outside to watch her children play.

She was on the phone when I returned an hour later.

"It is Michael and Rebecca," she said through tears to whichever relative she was speaking with. "They are alive and in New Cush."

I left the photo with her and went to bed.

The fog of numbness did not lift until the next day at school. When the reality that my parents were alive finally hit, it struck with such force, it nearly put me to my knees. I remembered my conversation with Adual in Bor, when I had asked her if my mama was alive.

When my husband was killed in the war, I knew he was gone because someone told me he had died. Has anyone told you your mama is dead?

No, but—

Then until someone tells us otherwise, your mama is alive.

No one had ever told me Mama was dead. After so many years of looking and not finding her, I had told myself she was gone. I had to in order to move on, but now everything had changed. Mama was alive, and so was Baba. I was no longer alone in the world, and yet, as I sat in my classroom, I felt utterly alone.

A month after I received the photo from Atem, I waited for my phone call to connect to New Cush Refugee Camp. Atem had scheduled another call with my parents, and I had purchased a five-dollar Hello Africa phone card to cover the charges.

It had been a long four weeks. I could think of nothing else. I hadn't been able to focus on my schoolwork, and my grades had dropped. But as anxious as I was to speak with my parents, I was grateful for the time. I needed it to process my conflicting emotions and think about what I wanted to say.

Over the weeks, my initial anger and feelings of abandonment had given way to understanding and forgiveness. My parents were living in a refugee camp, just as I had. I didn't know what had happened to them during the twelve years we had been apart, but they, also, had lived through the same horrendous war I had survived. I remembered how hard Adual had worked to care for me and how much Koko had sacrificed to keep me alive. I knew my parents must have suffered, too. Everyone in southern Sudan had. I owed it to them to listen to their story. And I owed it to myself.

The connection clicked, and a man's voice crackled from the other end of the line. "New Cush Refugee Camp."

"Hello. My name is Rachel Lual Deng. I am looking for my parents."

"What are their names?"

"Michael Lual Deng and Rebecca Agau Kuir Bul."

The man must have covered the phone because his voice became muffled, but I could hear him yell, "Michael Lual Deng and Rebecca Agau Kuir Bul!"

I waited, expecting to hear the voice of the man I'd spoken with a month earlier, the voice I now knew belonged to my baba, but this time, a woman answered.

"Rachel?"

I knew her voice instantly.

"I saw the picture," I told her, scrambling for some way to start the conversation. "You look a little different."

"I got older," Mama said.

"We both did."

Her voice wavered. "Yes."

"I looked for you everywhere," I said. "Every time they brought in new refugees to Kakuma, I looked for you."

I paused to see how she would respond. But she didn't.

"I need to know," I told her. "In all that time, did you ever think about going back for me?"

For a moment, I worried I had rushed the question and upset her. I feared the silence would never end, but then she began to speak.

"When we heard about the attack, the SPLA gave me

and the other women in Torit two options. We could stay under the protection of the military and move forward with our lives, without our children, or we could go back, on our own, and search for survivors. I chose to go back, Rachel. I needed to find you, so some of the other women and I left Torit in search of our children.

"We traveled southern Sudan for months, walking at night and hiding during the day. Everywhere we went, I asked if anyone had seen you and Koko, but no one had. And then we heard the people fleeing the rebels and GOS were walking to Ethiopia, so we headed east. It wasn't until 1996 when I finally found someone who had been in Pawel during the rebel attack."

Her voice caught, and she paused before continuing. "They said Koko and you had been hiding in her sister-in-law's hut when the rebels returned. They said the rebels shot everyone. They said there were no survivors."

Adual's words echoed in my mind. *I knew he was gone because someone told me he had died.*

"You believed I was dead."

"Never." Her response, spoken firmly, without hesitancy, left no room for doubt. "I never gave up, Rachel. When Atem came here and told us you were alive, I did not doubt him, not for one second. I knew you were alive. No matter what anyone else said, in my heart, I always knew you were alive and I would find you again someday. And when I heard your voice over the phone last month, I knew that day had finally come and my prayers had been answered."

My breath caught in my throat. She had been on the phone that day. Baba had not lied. During those long seconds of silence, she had been on the other line. I imagined her holding the phone and crying, unable to speak through her tears.

"Your voice," she said, "it's still the same."

"So is yours." I couldn't think of what else to say. I couldn't find the words to express everything I was feeling in that moment.

"This is hard for me, Rachel. You are my child, but you are grown now. You were forced to grow up on your own, without Baba or me. I understand if you never want to talk to me again, but I need you to know, I never wanted to leave you. When your baba was hurt, Koko and I discussed who should go to Torit to care for him. I thought it should be her. He was her child, but she told me to go, that she would watch over you. And she did."

"She sacrificed herself to save me."

Mama's breathing hitched, and when she spoke again, her voice broke. "She loved you very much."

Tears streamed down my cheeks. "For so long, I thought she was the only one."

"Rachel, it doesn't matter how many years or kilometers separate us, you are my child. You will *always* be my child. I love you. No matter what you decide today, even if you

333

choose never to speak to me again, know you are loved. I will always love you. I need you to understand I didn't choose your baba over you. You came first in my heart. Always. I'm so sorry I wasn't there when you needed me."

"This is not your fault, Mama," I said, my voice thick with unshed tears. "You didn't know, when you left to care for Baba, that the rebels would attack. No one knew. You did your best in an impossible situation. Baba was hurt. He needed you. And you left me with someone you trusted, with someone who loved me. You left me with someone who watched over me until the very end."

"You have her strength," Mama said. "Koko would be so proud of you. We are so proud of you, my brave girl."

I said goodbye to my parents that day with the promise that we would be a family again. But I was not naive. Promises, even ones made from the heart and spoken as truths, despite our best efforts, are sometimes broken. In my seventeen years, I had learned how unpredictable and cruel life could be. The journey ahead would not be easy. It could take years for me to reunite with my family, and there would be many difficult obstacles along the way. There would be those in the world who would not believe in me, those who would tell me to give up, it was too hard, and there would be moments I would be tempted to believe them. I would face failures that would make me question myself and my ability to go on. And there would be times I would want to stop.

But I never would. I would put one foot in front of the other and I would keep moving forward because I knew each step I took, no matter how small or painful, would bring me one step closer.

And I knew something else, something the rest of the world didn't.

I had survived worse. I would survive this, too.

CHAPTER 36

Kansas City, Missouri—May 25, 2010

Eight years after I heard my parents' voices over the scratchy connection from New Cush Refugee Camp, I sat in the crowded Kansas City Immigration and Naturalization Service (INS) office and waited for my number to be called. I was twenty-five years old, but my body hummed with excitement and nervousness, like a child awaiting her first day of school. I started to open the folder on my lap to review my supporting documents and application requirements but stopped. Chiding myself, I closed the folder. Nothing in it could have magically changed or disappeared since I had last checked it five minutes earlier.

Instead, I took the small ticket I had pulled from the dispenser at the office entrance from my pocket and glanced at the red number alit on the digital counter above the INS clerk's window. I was six numbers away from taking the next step in my long journey. Once the clerk processed my paperwork and I passed the citizenship test, I would be sworn in as an American citizen. As a citizen, I would be eligible to get my passport and travel to Kenya.

I was so close to seeing Mama again. It had been twenty

years since I last saw her. Twenty years since I had felt the warmth of her embrace. My eyes stung with unshed tears at the thought of feeling her arms wrapped around me, holding me close again. And I was finally going to meet Baba. Over the past eight years, we had spoken on the phone many times. We'd learned a great deal about each other during our talks. There had been much to share, including how my parents had survived the war and been reunited with other family members.

I was relieved to learn Uncle Abraham and Aunt Monica had escaped the Nuer rebels the night of the massacre by hiding in the forest, and I was shocked to discover they had been so close to where the SPLA soldiers kept me in Paliau those first days after my rescue from Pawel that they had heard the gunfire and artillery from the same battles that had kept me awake those nights. Years later, Abraham became a minister, like Auntie Martha. He and his wife had four children and would add three more to their family in the years that followed. They lived in Kakuma, but Abraham often traveled into southern Sudan to preach the word of God.

Monica was also married and had children of her own. She and her husband had suffered the loss of their first-born, a daughter, who was abducted in Bor before she was ten years old. My heart broke for my aunt. After searching for her daughter, Monica and her husband had settled in Kakuma, where they were raising two sons.

Abraham and Monica were not the only Deng relatives

whose families had grown in my absence. Mama and Baba shared the news with me that I was no longer an only child. My parents had six sons during the time we were apart. Four had survived. Mama made porridge every morning for their sons and any starving orphaned children who lined up outside their hut. I had also been blessed with two sons of my own in the last four years. My parents and I had exchanged photographs through the mail, but I couldn't wait to meet my brothers and Baba in person and introduce my parents to their grandsons, Deng and Kuek. When I closed my eyes, I could imagine myself disembarking the plane in Kenya and finding Mama and Baba waiting for me.

Finding my brothers waiting for me.

Finding my family waiting for me.

Finding my family.

I smiled, and a tear slipped down my cheek. I did not wipe it away. I had experienced so many tears in my life.

Tears born of fear and anger.

Tears born of pain and loss.

Tears born of regret and shame.

Tears born of hopelessness and grief.

But these tears flowed from a wellspring of joy and hope. I refused to hide them as though they were signs of weakness. My tears revealed my strength. I would wear them with pride.

The digits on the sign clicked to the next number. Five left. My knees bounced with impatience. Just that sign and a test stood between me and my dream of reuniting with my family. I took the study guide I'd received from my bag. Hoping the thick book of facts about the United States of America would help pass the time left before my number was called, I began to memorize facts about the US Constitution, the branches of government and their duties, American history from the colonial period to today, geography, and the names of my state's representatives. I knew I had to learn every fact before my exam, which would be scheduled for two weeks after my application was processed and accepted, but as hard as I tried to focus on what I was reading, my eyes kept sneaking glances at the counter.

"Watching it doesn't make it move any faster," the elderly gentleman seated next to me said. He'd been waiting with his own folder, study guide, and ticket when I'd arrived an hour earlier. "I should know," he added with a sheepish grin. "This is my fourth time."

"They don't make it easy, do they?" I said. I was now fluent in English. It had been difficult and taken me years to master, and my pronunciations still carried my Dinka accent, but I no longer worried about what others thought. Mr. Nguyen, my high school history teacher in Kansas City, had helped me shed that unearned shame, discover the pride in mastering another language, and embrace the beauty of my accent. Mr. Nguyen had immigrated to the United States from Vietnam and was an amazing teacher.

"I know you have a voice, Rachel," he'd told me one day after class, not long after I'd escaped Portland and arrived in Kansas City. He had noticed my reluctance to speak in front of others and recognized the reason. "Look at me. English is not my first language, but I am a teacher. You hear my accent when I speak, but you also hear my words. I speak because what I have to say is important. And what you have to say, Rachel, is important, too. Share your voice with us."

Mr. Nguyen taught me more than history that year. He taught me to speak so everyone could hear me. He taught me to share my voice with the world.

"No," the elderly man seated next to me said. "This has not been an easy process." Then he smiled at me. "But nothing worth doing ever is."

He was right. I thought of the other numerous, seemingly impassable barriers I'd faced in my long, difficult journey to get to this moment. It didn't matter if it took four or forty or four hundred attempts, I would pass this test, too. I glanced around the room, at the dozens of men and women waiting for their numbers to be called, waiting to face their next obstacle. I did not know their stories or what had driven them from their home countries, but I knew each and every one of them had faced their own difficult journey. "Where are you naturalizing from?" I asked the elderly man.

"Mexico," he said. "You?"

"Sudan."

He nodded. "Do you still have family there?"

The question should have brought fresh tears to my eyes, but instead it brought a smile to my lips. "Yes."

"So do I," the man said. "In Mexico, I mean. I hope to visit them if I get my citizenship. When," he quickly corrected himself. "*When* I get my citizenship."

"Me too. *When* I get my citizenship."

The digital counter clicked, and the clerk behind the window called out the next number.

The elderly gentleman checked his ticket. "That's me." A slight tremor took hold of his hands as he gathered his belongings. "You'd think after so much practice, I'd be ready."

"Good luck," I told him.

"Thank you," he said. "Good luck to you, too. I pray we will both be reunited with our families soon."

As he slowly made his way across the waiting room to the clerk's window, I closed my study guide and opened my folder. My test would not be administered for several weeks, but any missing documents could lead to further delays in the process or a denial of my application and loss of my filing fee. I could not afford another setback. I had waited too long and worked too hard to be denied now. I mentally ran down the application requirements checklist and carefully inspected each document.

Completed N-400 Citizenship Application—all twenty pages.

Check!

Photocopy of my green card, proof I had been a resident of the United States for a minimum of five years.

Check!

A photo ID—my driver's license with my name, Rachel Lual, verifying my identity, and my birth date, 1/1/85, proof I was eighteen years or older.

Check!

Receipt for the $675 application fee, which I'd worked two jobs to pay for, and that I would lose if my application or supporting documents were incomplete or missing or if I failed the test.

Check!

Fingerprinting completed.

Check!

The evidence of the last requirement was visible on my hands. Official fingerprinting had been my first stop at the INS office that day. Tucking the documents back in my folder, I inspected the remnants of the black ink clinging to every raised sweep and swirl of my fingerprints.

Through everything I had suffered and survived over my twenty-five years of life, with all I had lost and reclaimed and rebuilt, despite the countless ways my life had been altered by circumstances beyond my under-standing and forces beyond my control, my fingerprints had remained unchanged. Since the day of my birth, they had been uniquely mine.

Staring at my ink-stained fingers, I thought back to my early years in the village of Wernyol with Mama, Uncle Abraham, Aunt Monica, and Koko. Before the war came. Before everything changed.

For ten years after the attack on our village, life had chipped away at me, like an angry sculptor.

In hails of bullets.

Across unforgiving deserts.

Through starvation and illness and death.

In foreign lands with foreign tongues, it carved and gouged away parts of me.

Bit by bit.

Piece by piece.

With rough hands and cruel strokes, it had fashioned me into someone I had no longer recognized. Someone who cowered in a closet with a rope, a knife, and a choice.

And I had chosen. I'd chosen to no longer allow life to wield its knife on me. I had taken the knife and become my own sculptor. No one else would ever dictate who I was or who I could be.

I thought back on the people in my life who had shared their strength and helped me survive.

The women of Bor, holding up one another in prayer and grief and cobbling together the broken pieces of their lives to form a protective wall around us children.

Adual, taking my small hand, in the absence of Mama and Koko, and helping me escape a future of pain and death by giving me faith and hope.

Mama, promising me in the garden on the morning she left that she would return, and her voice, over the phone twelve years later, telling me, *I never gave up. I always knew you were alive and I would find you again someday.* I closed my eyes and pictured her walking hundreds of kilometers across the Sudanese desert, enduring the same unbearable heat and unquenchable thirst millions of others had suffered, in her fight to fulfill the promise she had made to her lost daughter.

Koko, shielding me from bullets, leading me through the darkness, teaching me in the garden, soothing my pain, and whispering words of love as I drifted to sleep.

Their voices and words carried me. Through forests, villages, and ambushes. Across rivers, deserts, and oceans. Over twenty years and thousands of kilometers. They had carried me.

There's always tomorrow, so there's always hope.

If we are to survive, we must keep moving forward.

With each step, no matter how small or painful, we are a step closer.

We just need to survive until morning.

No matter what happens, do not let go.

Don't look back, Achut.

You are loved.

You are strong.

Never forget who you are.

And I had carried them. Through death and grief. In moments of weakness and despair. To a new home and a new life.

Their voices became my voice.

Their words became my strength.

I would carry them with me. Always.

The counter above the clerk's desk clicked. I gathered my things and was halfway across the room before my number was called.

With barely a glance, the clerk took my receipt for the application fee and the photocopy of my green card. She then scanned my license before thumbing through my twenty-page application to make sure no lines had been left blank.

When she was done, she pushed it back across the desk and said in a bored, monotone voice, "Please review this information and let me know of any errors. If you want to change the birth date, you will need to provide an official birth certificate from your home country. Consider each of your written responses carefully. Once the paperwork is processed, no changes may be made."

I checked every line twice to make sure I hadn't miss anything before handing back the application.

"Is everything correct?" the clerk asked without looking up from her work.

"No." I pointed to the first line on the first page. "A mistake has been made."

The clerk glanced at the line, checked it against the scanned image of my license, and then looked up at me, confusion wrinkling her brow. "Your name is not Rachel?"

"No."

I lifted my chin and smiled as tears born of strength and pride ran down my face.

"My name is Achut."

A LETTER TO THE READER
FROM ACHUT DENG

When I was first approached by Farrar, Straus and Giroux Books for Young Readers about sharing my story, I was hesitant. I had never shared all the details of my past with anyone before and was afraid to revisit the memories I'd left behind. In order to survive the traumas I'd faced and build a life for myself and my family, I'd had to leave my past in the past so I could keep moving forward. What I realized, while considering sharing my story, was even though I'd shut my mind to the painful memories of my past, my heart and soul were still suffering. The traumatized girl I once was had never healed. I continued to carry her with me. I also knew there were others like me who were suffering in silence, so I chose to tell my story to heal myself and to hopefully help other girls and boys who are hurting. I want them to know they are not alone. I also wanted to tell my story so my sons will know their mother. I hope by sharing my story with my boys, Deng, Kuek, and Mayom, they will better understand the life I lost, the life I left behind, and the life I reclaimed for myself and for them.

Part of the life I'd lost and left behind, I was able to reclaim in 2002 when I discovered my parents were alive.

My family and I have stayed in contact since that first phone call with my baba. Eleven years after I left Kakuma, I returned to Kenya, where I was finally reunited with my mama, Uncle Abraham, and Aunt Monica and where I met my baba again and my brothers for the first time. There were many hugs and tears. There were also many smiles. It was difficult to leave my family in Kenya, but I was able to visit again a couple of years later.

Since 2002, I have supported my family in Kakuma and financed my brothers' educations while also following the legal procedures with the hope of bringing my family to America someday. It has been a long and difficult process, with many setbacks, but we keep moving forward, and on July 5, 2021, my three sons and I, surrounded by friends, waited at the Sioux Falls Regional Airport to welcome my mama to the United States. She was the first family member I was able to bring to America. My baba joined us on May 23, 2022. They are living in Sioux Falls, and we are continuing to work hard to bring my brothers over, too, so my family will all be together again. I purchased a small plot of land next to my house so Mama can plant a garden like the one we tended together when I was a child in Wernyol. I have also remained in contact with Andrew, Thomas, Deborah, and Sarah. Though we live in different states, we still talk frequently to share updates on our lives and families.

Working on this memoir has been one more step on my long journey. It is a step toward healing. It is my hope that just as I drew strength and faith from Koko, Adual, and every person who helped carry me, my story will help carry you. I pray it provides you some light when the nights are too long, and the darkness is too heavy.

You are strong. Don't let go. And never forget who you are.

ACKNOWLEDGMENTS

ACHUT DENG

To my beautiful friend, inside and out, Keely Hutton, our work on my memoir started as a business partnership, but it quickly grew into a friendship. I consider you my best friend. When I talk to you, I feel better. Thank you for helping me tell my story.

To Molly Ellis, for reading my interview and believing I had a story to tell.

To my amazing editor, Joy Peskin, for believing in me and bringing this amazing team together to help me share my story with the world.

To the FSG BYR Team, including Molly Ellis, Asia Harden, Elisa Rivlin, and Mallory Grigg, who designed the beautiful cover for *Don't Look Back*. Thank you all for working so hard to bring my story to readers.

To my awesome agent, Soumeya Roberts; her assistant, Hannah Popal; and HG Literary, for your ongoing support during this totally new process for me. Soumeya answers all my many questions, always has my back, and even sends me cake, which my boys loved.

To Awak Bior, for reviewing my memoir and sharing her insight.

To Caitlin Dickerson, for introducing me to the world and encouraging me to share my story.

To the *Daily* podcast staff, Clare Toeniskoetter, Eric Krupke, Sydney Harper, and M. J. Davis, for providing me a platform to share my voice and story.

To the Lipsky family, Laura, Mikayla, Aliyah, and Jason; Walter Groff; Paul Lazar; and the many generous people who reached out to me after reading the *New York Times* article, for giving me support and words of encouragement and letting my family and me know we are not alone.

To my friends Deborah Ajak, Monica Manchol, Kirsten Dunlap, Jakoma Kona Machok, Mr. Nguyen, Briana Johnson, Cathy Duffy, Sarah Ayual, Joseph Lual Deng, and Arok Thon for the support, understanding, and encouragement you have provided my boys and me over the years.

To Musa Dibba, who has been a true friend to me and a positive role model for my sons.

To Atem Deng Atem, who found my parents and reunited my family.

To my family: to my mama, Agau Kuir Bul, and to my baba, Lual Deng Ater, who never gave up on finding me and never stopped loving me. To my brothers, Deng, Dhieu, Aruai, and Ajak, who gave me a sense of family and belonging. To Garang Deng Ater, Amam Deng Ater, Peter Kuir, John Giel, Akuch Giel, Akoi Mayen, Daruka Ajah Mayen, and all my aunts, uncles, and cousins—no matter the time and distance between us, I hold you all close to my heart.

To my koko, Abul Deng Goch, whose love and strength saved me in Pawel and continued to save me throughout my life.

To Adual, whose faith and kindness carried me across Sudan and continues to carry me today.

To my sons, Deng, Kuek, and Mayom, for giving me the courage and strength to face my past and the love and hope to embrace our future together.

KEELY HUTTON

My heartfelt thanks to the team of amazing women who helped bring *Don't Look Back* to readers.

To Achut Deng for her trust, time, and truth. I am honored to help tell her story and blessed to call her my friend. The months I have spent talking with Achut are a gift, for which I will be forever grateful.

To my agent, Soumeya Roberts; her assistant, Hannah Popal; and everyone at HG Literary. Soumeya swoops in to save the day with good advice, honest editorial feedback, help navigating the publishing world, and chocolate cake. Even without a cape, Soumeya is a true Super-Agent.

To my fabulous editor, Joy Peskin, and her editorial assistant, Asia Harden. Joy's passion for this project was evident from our first Zoom call. Her insightful editorial feedback was infused with equal measures of guidance and enthusiasm. Achut's memoir could not be in better hands.

To FSG BYR publicity director Molly Ellis, who discovered the interview with Achut Deng in the *New York Times* and, recognizing the potentially powerful story Achut had to share, brought it to the attention of Joy Peskin and her team.

To FSG BYR art director and cover designer, Mallory Grigg, who perfectly captured Achut's vulnerability and strength in her powerful cover design.

To Elisa Rivlin and the FSG BYR legal team for their support and guidance.

To our terrific team at Farrar, Straus and Giroux Books for Young Readers. All the contributors from copy editing to the art, marketing, publicity, managing editorial, production, and audio departments have poured their talent and hearts into Achut's memoir. Working with the staff at FSG has been a true collaboration.

To Awak Bior, who reviewed a draft of *Don't Look Back* and provided invaluable feedback based on her knowledge of and experiences in South Sudan.

To Caitlin Dickerson, whose interview with Achut touched the hearts of many readers and was the first step in bringing Achut's inspiring story to the world.

To my critique partner, Eboni Collins, who never pulls her punches and generously shares her brilliant editorial advice. I cherish our friendship and am grateful for the conversations and laughter we have shared.

To my incredible network of writing friends: Donna Farrell, Kathy Blasi, Andrea Page, Sibby Falk, Marsha

Hayles, the Rochester Area Children's Writers and Illustrators (RACWI) group, Fiona McLaren, and the writers and illustrators I've connected with through social media platforms, conferences, and workshops. I am inspired by your passion, perseverance, and creativity.

To the brilliant composers Hiroyuki Sawano and Kohta Yamamoto, whose powerfully emotional scores for Hajime Isayama's *Attack on Titan* accompanied my many hours of writing and revising.

And last, but not least, to my family. To my husband and best friend, Greg, whose love and support gifted me the time and confidence to pursue my dreams. To my sons, Aidan and Colin, who inspire my words and sprinkle pixie dust on my life. To my mother, Sheila, who nurtured my imagination and lifted my dreams. To my father, Mick, whose love of language and books made writing musical and storytelling magical. To my brothers, Grady and Patrick, natural storytellers who bring our childhood memories to life with love and laughter. To my aunts, uncles, cousins, and in-laws, Carolyn and Mike, for their encouragement and support. And to my adorable dog, Maximus, who provides endless cuddles and reminds me daily of the importance of stepping away from work occasionally to play.